KEY ISSUES IN BUSINESS ETHICS

KEY ISSUES
IN BUSINESS ETHICS

JOHN DONALDSON

ACADEMIC PRESS

Harcourt Brace Jovanovich, Publishers

London San Diego New York Berkeley
Boston Sydney Tokyo Toronto

ACADEMIC PRESS LIMITED
24–28 Oval Road
London NW1

United States Edition published by
ACADEMIC PRESS INC.
San Diego, CA 92101

British Library Cataloguing in Publication Data
Is available

ISBN 0-12-220540-5 (cased)
0-12-220541-3 (p/b)

Typeset by Bath Typesetting Limited, Bath
Printed in Great Britain by St Edmundsbury Press Limited, Bury St Edmunds, Suffolk

CONTENTS

v

FOREWORD
AND METHODOLOGICAL NOTE

Key Issues in Business Ethics offers constructive proposals towards raising standards of conduct on all sides of industry and business. It is *non-dogmatic* in that it recognizes value in rival doctrines. It is *pluralist* in that it sees no defensible grounds for enforcing the *mores* of any one group, class or creed on others; it is *objectivist* in that it seeks to demonstrate that particular beliefs and practices can be defended or discredited by reference to *rational argument*, grounded in experience using principles that are independent of time and place, even though the applications are profoundly influenced by the contingencies of time, place and much else. It is *positive* (though not 'positivist') in that it seeks to demonstrate that *improvement* is both meaningful and possible.

Practice in business can be seen to be neither uniformly deplorable nor beyond reproach. Approaches to such a highly charged subject are, not surprisingly, highly varied. The more uncertain the issues, the more contemptuous and intolerant some people appear to be in the face of alternative views. Such closed-mindedness, as in other disciplines, is the most serious enemy of rational, consistent conduct. There are enough examples to show that such closed-mindedness is not an inevitable and universal human experience. The main, rival, approaches to both the substance and methods of business, and of ethics based on *utility, duty, group interest, individual interest, consent* or *history*, though often incompatible with each other, seem to be at the same time necessary for orderly, rational conduct of business life. There is, fortunately, little likelihood of any one outlook refuting all others. Ethical arguments and issues are not like that. The dangers of such outlooks dominating others by non-rational and improper means have been all too apparent throughout history, and not least in the twentieth century.

Moral reasoning has at the most the power to persuade. The enforcement of morals is necessarily a denaturing process, although inevitable at some level. The balance and boundaries between law and morals, being closely related to the traditional dilemmas faced by attempts to balance freedom and other values, must constantly change, but enforcement takes many forms other than the law. Such processes, such as group pressures, are major elements in ethical issues, including those of business ethics. What Orwell called 'Groupthink' is pervasive, and more often than not as baleful as Orwell described it in his book, *Nineteen Eighty-Four*.

This book attempts to show that it is possible to be constructive, tolerant, practical and principled and willing to admit to mistaken judgement. Some people and practices achieve this. More could and should do so.

Methodological Note

The most salient features of moral or ethical arguments are their complexity, their ability to attract rival stances, and the variety of such stances. This has led many to believe that moral matters are incapable of settlement, on the grounds that they are subject to time, place, taste, experience, hidden motivations and much else. There is no doubt that these matters do influence people's views. People cannot time-travel, because of *time's arrow*. People cannot have themselves brought up in different circumstances to test for the effect of time and place. People cannot exchange identities with others in order to find out whether their perceptions and values differ or are identical. No experiments could ever be conclusive in relation to general theoretical stances in ethics, or in any other area for that matter. The complexity of ethical matters can be brought out by means of case studies, but cases are notoriously difficult to generalize, one to another. Surveys of opinion can shed some light on people's beliefs, but can be systematically misleading and often superficial, though having merit in adding some numbers to what has traditionally been a literary and conceptual as well as directly practical set of ideas. The variety of views and the formidable problems of evidence and of explanation of behaviour do not prove that ethics is 'subjective', or merely a matter of opinion. What they do prove is that the subject is very complex, perplexing and at times difficult to understand. They prove also that it is unlikely that any knockdown arguments can be found against any major school of thought, even if particular arguments within such schools can be refuted, discredited or given persuasive advocacies.

The variety and complexity present problems of exposition. Lengthy tracts of theory rightly attract the criticism that they are excessively abstract, leaving no 'handle' for readers to use in judging the validity of the argument. Detailed descriptions of cases leave readers rightly wondering when the author will come to the point. Most of the key words are either technical terms in philosophy or in business, open to accusations of 'jargon', or are controversial or ambiguous in their own right. Some technical terms are essential. Ethics cannot be discussed without using the traditional labels of the main schools of thought, such as those of 'utilitarianism', 'deontology', 'egoism' or 'prescriptivism'. Many people, in discussing such matters, demand that the terms can be defined in advance of the discussion. However, this stance expresses a particular view of the nature of words and language, and of the nature and functions of definitions. As a result, discussions end up, often, in semantic morasses. 'Semantics' itself has legitimate uses, but is sometimes used as a term of abuse, as when issues of substance are dismissed as being 'mere semantics'. As it happens, there are many well-developed arguments not only on the nature of language, but on the nature and functions, uses and abuses (or limitations) of definitions, and of such general terms as 'good', 'right', 'wrong', 'true', 'false', 'moral', 'ethical' or 'ought'. Even the labels for the main schools of thought are portmanteau expressions. For example, the utilitarianism of the elder and younger Mills (James Mill and John Stuart Mill) is dramatically different at some points. Even the process of labelling is itself capable of being used to evade issues, dismiss arguments improperly, or even to deprive people of rights.

In writing the book, I have tried to resist the temptations to offer a precise definition of every term that arises as soon as it arises. For some terms, their power lies in their ability to evade precise definitions or simple usages. 'Democracy', 'truth', 'freedom' are classic examples: delegates at party conferences can cheer, stamp their feet and give standing ovations on hearing some of these terms, and can continue to do so as long as they all mean something different by them. The vagueness of moral terms and their ambiguities are part of the explanation of the power of persuasion (and its less reputable counterparts of propaganda and brainwashing). Their vagueness, ambiguity and power to persuade are, along with norms of secrecy and control of communications, major tools which are used for control purposes in business, administration and the unions. Their illegitimate uses trade on their legitimate ones; their emotive meanings sometimes dominating their rational ones.

These 'moral manipulations' do not form a dominant theme in the book. They are pathological, and the book is not a study in the moral pathology of industry.

For purposes of exposition, the temptation to make cross-references to arguments already expressed or yet to come cannot always be resisted. As a rule, controversial and radically ambiguous terms are printed in quotation marks or italics at their first appearance, but references to authors are used to indicate where a fuller treatment of the term appears. This is supplemented by a glossary and a full list of references.

For the most part, every attempt is made to use words and language in a way that conforms to the usage in the *Concise Oxford Dictionary*, sixth edition, 1976. An attempt is made to maintain, for purposes of exposition, a balance between 'abstract theoretical arguments' and discussions or expositions of evidence, including that of attitudes and opinions of business people, administrators, or others who have to do with industry.

The minimum of technical terms and special usages of words will not, it is hoped, put non-specialists off from thinking about the subject. Ethical argument unfortunately does require some specialized vocabulary and some labels for schools of thought. My own experience on all sides of adult education and industry tends to the conclusion that people will master the technical terms if they are interested in the subject. In particular, it is hoped that 'practical managers' who tend to be suspicious of academic language, and others, who are often sceptical about managers and academics alike (sometimes with ample justification), will not be put off by the theme and the terminology. Some of it is their own.

The book claims to have identified the key issues in business and industry to which moral or ethical reasoning can be fruitfully applied by the various participants, and to have identified possible ways of structuring the debates and the practices that should follow from consideration of them. Students on courses in business and management or preparing for professional or general examinations should find the amount of detail in the cases useful in providing material with which to support their arguments. The book is not intended as a summary of the introductory texts in either general ethics or in business ethics, such as those featuring in the discussion, but it is hoped that it will be helpful for people who wish to attempt a synthesis of theory, description, analysis and prescription.

It differs from some other materials in the area in that it includes an attempt at providing criteria for improvement, with proposals based on them. It also offers a critique of trade unions in ethical terms, set against discussion of firms and corporations and their behaviour. An attempt is made also to include some running themes that recur in different contexts, such as issues of inflation, pay and price control, as well as methodological themes such as positivism, scepticism and progress (and its equivalent notions).

GLOSSARY

The expressions listed below summarize the concepts and ideas which I consider to be basic to constructive debate on business ethics. Most of the words have several levels of meaning, and many uses—descriptive, emotional, prescriptive, persuasive (for example)—and many 'overtones'. They are thus theory-loaded, and can give rise to much argument at cross purposes, and to much wandering from the points at issue. This is in the nature of the subject. The uses in the text are, unless otherwise stated, those of the *Concise Oxford Dictionary*, and non-technical uses are preferred to technical ones. Where the words have many meanings, such as in the case of the word 'key' or the word 'issue', it should be clear from the context which one is intended. In some cases the expressions are used in a way that is inclusive of several shades of meaning. The definitional precision often sought in arguments on moral issues is not always appropriate. It is not easy to achieve consistently, and in my experience is least often achieved by those who tend to be most insistent upon it. Using words carefully is always a better alternative than spurious precision or fake hard-headedness.

Further details of usage can be found in any general dictionary or in a dictionary of philosophy, for example, Flew (1984).

agapism   An influential notion often neglected in theoretical work, agapism is the idea that there is only one truly general ethical imperative: to love (God, one's fellows, or the whole of nature, etc.).

analysis/analytical   Generally taken to mean breaking down complex ideas into simple ones. Can be used more generally to refer to drawing out the implications and ramifications of ideas, doctrines or situations.

analytic   A technical term used in logical theory to refer to the idea that some truths are independent of the state of the universe. An example is $2 + 2 = 4$. Often means 'true (or false) by definition'. An essential element in the doctrine of logical positivism, which is discussed in the text. The whole of mathematics would usually be taken to be analytic. The notion usually forms one part of a dichotomy. Its partner is 'synthetic', which means 'true (or false) if it is supported (or not supported) by the evidence'.

autonomy   The right of self-government. Extended to mean that people are, or ought to be placed in, a position to be able to make up their own minds about moral issues. It implies an appropriate level of knowledge and a supportive institutional framework.

business ethics   Explained in detail in the text. In short it can be described as the systematic study of moral (ethical) matters pertaining to business, industry or related activities, institutions or practices and beliefs. Can also refer to the actual standards, values or practices—or beliefs. An example of the latter use is seen in the title of Max Weber's book, *The Protestant Ethic and the Spirit of Capitalism.*

casuistry   Sometimes used in a derogatory sense to refer to an alleged quibbler or sophist, with the implication that the casuistry is insincere, or ignores major matters in favour of trivial ones. In the text the expression is used to refer to the systematic discussion of the application of general moral laws to particular courses of conduct, or to accommodation to new ideas that enter and challenge the social order (Flew, 1984).

collective bargaining   The practice in industrial relations of negotiating pay and conditions by representatives on behalf of an indefinite number of employers and employees, usually members of organizations to which the bargainers belong.

collective rights   A term used in industrial relations, implying the belief that some *rights* are attributable to groups as opposed to individuals. The concept is not recognized in law.

definition   A process or expression that provides the precise meaning of a word or phrase (Flew, 1984). Much has been written on the nature and value of definitions, occupying much time in formal and informal logic. In moral matters, the precision of definitions can be preserved at the cost of rendering them worthless in practice, or of making them so broad that they are hopelessly ambiguous. Three kinds of definitions are worth noting:

lexical   reporting on how expressions are in fact used

prescriptive   recommending a use for an expression (a procedure that is often difficult to maintain consistently)

persuasive   a definition in which emotive overtones dominate the logical or factual content.

Much moral reasoning is at cross purposes as a result of confusion between these forms of definition, and as a result of popular misconceptions such as that moral argument must begin with definitions.

deontology   The doctrine that ethics is grounded in notions of duty; that some acts are morally obligatory regardless of consequences in terms of practice. One of the major doctrines in ethics.

democracy A notoriously ambiguous expression. Broadly refers to the idea that the people affected by a decision, government, practice or institution should have an equitable say in the processes leading to the decisions, etc. Various theorists of democracy use different principles on which to ground their conclusions. In general it should be recognized that people can appeal to different *principles* and to different *institutional arrangements* in referring to democracy. Its emotive appeal often obscures the fact that democratic states, businesses and processes can be very different, with little in common. Both the *principles* and the *arrangements* need to be specified.

descriptivism The notion that moral judgments are derivable from facts. Sometimes referred to as *naturalism.*

determinism The doctrine that human action is not free but determined by motives regarded as external forces acting on the will (*COD*).

Deus ex machina Power or event that comes in the nick of time to solve a difficulty. More loosely can refer to an unexplained method of solving a perplexing problem.

egoism The belief that self-interest is the foundation of morality.

ethics Moral philosophy (q.v.). Can also refer to the customs or standards which a particular group or community acts upon (or is supposed to act upon). Thus it refers to the codes and practices and to the principles by which they can be analysed or criticized, positively or negatively. Derived from the classical Greek, meaning the characteristic beliefs of a people.

essentialism A variety of doctrines. In ethics generally taken to mean the idea that concepts have an indispensable or fundamental element, which is necessary to establish the presence of a concept or its use. For instance, in economics, inflation is sometimes thought to be 'essentially a monetary phenomenon'.

first order (and higher order) A logical distinction. A first-order proposition would be: 'management has a right to manage'. For the second-order we might say: 'The idea that management has a right to manage is ambiguous'. At the third-order we might say: 'the ambiguity is not in question'. At the fourth-order we could say: 'Your statement that the ambiguity is not in question is misleading'. There is no limit to the number of orders of analysis. In practice the distinction between first-order and second-order is sufficient.

freedom An ambiguous concept. It broadly means the same as liberty. It is usual to follow Sir Isaiah Berlin and distinguish between positive freedom, e.g. to do things, and negative freedom, to be free not to do them.

free will Sometimes called libertarianism. It broadly means that people are able to decide for themselves what they believe and what they do. The doctrine can be modified to hold that the freedom operates within the laws of nature.

golden rule   Do as you would be done by. Various expressions for this fundamental moral rule are to be found in most religions and creeds through the ages, testifying to its universal applicability (Flew, 1984).

groupthink   The idea originated in George Orwell's novel *Nineteen Eighty-Four*. In general it refers to what are called group norms, though usually referring to those norms which do not admit challenge or amendment. Individuals are required to believe what the group thinks, suppressing or exchanging their own views in favour of the official view of the group. Very widespread.

ideology   Manner of thinking characteristic of a class or individual. Set of ideas as a basis for a political or economic system (*COD*). Sometimes, apparently, believed to be (a) essential to any system, (b) beyond rational debate between systems, or (c) rendering ethics impossible.

improvement   Making something better or adding value to it. Views differ as to whether a change is an improvement or not, hence the need for criteria.

issue   Any affair in question or any important topic for discussion.

jargon   Mode of speech familiar only to a group or profession. Often used derogatorily to indicate that expressions are meaningless, worthless, or unnecessarily obscure.

kangaroo court   Improperly constituted illegal court held by strikers, etc.

labelling   Literally, attaching labels. Figuratively, it refers to the use of short classifying phrases with intent to persuade self or others to accept a description that may not be accurate. For example, 'freedom fighter' or 'terrorist' are labels that purport to describe the same activist. Labelling is a subtle process with many moral overtones and implications.

meta-ethics   Any higher order statement concerning ethics, e.g. "All ethical theories are incomplete", is a meta-ethical statement.

metaphysics   Branch of learning, currently unfashionable, that is taken to refer to attempts to identify the fundamental realities, or 'God', 'Freedom' and 'Immortality' (Kant); or the absolute presuppositions of our (or any other) age.

methodology   Refers to (1) the list of methods used in an enquiry and/or (2) the analysis or critique of the methods that are, or can be, used in an enquiry.

moral   Synonymous with 'ethical'. Refers to the customs, values, standards, practices of a group, age, or of a theory intended to be timeless.

Refers also to the way in which they are, or can be criticized constructively or destructively. From the Latin *mores*, meaning customs. (See also 'Ethics'.)

moral concepts Key concepts include 'good', 'bad', 'right', 'wrong', 'just', 'unjust', 'proper'. Their importance, meaning and use are viewed differently by the different theories of ethics, such as those discussed in the text. As concepts they are interrelated, and in part, often take their meaning from each other.

objectivism The belief that there are at least some moral truths that would remain true whatever anyone or everyone thought. A version is the idea that at least some moral arguments are capable of proof or refutation in the same way as mathematical or scientific arguments are. Objectivists do not necessarily claim certainty or infallibility, only that some ethical issues are decidable. Objectivists differ in their use of the term and in the extent to which they are willing to qualify the doctrine.

pathology Adapted from the medical use. In the context of business, often used to refer to systems or practices that deteriorate or cause deterioration in performance.

pluralism The view that the world contains many kinds of existent, which in their uniqueness cannot be reduced to just one (Flew, 1984). In moral and political theory it is the view that there can be more than one focus of loyalty for an individual, and that different institutions with opposing views and different opposing theories or beliefs are permissible or desirable.

positivism The philosophical system of Auguste Comte, recognizing only positive facts and observable phenomena, and rejecting metaphysics and theism (*COD*). The doctrine pre-dates Comte. Despite its rejection of metaphysics, positivism is a metaphysical doctrine.

prescriptivism The view that the primary function of moral judgment is to prescribe courses of action (Flew 1984). The term was coined by the contemporary British philosopher, R. M. Hare.

progress Move forward or onward; advance to a better state (*COD*).

relativism See 'Subjectivism'.

rights A person's entitlements as a member of society, and including liberties such as the right to use a public highway, and 'claim rights', such as the right to a defence counsel (Flew, 1984). Few people would deny that rights exist; but the sources are in dispute. Views range from rights as grants from the sovereign or from the law, to natural rights, upon which the law is thought to be based.

science A general term whose use has varied in different historical periods. In contemporary thought generally taken to refer to organized studies or research in physics, chemistry and other disciplines where principles and evidence bearing on them are thought to be capable of rigorous proof and testing. There is no single theory of science. The expression is sometimes used to mean organized knowledge of any kind. The social sciences are often referred to as though they are not really sciences at all. On the whole it is probably more defensible to distinguish between high-grade rational enquiry, some of which is scientific, and other forms of activity. On this view, not all science is high grade or rationally defensible.

scientism   Method or doctrine deemed to be characteristic of scientists. Often used pejoratively to indicate a belief that scientific modes of thought in a particular case are being applied though inappropriate to the question in hand.

sciolism   Superficial pretence at knowledge.

social/society   The words are notoriously ambiguous. 'Society' can mean the rich at play, or be taken to refer to the people within a national boundary. Following Russell, we can refer to society as a logical construction out of individuals. This implies that society is an abstraction with no claims over individuals. At a more neutral level it is perhaps best to treat 'society' in the same way as 'democracy' or 'freedom' and regard it as a weasel word until a defensible use is offered.

subjectivism   In its simplest form, the position held by someone who believes that all moral attitudes are merely a matter of personal taste (Flew, 1984). Generally held to be the antithesis of objectivism. Cognate forms include relativism, the idea that moral values are valid, if at all, only for the groups who hold them or for a particular epoch.

truth   There are many theories of truth, none of which is satisfactory. Theories include the correspondence theory, the pragmatic theory and the coherence theory. Particular truths are less problematic than truth in general. It is probably advisable to discover the particular requirements that people have for the concept in a particular context. Some require truth to be certain and infallible; others are prepared to settle for probability. It is usually possible to tell whether people are lying or reporting accurately. The problem is not, in my view, of discovering what truth is, but of why we should feel a need for a single word to cover such a wide variety of matters.

utilitarianism   In general the notion that an action, state, process, etc. is good or right insofar as it causes more good than ill to be produced. Some see the end as pleasure; Bentham saw it as utility. This last has had a profound effect on economic theory with frequent changes of alias. One of the major doctrines in ethics.

values   A general term referring to those things which people regard as good, bad, right, wrong, desirable, justifiable, etc. We can speak of 'truth values' ('true' or 'false'), and of value judgments which are statements about what is valued, sound, deplorable, skilled, etc. It is useful to distinguish between technical, prudential and moral values.

weasel word A word used for the purpose of removing any real force from the expression containing it (*COD*). Many of the key expressions in ethical discourse can be, and often are, used as weasel words. The process is creative and sometimes difficult to pin down.

PREFACE

The systematic treatment of industrial values, or *business ethics*, has been relatively neglected in Britain, where the Industrial Revolution is generally considered to have originated. This relative neglect applies in other mature economies. A great deal more work on the subject has been done in the United States of America, the richest large industrial power, where there are hundreds of courses on business ethics taught to managers and to students of management. Nearly all the books on the subject (and there are relatively few of these) are published in America, although interest, for example, in The Netherlands can be seen from a conference at Nijenrode (Van Dam and Stallaert, 1978). The reasons for this relative neglect at one level are not difficult to find. One such reason is that the rise of the *social sciences* has been seen as replacing the literary and philosophical speculations that were common until the early decades of the present century. The field, which had been left to historians, radicals and apologists, came to be dominated by an urge to describe, measure, count and model. Political economy (despite occasional attempts to reassert itself) has been replaced with economic science, econometrics and positive economics. This last outlook has dominated economics at least since the 1960s, though it has never been without serious critics (Mishan, 1981; Sen, 1987). Social scientists have covered the field of practices in industry in their analysis. Economic, social, political and organizational studies have produced rich insights and much counting and measurement. From time to time, writers have drawn attention to what they saw as biases inherent in the scientific tradition in these matters (Winch, 1958; Silverman, 1970; Routh, 1984). It is not obvious that the performance of industry on any measure has been enhanced by this knowledge, but the contrary is not obvious either. How industry would have fared without the benefit of economic models and econometrics, management techniques, or social survey analyses is subject to much debate, but even if there were definitive ways of estimating the overall effects over time of particular techniques and policies, such as economic demand management techniques, group dynamics or 'management science' techniques, or for that matter 'incomes policies', the problems of 'historical explanation' (Dray, 1957, 1964, 1980) are serious enough to indicate that the limitations of these recent fashionable modes of thought are severe. The difficulties are compounded by the largely unre-

xix

solved problems of 'counterfactual conditionals'—the problem of what would have happened if certain policies had not been pursued or certain techniques used or not used (Goodman, 1965). The problems raised go to the centre of matters related to industrial growth and performance: would pay and costs have been lower if unions had been weaker in the 1950s and 1960s? Is 'incomes policy' counterproductive? Does the 'welfare state' undermine people's self-reliance? Have unions redistributed income? Has the contemporary weakening of trade unions through unemployment and regulatory legislation, particularly in Britain, effectively controlled inflationary pay rises? Has inflation been controlled? Simply putting the question raises a complex mixture of fact, myth, fiction, forecast and ideology, all of which are intermingled with many values at many levels; technical, prudential and moral (including moral values relating to the biases in collection, presentation and use of statistical, and therefore supposedly 'empirical' data).

The general justification for the modes of thought that exclude the systematic handling of values is that of *positivism* and its cognate ideas, i.e. that the prediction of the behaviour of 'variables' is possible and sufficient, and free from values of any kind. Values, when they are admitted to exist, are seen on this theory as the ends of action, and the proper province only of politicians and the electorate (or occasionally of the professional analysts when they speak in a private, not a professional capacity). They are seen as so because values are held to be incapable of scientific or objective analysis, matters of opinion to be left to others than scientists. As it happens, there has been a very detailed debate on these matters, not only in business affairs. It is a central issue in the philosophy of science and can be traced back for a couple of millennia.

Values, technical, prudential and moral, *can* be treated systematically and this book attempts to do so. It draws upon the management tradition in various disciplines. The tradition is usually thought of as originating in responses to the rapid growth of bureaucratic forms of organization in the nineteenth century, but not analysed systematically until Max Weber's work, which was not incorporated into the management literature until the mid-twentieth century. The major point of departure for management thought is usually taken to be the work of Frederick Taylor in the early twentieth century. Taylor was a practical engineer, a management writer, a campaigner for 'scientific management', and a major influence (Sofer, 1972). Taylor himself did not claim that values could not be treated systematically. He did treat them as obvious and linked to the common *goals* of prosperity and *efficiency*. A great deal of management thought is derived from Taylor's work, or is a reaction to it. The book draws on these lines of analysis. It also draws upon the economic tradition and on the ideas of moral philosophers and others. The theoretical arguments and the detailed case material bring out the complexity of the issues and their sheer variety and pervasiveness. The variety and complexity of issues in business ethics suggest that an attempt be made to reduce them to a manageable number. This can be done in a variety of ways, and can be as a major function of theories in the area. The number and variety of theories themselves is, unsurprisingly, an issue in itself, or rather raises a number of issues. Each theory can be regarded as a way of resolving issues, or of drawing boundaries in such a way that the number and variety are reduced to manageable proportion. The complexities of the substantive issues and the problematic nature of attempts to reconcile rival theories or to assert the dominance of one over the other calls, I believe, for an attempt to reduce the practical and theoretical issues to manageable levels in ways that are capable of identifying criteria and methods for *improvement* of industrial practice. Any attempt to do so must, of necessity, meet the criticism that it is presumptuous to attempt to tell business people and trade unions (for example) how to go about their business. On the other hand, what they do affects the rest of the community, and it is arguably irresponsible for academics to take one side or another when a duty is owed to both at the least. Theorists and teachers of business ethics can justifiably show how reconciliation of differing viewpoints can be achieved, or point to ways forward that are unseen by practitioners. It is possible to be impartial and objective without being irresponsible. Since the issues are complex, an attempt is made to take representative issues from a smaller number of detailed cases. The book should be accessible to managers, trade union members, shop stewards, administrators, and students on business courses ranging from professional examinations to postgraduate courses in business administration.

The main argument in the text is that values, moral and non-moral, can be handled systematically, and that business and industrial practices can be objectively evaluated from a moral (ethical) point of view. For instance, it will be argued that the behaviour of nineteenth century industry can be evaluated in moral terms. The notion that only the standards of nineteenth century are relevant to such as evaluation will be shown to be inadequate. Contemporary industrial practices in 'free market' and in 'centrally planned' economies are equally capable of evaluation against a common standard. The analysis can extend to 'macro' issues (i.e. large-scale matters) such as the distribution of income and power, the closed shop, union democracy, the control of employment levels, and of the control of the financial system, where there has been a recent explosion of moral issues in business.

Business ethics is by no means only about malpractice or pathological conditions in business. We can say, with John Hospers (1978), that for all its faults the free market, or capitalist system, is superior to a totalitarian one, or with the 'industrial democrats' that the imbalance of power inherent in current company law can be countered efficiently and fairly. The matter of whether industrial practice improves over time is decidable. The tolerance of different institutions, such as pressure groups, consumer associations and independent trade unions, can be cited in support of the view that improvements do occur. Many firms make provision for the use of management principles that are held to be 'enlightened' in governing the relationships between companies, consumers, employees and public. Thus I hold that business, government and trade unions are neither generally corrupt nor able to provide general grounds for complacency. The successes in investigating behaviour and in finding methods of technical improvement by material technologists and social scientists are identifiable (if not measurable) in terms of their general impact. They need to be supplemented by *moral* investigations. This is the stuff of *business ethics*.

The question of whether firms will do good by doing well, or vice versa, is sometimes asked and sometimes dismissed; there is much scope for rational argument here. It is not obvious that high ethical standards are too expensive to acquire, or without costs in efficiency terms.

One of the core propositions of the book is that it is possible to give an *objective* (in several senses of the word) analysis of business standards—that business ethics is not just a matter of taste. Ethical arguments vary in quality and plausibility. Alternative options can and should (in my view) be welcomed, as should differences in values and preferences, but there are limitations, not least of a logical kind, to what is reasonable. Thus to claim that objective analysis is possible is not the same thing as taking sides in a debate with subjectivists, or to claim that all issues are decidable on present knowledge.

The analysis in the book will show, I believe, that improvement is possible, and that there is no adequate general ground for 'forlorn scepticism' or cynicism in relation to business and industrial (including industrial relations) practice, any more than there is ground for complacency in these matters.

The recent growth of the specialist literature in business ethics is encouraging, but carries dangers with it: business ethics could become an isolated specialism with little influence on decision makers. It would not be the first to suffer that fate. From time to time the literature in industrial relations, personnel management, operational research (now known more usually as 'management science') and organizational behaviour carry debates on the 'low rate of take-up' of their ideas, the ignorance of them at the top levels of management, or the isolated and mistrusted position of specialists. There is little evidence as yet of business ethics becoming integral to even the most closely related managerial and business literature, such as that of organizational behaviour, industrial relations or marketing or finance. Much, though by no means all, of what does appear has a clear 'prudential' tone, suggesting that industry and unions should act ethically out of self-interest, rather than principle. As it happens, the relationships between matters of interest and matters of principle are complex, and merit much close attention. Emphasis on 'pure' business ethics, perhaps as a manifestation of fear of 'casuistry', will lead to a retreat to the infamous 'ivory tower', whence the influence and impact will be negligible (Mitchell, 1968; Donaldson and Waller, 1980). Scholarly disciplines tend to draw boundaries that can be indefensibly narrow (Flew, 1973; Lupton and Donaldson, 1985) favouring some kinds of data at the expense of others. Thus 'mainstream economics' tends to identify 'statistical' with 'empirical', and to exclude all other kinds of evidence other than other writers' opinions, and to insist that only some kinds of methods are proper (or, more usually 'scientific'). The word 'scientific' all too easily can become a 'weasel word', full of emotive meaning but devoid of sense. Such paradigms of substance and methods are restrictive in nature, and patently do not fit the requirements for coming to terms with major changes in circumstances. In industry it has clearly led to the resistance to change so eloquently documented in the management literature. In the literature it has led to some obvious biases: managerial, manufacturing and methodological (Donaldson and Sheldrake, 1987).

Much of the impetus for the growth of the literature and for explicit incorporation of values in business practice has come from religious, and in Europe and North America, specifically Christian sources. It will be clear I hope from the text that I am advocating a pluralist stance, which recognizes and welcomes diversity of values, beliefs and conviction, but also recognizes the age-old problems of reconciling freedom and order (Hobbes, 1651; Rousseau, 1972; Hare, 1963). There are enough uncertainties to warrant a degree of scepticism about most systems of belief, but as Hume long ago pointed out, even the most committed sceptic must make some unproved assumptions (Hume, 1779).

In business ethics there *are* arguments that I believe to be compelling and some major issues that I believe to be incapable of resolution. Moral codes and other sets of norms are in fact enforced, for example by the state, in legislation, and by groups at work, as well as by a variety of institutions (Roethlisberger and Dickson, 1939; Brown, 1954; Cartwright and Zander, 1962). This is inevitable, but the problem is not whether such processes occur, but how they can be guided constructively. This may involve recognition of inevitable conflicts, and the skilled handling of them. The alternative, favoured by human relationists, of trying to eliminate conflict, and that favoured by most management custom and practice, of not facing up to it until it is too late, are clearly inferior to the systematic handling values. All these practices are capable of constructive moral evaluation. Codes, once enforced, can lose their moral status. They need to be renewed by critical evaluation, and proper procedures for amendment. The variety in business in these matters demonstrates that some at least are conscious of it.

The manifold issues and ways of dealing with them can usefully be reduced to a number of 'key issues'. The answers given to these determine the kinds of issues that can be raised or are judged to be beyond the scope of the subject, the kinds of evidence that can be accepted, and norms of relevance. The need to identify such key issues arises from consideration of the role of the study of business ethics and the consequences for its status and influence of drawing its boundaries too narrowly or too broadly. Drawn one way, business ethics would necessarily retreat to the ivory tower. Drawn another it could be put to the service of particular interest groups or ideologues. Scholarship requires the constant review of discipline boundaries and of favoured methods if these consequences are to be avoided. Business ethics is too new for any of these failings to have become manifest, and may yet manage to evade them.

PART ONE

The Ground Rules

CHAPTER ONE

Standards and Values in Business and Industry

The Scope for an Ethics of Business

Business practices and standards of conduct vary from time to time and place to place. On the whole, factories, mines and offices are safer in such developed countries as those of Western Europe and North America than they were in the nineteenth century. Other conditions of work have improved dramatically, as hours of work have fallen from typically in excess of 60 per week in the mid-nineteenth century to less than 40 hours now. Lord Shaftesbury's 'Ten Hours' legislation was introduced to the British Parliament in the 1840s and effectively passed, amid much opposition and after much campaigning.

The following example of office regulations, dating from 1852, gives the flavour of commercial attitudes and life in what were no doubt some of the better establishments.

OFFICE STAFF PRACTICES

1. *Godliness*, *Cleanliness* and *Punctuality* are the necessities of a good business.

2. This firm has reduced the hours of work, and the Clerical Staff will now only have to be present between the hours of 7 a.m. and 6 p.m. on weekdays.

3. Daily prayers will be held each morning in the Main Office. The Clerical Staff will be present.

4. Clothing must be of a sober nature. The Clerical Staff will not disport themselves in raiment of bright colours, nor will they wear hose, unless in good repair.

5. Overshoes and top-coats may not be worn in the office, but neck scarves and headware may be worn in inclement weather.

6. A stove is provided for the benefit of the Clerical Staff. Coal and Wood must be kept in the locker. It is recommended that each member of the Clerical Staff bring 4 pounds of coal each day during cold weather.

3

7. No member of the Clerical Staff may leave the room without permission from Mr Rogers. The calls of nature are permitted and Clerical Staff may use the garden below the second gate. This area must be kept in good order.

8. No talking is allowed during business hours.

9. The craving of tobacco, wines or spirits is a human weakness and, as such, is forbidden to all of the Clerical Staff.

10. Now that the hours of business have been drastically reduced, the partaking of food is allowed between 11.30 a.m. and noon, but work will not, on any account, cease.

11. Members of the Clerical Staff will provide their own pens. A new sharpener is available, on application to Mr Rogers.

12. Mr Rogers will nominate a Senior Clerk to be responsible for the cleanliness of the Main Office and the Private Office, and all Boys and Juniors will report to him 40 minutes before Prayers, and will remain after closing hours for similar work. Brushes, Brooms, Scrubbers and Soap are provided by the owners.

13. The New Increased Weekly Wages are as hereunder detailed:

Junior Boys (to 11 years)	1/4d
Boys (to 14 years)	2/1d
Juniors	4/8d
Junior Clerks	8/7d
Clerks	10/9d
Senior Clerks (after 15 years with owners)	21/-d

The owners recognize the generosity of the New Labour Laws but will expect a great rise in output of work to compensate for these near Utopian conditions. The above were the regulations for a Burnley cotton mill office in 1852.

Source: Anon.

Legislation to control conditions in factories was slow in making its appearance after the onset of the Industrial Revolution. The first factory legislation in Britain, introduced by the elder Sir Robert Peel, was entitled 'The Health and Morals of Pauper Apprentices Act', in 1802. According to J. Wesley Bready:

> In 1802 Peel passed an act to protect little "apprentices"; it, however, had no application to any children save cotton mill "apprentices", all other young-sters being left "free" to make their own bargains and to work twenty-four hours a day if the masters so desired. This measure limited apprentice labour to twelve hours daily, exclusive of meals, and forbade night work, but the masters greeted it with a storm of protest, crying loudly that they would all be ruined. It was soon discovered, however, that no effective means were provided for enforcement: the Act had no teeth, and because of this deficiency it was doomed to be worthless. (Bready, 1926, pp. 175–176.)

The same fate, for no fault of Peel's, befell his later attempt, in 1819.

The contemporary combination of statutes and regulations governing shops, offices, mines and vehicle conditions is complex and voluminous. The British Health and Safety at Work Act (1974) combines regulation, codes and representative committees and incorporates the former inspectorate within the Health and Safety Executive. The Act requires employers whose business is over the minimum size to set up safety committees through the trade union machinery. The Act, passed by a Labour Government, was retained by the Conservative one that followed it.

Suffering a major setback in the 1980s' recession in terms of numbers, the British trade unions have grown in size and influence to the point at which membership is effectively total in some industries. It is indeed quite common for British commentators to suggest that trade unions, having played an important role in checking the excesses of rapacious nineteenth century industrialists, have now pushed the balance in the opposite direction, and have thus outlived their usefulness. They have been criticized on many ethical grounds throughout their history, albeit with varying conviction and popularity. Issues surrounding the trade unions figure prominently in subsequent chapters. For the present it is sufficient to note that their growth in Britain and USA and Western Europe at least has been associated with improvement in working conditions. Whether the link is causal, and in which direction the causality runs, is also a matter for later discussion. The growth in unions has been associated also with legislation. The British Trade Disputes Act of 1906 essentially set up a system of immunities, which have been eroded, partially restored, or removed via statutes, decisions of the courts, and policy measures by governments. The American system of positive legal rights for trade unions dates from the Wagner Act of 1935. Recognition cannot be enforced in Britain, as demonstrated by the Grunwick dispute of 1977 (Rogaly, 1977). These differences in legal position account, in part, for some of the forms which ethical discussions have taken in the two countries.

The development of collective bargaining has reduced the arbitrary treatment of employees by managers and employers. Most managers, in large organizations at least, seem to welcome this development in Britain, though 'most' would be a serious exaggeration in America. There are signs that some observers think that the process has gone too far, though class warriors on both sides have long held strong and opposing views on the matter. In 1980 a British Minister for Employment indicated in a television enquiry that the only reason (ironic in his view) why people could be sacked was for refusing to join a trade union.

Unemployment has generally shown a downward trend during most of the twentieth century, despite reversals in the inter-war period and in the 1980s. Even though the precise effects of the presence of social security systems is controversial, there is a substantial consensus that some provision should be made. A thoroughgoing 'Social Darwinism' that advocates the 'survival of the fittest' can be safely regarded as outside the mainstream of opinion. The list of achievements in relation to conditions of employees, customers, third parties and investors in relation to business is easily verified. The same applies to matters which affect industrial performance but are not directly related to business practice: public health provision, eradication of diseases such as smallpox, cholera and tuberculosis. These are substantial achievements. None of these has been uncontroversial at all times, and many have had persistent opposition from pressure groups. For instance there has been opposition to inoculation on religious grounds and to provision of fluorides in public water supplies on grounds that vary. The matters have nevertheless been or become accepted as part of the consensus of opinion. The fact of 'improvement' has been relatively uncontroversial, although there have been many serious critics of the manner in which the improvements have been achieved. This relative lack of controversy on many of the (non-industrial relations) issues can be easily explained by reference to three factors.

First, and most importantly, there is a wide measure of agreement that these things are worth having—the 'ends' of health, freedom, high income and safety are valued virtually universally. Most of the items can be described and evaluated statistically in ways that make it impossible to doubt sensibly that improvement has been substantial. There is much historical evidence which compares conditions and relationships over time, from the use of labour-saving domestic appliances to improvements in the housing stock, freedom to take holidays abroad, and much else. The persistence of poverty, arbitrary treatment, exploitation, occupational ill-health, and indeed the return of some of these recently in areas where they were thought to have been eradicated, are matters on which concern is frequently noted, but the absence of benefits in one place does not invalidate arguments for their presence in others. The distribution may be problematic, but the existence of improvements is not.

Second, the statistical evidence of reduction of working hours and of the incidence of the diseases mentioned, of growth of income and reduction of unemployment and its reversal, is powerful enough to establish the general proposition.

Third, the improvements are often within the memory of the public. To deny the fact of progress in many areas would be to go against the common experience of many people.

The rapacious industrial system of the early nineteenth century has thus been reformed, and the reforms have worked within what is usually held to be basically the same 'free market', 'enterprise', 'free enterprise' or 'capitalist' system. At this stage in the argument, objections might be raised to the use of such expressions as 'progress', 'improvement' and 'rapacious industrial system' as tendentious. Would it not be better, or at least more appropriate, to speak in more neutral terms, of 'expansion of incomes', 'eradication of epidemic diseases', or 'growth of collective bargaining'? The answer is that it would obscure the issues rather than clarify them to do so. The notion of 'appropriate' implies values or norms of relevance, fitness for purpose, and implies agreement on purposes. Growth of income is growth of those things that are held by those who compile the figures to be worth counting and measuring, and are much to do with the concerns of administrators, thus being far from neutral. It cannot be taken for granted that the data collected and the picture given by administrators is neutral between their interests and values and those of the people subject to their decisions. At the gross level, it is possible to argue that growth as measured does in fact represent the values of administrators and public, but we *are* dealing with values, rather than neutral 'data'. My argument is that on the whole the various indicators do amount to a generalized meeting of values held by people, and that the values are defensible—but this is a far cry from taking it for granted that to say that there is more of something is to say all that needs to be said. The logic of these matters is that of the prescriptive use of language. The prescriptive issues do not disappear when masked by superficially neutral language or grammatical forms that seem to imply neutrality. 'Growth', 'income' and 'progress' are terms that have evaluative components as well as descriptive ones. It does not help to substitute 'scientific' for 'appropriate' in these contexts. 'Science' and 'appropriate' are expressions with very many uses, overtones and meanings: to prescribe a use is a value process. It is better to stick to plain language, and speak of 'progress' or 'improvement' as useful but problematic expressions—as are 'science' and related notions.

One of the most widely discussed topics in business ethics in America has been whether the capitalist or free enterprise system (the terms are often used interchangeably) can be shown to be the embodiment of justice, in addition to producing an impressive flow of goods and services. The topic will be raised in later chapters, but for the present it is sufficient to note that the system has shown itself to be capable of reform and improvement.

The consensus begins to break down when we consider the explanation—the causes and significance—of the rise in industrial and economic standards. Some countries have not achieved many of the standards visible in America, West Europe and Japan, despite, in some cases, strenuous efforts and much assistance to do so. This is particularly true of some 'developing' countries, where economic development has been elusive. In others, the development effort has extended little further than extraction of resources. Where this is so, the ethical issues are a good deal clearer than in the cases where development effort has been substantial and unmatched by achievement. It is important to note that 'free enterprise' is no automatic producer of growth, or of welfare, reform, or of any particular set of values or ends. It produces no value-free techniques that guarantee or even make probable the attainment of agreed 'ends'. The techniques it does produce, of production or of management and administration, are associated with a highly varying rate of economic growth between countries. If growth produces welfare, without the intervention of values, then the system is an uncertain producer, and the causes of differences in rates of growth are unknown, though often guessed at. To say that the free enterprise system does not automatically provide for the principal values held by communities is not to say that it is not a morally 'good' system, because to say so is not to make any moral evaluation at all about it. What can be said is that the system may be judged fairly, according to technical norms within economic theory, to be an uncertain provider of those goods and services that are relevant to ethical matters of lifestyle. It cannot be said that it produces the moral or ethical ends desired by any community. This is so for a large number of reasons: the ends themselves cannot be deduced from first principles or 'from common sense' as much of economic reasoning tries to do. The ends can easily change, and there is no known way of estimating whether any large-scale system can meet all the ends, or can be consistent with any universally held system of values, even if we assumed them to be constant over millennia. Another ground is that, for cogent reasons, the law has always claimed precedence over contractual relationships, including implied ones, such as occur in economic interactions (Devlin, 1965).

The issue of whether the economic system can provide a set of technical concepts pointing to mechanisms that generate values universally held, or at least which *ought* to be universally held, though important, cannot be solved by avoiding value-laden language. If it can be solved at all, the problem will be solved by reference to value concepts and the evidence bearing on them. Thus, the notion that standards can and do rise over time, within the free enterprise system, can be assented to. At the same time, someone assenting to the proposition can logically take a wide variety of stances on the system itself, including enthusiastic support, indifference or hostility. The issue is live, but not, in my view, a 'key issue' in business ethics.

Standards, then, can and do rise over time, but they vary over time and between countries. Historical and international comparisons are made between growth rates, between alternative institutional arrangements and between economic systems. Such comparisons are legitimate, though much more problematic than supposed by those who seek to transplant, say Swedish or Japanese industrial relations practices in Britain. In sum, standards do rise, but the discussion of them is a matter for moral as well as technical reasoning. Progress (however unfashionable the word happens to be currently) is implicit in notions of growth and in arguments about whether or not the free enterprise system is the embodiment of justice, as can be seen from the stimulating discussion of the subject by Hospers (1978).

When attempts are made to *explain* the rise and variation in standards, the consensus gives way to what can best be described as a tangle of difficulties, against which the technical problems of comparing growth rates or transferring institutions are comparatively simple, though not trivial. These difficulties are illustrated by means of a number of arguments that are often used in conversation, and in some cases frequently appear, in one form or another, in the various literatures. They are introduced in the next section.

Is Business Ethics Possible?—Some Sceptical Arguments

The Argument from Special Circumstances
It is possible that the standards attained at some times and in some places are unsustainable. Many economic commentaries now regard it as beyond doubt that the high employment levels of the 1950s and 1960s resulted from techniques suggested by Lord Keynes in the *General Theory of Employment, Interest and Money* (Keynes, 1936). Keynes' notion of 'the demand gap' indicated that unemployment in a recession or slump could arise from a deficiency of income, so that, given slack resources (unemployed people and equipment), an economy could be expanded beneficially, at least up to the point at which unemployment is low, after which serious problems of inflation (rising prices) would follow. It was believed in the 1960s quite generally, if not universally, that the Keynesian system had eliminated the trade cycle and abolished high levels of unemployment. Worries began to develop that Keynes' methods led to insoluble problems of inflation and, indirectly, to industrial decline, as well as to 'excessive union power' derived from labour shortages. The inherent faults thought to reside in the Keynesian system together with the rise of Far Eastern economies, such as those of Japan and Korea, are held to demonstrate that the standards achieved in the 1960s are unrepeatable and arose from the use of an economic policy derived from Keynes that could only work

over a short period, and only once. It is true that the argument is often accompanied by propositions to the effect that some of the values and standards achieved by Keynesian methods can be achieved by 'better' methods, such as a firmer commitment to enterprise, but in the context of the present argument such notions tend to be accompanied by an insistence that some at least of the old standards must be sacrificed to these ends. They include the levels of unions' control over workplace practice (especially in Britain) and expectations of secure employment. The argument is typical of moral arguments, in that the ends held to be desirable and the means held to be necessary to achieve them are all in dispute. The means themselves take on also the character of values in themselves.

In brief, the argument from special circumstances holds that the rise in standards is technically determined, and in some circumstances can only be partially retained by sacrifice of some values, moral and technical, and their replacement by others. In the hands of politicians, this tends to degenerate to the undebated replacement of one set of values by another, on the grounds that the favoured set (favoured by the politicians) is one that is technically imperative, and happens to be a better set of values anyway. The rise and decline of Keynesianism and the rise and decline of its rival, 'monetarism', provide fascinating examples of slithering between advocating 'technical necessities' on moral grounds and dressing moral arguments up as technical ones. The technical merits of the arguments are beyond the scope of this book. Excellent expositions in technical guise of the main contending arguments can be found in the standard economic textbooks, and of other analyses of the state of industry in relation to the prospects for economic growth. The reader is referred to them (Lipsey, 1963; see also Blackaby, 1981; Elbaum and Lazonick, 1986.) On the basis of the argument from special circumstances, progress has technical limits, and is perhaps seen as not really progress anyhow. Whether progress (or its fashionable substitute expressions) has technical causes and only technical causes, as well as technical limits, is a different line of argument, discussed next.

The Argument from Group Interests
The growth of joint regulation of work by managers and trade union representatives has been a virtually universally acknowledged, if not necessarily approved, feature of the industrial process. It would be wrong to give the impression that the growth of unions has been either universally opposed or universally welcomed by managers. Indeed, the growth has been strenuously resisted by some managers, some firms, regions and industries. The growth has made more headway in Britain than in America. Unionization of the British labour market at its peak reached

somewhat over 50% before the onset of the recession in the early 1980s. Unionization of the American labour force is currently estimated at less than a third, and commonly thought to be falling. Not all observers are so certain of the decline. Speaking particularly of the private sector, Freeman observes:

> Will the proportion of the private work force that is organised continue to decline in the remainder of the twentieth century or will unionism grow once again? It is difficult to answer this critical question because union growth has rarely taken the form of a readily predictable gradual increase. Unionisation tends to occur in sudden sharp spurts as in the 1930s, often when analysts are belaboring the loss of union vitality. (Freeman, 1979, p. 156.)

In Britain at least, the argument that unions have forced standards and therefore costs that cannot be afforded on industry has commanded widespread support. We are not concerned here with the truth or falsity of the argument, but only with noting its influence. What I have called "the argument from group interests" is the idea that standards, such as those governing health and safety, hours of work, pay and other conditions, are determined in the long run by the interplay of power strategies and tactics. Thus, in the 'Keynesian' era, unions could enforce 'overmanning' and favourable *contracts* (America) or *agreements* (Britain). By the 1980s power had swung to the employers, and a few old scores were settled. In Britain, the 'Salford Plastics Dispute' in 1987 gives a dramatic example of a reversal of union power, as shop stewards were fired and safety standards (according to contemporary press reports) fell dramatically (Foot, 1987).

Again, the merits of the case are not under discussion here. The argument under discussion is that standards are determined by the requirements of whoever has the power to enforce them, or, as Thrasymachus puts it in a famous passage in Plato's *Republic*, "justice is the interest of the stronger". The idea that the standards of the 1960s and early 1970s were temporary is further reinforced by the development of robotics and other forms of 'new technology'. These are widely held to make high levels of unemployment inevitable for ever. The argument from special circumstances and the argument from group interests thus reinforce each other.

The Argument from Technique
A third modern line of approach is sometimes taken. Though it is difficult to find definitive expressions of it, the argument is influential. On this view, the idea of progress is itself seen as an illusion. Classic statements can be found in Rousseau's *Social Contract* (Rousseau, 1762). As Plamenatz puts it:

> In the eighteenth century, as never before, men had come to believe in progress. They were exhilarated by the quick growth of their knowledge,

their power over nature and their wealth. Mandeville, Hume and the Utilitarians in Britain and the Encyclopaedists in France welcomed this great accumulation of knowlege and wealth. They did not deny that knowledge and wealth... were still confined to the minds and pockets of only a small part of the community; they even admitted sometimes that men were more unequal in their day than they had been in the past. But this inequality did not disturb them, for they believed that all classes were gainers... (Plamenatz, 1961, p. 419.)

Plamenatz sees Rousseau as reversing the earlier, mediaeval argument that inequality (for example) is an effect of 'man's corrupted nature': corruption was an effect of inequality:

How, according to Rousseau, does inequality corrupt? It magnifies vanity and its evil effects, and it also makes the poor subservient to the rich. It creates such differences between men, exalting some, and debasing others, that they are driven to care more for how they stand in relation to one another than for getting what will satisfy them. (loc. cit.)

In the Rousseau version, the development of modern states and techniques has enabled some to amass wealth, and has encouraged the growth of interest groups but has diverted mankind from realizing its potential by preventing people from giving effect to free choices, which would spring from the natural sympathy which he believed people have for one another, which enables them to work together to provide a rational balance between individual whims and the need for law and order. What would normally be taken to be 'progress', i.e. what we would now call economic and industrial growth, Rousseau saw as having retrograde effects: technical development or amassing of technical knowledge and economic wealth were inimical to progress, not providers of it. Levi-Strauss, the anthropologist, provides a twentieth century version of at least part of the Rousseauan view, that the descent of people from savage ancestors has not been a matter of development from primitive minds or primitive moral ideas to more advanced ones, but that technical change has occurred to people who were fully developed morally and intellectually in the stone age (Levi-Strauss, 1958).

The argument from technique can be seen at work in the writings of Auguste Comte, the nineteenth century philosopher. Comte held that mankind did develop intellectually, passing through a state in which phenomena (including social and political ones) were explained in theological terms, a stage in which religious explanations were replaced by philosophical speculations, and finally to a state "where people... come to see that to 'explain' is simply to describe relations holding between phenomena" (Passmore, 1957).

This notion of Comte's was to become known as *positivism*, which, as will be seen in Chapter Two, takes many forms, all of which exclude the possibility of systematic treatment of values, since the ultimate stage of development was to be descriptive, whereas values are prescriptive. The doctrines that fall under the general heading of positivism are very old. Comte's application to human affairs, if not wholly without precedent, was clear, and thoroughgoing. It allowed for progress, but only of a scientific kind, so that what might appear to some to be industrial progress or moral development could only be a kind of scientific growth, if it were to be admitted at all. It should be noted in passing that the notion even of this limited 'scientific' progress is heavily value laden. Comte's own commitments turned out to be passionate enough to found a 'positivist church' in which to worship science. Few followed him in practice, though the spirit can be seen in much of the 'scientific' literature.

It is possible to view what is thought of as 'progress' as really the outcome of people pursuing what is no more than their own self-interest. This is not the 'hidden hand' theory of economic growth, but a proposition in moral psychology. It might be argued that Sir Edward Jenner, in finding a method of inoculating people against smallpox, was pursuing what amounts to a sophisticated curiosity. It so happened that the process was useful to people, who, after a great deal of resistance on technical, philosophical and moral grounds, were prepared to adopt his methods. On this view, the process was one of the serving of mutual interests. A development of this line would be that Lord Shaftesbury, in introducing factory reform, was no more than satisfying his self-esteem, or pursuing his religious beliefs, to achieve psychological comfort. This ancient argument appears in Plato's *Republic*, in Rousseau's writings and in Bentham's:

> Nature has placed mankind under the governance of two sovereign masters, *pain* and *pleasure*. It is for them alone to point out what we ought to do as well as to determine what we shall do. On the one hand the standard of right and wrong, on the other the chain of causes and effects, are fastened to their throne. They govern us in all we do, in all we say, in all we think: every effort we make to throw off our subjection, will serve but to demonstrate and confirm it. In words a man may pretend to abjure their empire: but in reality he will remain subject to it all the while. The *principle of utility* recognises this subjection, and assumes it for the foundation of that system, the object of which is to rear the fabric of felicity by the hands of reason and of law. . . By the principle of utility is meant that principle which approves or disapproves of every action whatsoever according to the tendency which it appears to have to augment or diminish the happiness of the party whose interest is in question. (Bentham, 1789.)

This statement, which establishes at least as strong a claim for Bentham as for Adam Smith as a founder of economic theory, has been subject to several cogent criticisms: for example, the argument is circular, has no independent method of ascertaining what motives in fact prompted actions, and provides no basis for preferring the explanation to alternatives such as altruism and what we would now call 'brainwashing'. It is unhistorical in that it assumes a notion of self that is far from universal in history, as opposed to less individualistic notions, some of which take modern expression in notions of 'the selfish gene'. Thus there are many rival models, often of a circularity similar to that of Bentham's.

A development of the argument is the idea that, for example, the acceptance in the nineteenth century of public health measures, such as municipal drainage, was motivated by fear of epidemics, not by any notions of progress or responsibility, noting the influence of the Benthamite reformer, Sir Edwin Chadwick, on these measures. It may well have been so, but the presence of prudential, self-interested motive does not prove the absence of others.

The Misanthropic Argument

A fourth line is to accept that there have been improvements in public health, employment practices and consumer protection, but to interpret them as aberrations, probably arising as people get richer, allowing benefits to be distributed more widely. This view sees the existence of greed and malpractice as the normal state of mankind. Impressive lists can be constructed: insider trading in city finance houses and companies, bribery and corruption in high office, cover-ups—indeed, a rising tide of financial, administrative and business scandals is clearly visible in the 1980s. Corruption in unions, enforced membership, sell-outs, kangaroo courts and industrial disputes that do much harm to third parties can all be identified or cited as indicating the corrupt nature of people, indulged in when the opportunity arises. This, too, is an old argument, illustrated in Plato's story of the Ring of Gyges (which others did not know he possessed, but which conveyed invisibility on the wearer, who could operate the ring to return to visibility as required). According to the story, Gyges, a shepherd:

> ...managed to get himself included in the party that was to report to the king, and when he arrived seduced the queen and with her help attacked and murdered the king and seized the throne! (Plato, *The Republic*, Part One, Book Two, pp. 90–91, Penguin Edition, Ed. H. Lee, 1959).

The misanthropic argument holds that people act not only from self-interest rather than other-directed principle, but that these self-interests are necessarily destructive of others. On this view, when a business speaker shows concern for industrial growth and prosperity, this is really a coded way of demanding the opportunity to make more profit at everyone else's expense. When a trade union speaker appeals to 'the brotherhood of man', this is no more than a cynical way of manipulating people to favour the speaker's group, rather than some other. It would be pointed out that the British trade unions pass resolutions at the Annual Trades Union Congress to help the low paid employees and to move towards equal pay for women, and have done so for decades, without following the resolutions with action (*The Guardian*, 7.10.87 p. 2). Such changes as have occurred are seen as resulting from equal pay legislation, European Court rulings, and domestic court decisions. The effectiveness of American Civil Rights legislation would be seen on this view as merely the result of civil action, the subsequent legislation and action to enforce it. Assuming that there is truth in the above account of the processes by which 'progress' occurs, the implication would appear to be that people take the interests of others into account only when forced to do so, and give way on prudential grounds.

Some versions of all of the above arguments, from special circumstances, group interests, technique and misanthropy, frequently appear in what people say and write, and are often implied in what they do. They are all *ethical* arguments in that they express or imply an ethical theory or make ethical assumptions. The argument by Auguste Comte is one of the few which explicitly tries to show that *ethics* is somehow bogus, or at least replaceable by something better, namely science. As will be seen, it is no more plausible to deny the reality of ethical reasoning than it is to deny the existence of language. Ethical reasoning includes arguments as to the nature of ethical arguments and is thus self-critical.

It is suggested here that when people say that "business ethics is a contradiction in terms", or say that it is naive to suggest that business can be conducted on ethical lines, they are sometimes adhering to the 'theory-in-use' that ethical standards are very low, and that this is not surprising, given the corruptibility of people. To my knowledge, there has been no published attempt at a sustained argument to show that business ethics is not logically possible, or that standards and values of an ethical nature do not exist. As it happens, the power of group pressure and of persuasive language have been demonstrated by many psychological experiments. People are moved by appeals to freedom, democracy, loyalty and many other abstractions. Chauvinistic emotions can be stirred and people can be manipulated because of the moral persuasiveness of these concepts, not only because they pay cynical lip service to them. The particular concepts may be vague and unanalysed in most uses, but people can be manipulated by use of these concepts because they believe in them. This is one of the many versions of the 'liar paradox': if people always lied, then the truth would be generally deducible from what they said, and therefore the lies would not achieve their purpose. If people only pretended to be honest and to honour contracts and respect other people's rights, there would never be a basis for trust, and frauds and confidence tricks would be impossible. People get away with misconduct because most people are honest. Whether the force of moral obligation has its origin in a specific 'moral sense', or religious or metaphysical conviction, or in a notion of self-interest is a matter for discussion. It may well turn out to be the case that the determinants of ethical conduct involve all of these, or some mixture of some of them. The notion that rule-governed and moral behaviour stems only from self-interest is an exceedingly narrow view, with little support from experimental psychology, and no evidence of its own. It relies on an interpretation of events, states and processes in the same way as Bentham's 'principle of utility' does.

The most likely explanation of the 'progress' and rise in standards that have occurred since the beginning of the industrial revolution may well include a complex mixture of motives, chance, technique, scientific knowledge, ideology, law, and much else. What I hope the foregoing has shown is that there are no compelling reasons for excluding beliefs in ethical standards, or for believing that the processes cannot be subject to analysis and criticism in terms of specified values and the extent to which industrial practice on all sides satisfies them.

Some Standpoints in Business Ethics

The above arguments for moral scepticism are diverse and lack coherence. It would be absurd to claim that there is no truth in them. They may express some truths about how the development of the modern industrial and business system has come about and operates now. Those who argue for business ethics as a matter to be taken seriously, providing practical business guidance, can also be seen to show a diversity of opinion as to the nature of business and of ethics. 'Supporters' of business ethics include groups or schools of thought which are in fundamental disagreement over some major matters. These schools of thought reflect age-old divisions, and will be discussed in various detailed aspects in relation to business practice in later chapters. But business ethics is by no means unique in the existence of basic disagreements: they exist too on the foundations of mathematics (Korner, 1960; Wittgenstein, 1964; Flew, 1973), where there are at least three fundamentally different, rival theories: intuitionism, formalism and logicism. The plethora of theories and conclusions in economics is the subject of some well-known business jokes, and of presidential addresses of the major learned societies in economics, and of not a few books charting the 'crisis in economic theory' (Bell and Kristol, 1981; Mishan, 1981).

In the theory of organizations there are dozens of different and only partially reconcilable theories. Some authors speak of "The Organizational Theory Jungle" (Koontz, 1961). The position has changed little since then (Woodward, 1965; Morgan, 1986).

It seems clear enough that the existence of basic disagreements is a sign of vitality in serious thinking about such matters. The alarm bells should ring when attempts are made to turn these subjects into dogmas, or rival factions; such attempts are plainly visible in economics, with 'classical theorists', neo-classicists, Marxists, Keynesians and monetarists vying for supremacy, with varying degrees of dominance and oblivion in different countries.

Thinkers in business ethics do have some shared beliefs and assumptions, and despite some disagreements would probably assent with varying degrees of commitment to the proposition that business ethics can have useful practical applications, that there are at least some values that are widely enough shared to be worth analysing and even recommending. These would include, for example, the idea that the state (or 'the company') is a logical construction out of individuals. 'The company' would thus not have primacy over individuals, since it is an abstraction, used for the service of people, and not vice versa. The notion of progress would be unlikely to be lightly dismissed. Consistent with this view is the acceptance that progress is not inevitable, that falling standards, or *regression*, can occur. The possibility of new areas of application would be generally held to be open, as for example in discussion as to whether there is any obligation on business to help to preserve the earth's ecosystem.

It is not claimed here that the existence of such shared beliefs proves that they are correct or true beliefs. They are testimony to the presence of a mode of thought that is sufficiently integrated to be able to address our first theme or *key issue*, "Is business ethics possible?" This body of thought offers an affirmative answer that explains at least some behaviour in terms other than expediency, or group interests, without insisting that *improvement* and *progress* in industry are wholly determined by the application of science, technology or management technique.

As already hinted, within this area of agreement on what needs to be discussed are some major differences in approaches towards explanation and in outlook. These are based mostly on a mixture of both *substantive* and *methodological* grounds. The standpoints can best be interpreted in relation to the question: "why should some actions, states, processes, omissions or prohibitions be held to be *moral* or *ethical, good, right, proper, justifiable, correct,* or their opposites?" According to various schools answers can be offered variously as: ". . . because *ethics* is about seeking (or maximizing) the 'goods' or 'ends' that people think to be worth pursuing, such as happiness, utility, freedom, or health, which are self-evidently integral to human well-being." This *utilitarian* doctrine has many forms and has been highly influential even outside ethics, in politics and economics in particular. Its classic exponents are Bentham (1789) and Mill (1861). Opposing the *utilitarians* are those who would say in answer to the question something like, ". . . because people have a *moral sense* or *sense of duty.*" It is discoverable what actions, omissions or prohibitions, etc. are *right*. Being right is a necessary, and often a sufficient ground for doing something. Thus it is on this view morally right to obey the laws and codes or practices that have been properly made or decided. The *moral law* in particular is to be obeyed out of reverence for the law itself. This is seen as derived ultimately from a 'moral sense'. This view is known as *deontology*, and, like utilitarianism, takes many forms. A classic statement is to be found in *Groundwork to the Metaphysic of Morals* (Kant, 1785) and in Hare's *Freedom and Reason* (Hare, 1963).

Other grounds include: self-interest (egoism), love (agapism), need to conform to group norms or codes (a variant of egoism and self-interest), and many more. When it comes to theoretical ethics, the core question can be summarized as: "How can the substantive claims, or the specifics of ethical action or prohibition be justified?" Here the answers range from "by intuition" as proposed by G. E. Moore (1903) in the influential work *Principia Ethica*, or by Sir David Ross's Gifford lectures in (1939) *The Foundations of Ethics*. An alternative answer is the emotivism expounded by C. L. Stevenson in *Ethics and Language* (1945) or by A. J. Ayer in *Language, Truth and Logic* (1936). By the 1960s, some considerable synthesis had been offered by R. M. Hare in *Freedom and Reason*. Hare's grounds are several, but importantly include both the notions of duty and commitment as logically based. This work was much influenced by the formative work of Immanuel Kant, in the *Groundwork to the Metaphysic of Morals*. Yet further explanations of the grounds include the linguistic philosophy which has been influential in Oxford for some decades, for example. Exponents of this line can be found in Phillipa Foot's *Theories of Ethics* (1967); see also G. J. Warnock's *Contemporary Moral Philosophy* (1967). Yet another line is derived from the doctrine of natural rights. Early modern examples are supplied in Tom Paine's *Rights of Man*, and later expositions, based in jurisprudence, can be seen for instance in Finnis' *Natural Law and Natural Rights* (1980).

Clearly, the variety of outlooks in ethics as in other disciplines is indicative of its continued vitality, and is not a reason for abandoning the subject as too uncertain to use.

The purpose of introducing these ethical outlooks at this stage is not to attempt to reconcile the different outlooks or to adjudicate between them. The extent to which that is possible is taken up in Chapters Three and

Four. The main purpose at present is to give the flavour of the kinds of problems of substance and method that must be faced in any attempt to apply ethical values consistently to business practice.

Readers who are not familiar with the various schools of thought may wish to consult some of the texts mentioned above, or some of the introductory expositions that are listed in the bibliography, such as Frankena's *Ethics* (1963), Grayeff's *A Short Treatise on Ethics* (1980), or Finnis' *Fundamentals of Ethics* (1985).

The discussion so far has been conducted with a view to answering the first of the *key issues in business ethics*: "Is business ethics possible?" The answer offered is the affirmative one: business ethics, despite differences in standpoint among writers and practitioners, is in no serious sense a contradiction in terms: whether standards in business are high, low, rare, inconsistent or confused, it still makes sense to compare and evaluate them. Whether these comparisons and evaluations hold over long periods of time or in relation to different cultures, nation-states and groups is subject to debate, and is indeed a current issue in general ethics. A thesis of this book is that different culture at different times and places can be compared against common criteria, and that there is some point in doing so: right and wrong in business practice are not dependent upon the particular customs adopted by a particular set of people at a given point in time. The arguments surrounding the proposition are complex, and form part of Chapter Four and the theme of 'objectivism versus subjectivism'. The standpoint adopted here is by no means universally held in work on business ethics, or in ethics generally. The division between 'objectivists' and 'subjectivists' is of very ancient origin, and the terms of the debate have recently been rejected, for example by Hare (1981/1987). That neither side has been able to provide 'knock-down arguments' is testimony to the complexity of ethical ideas.

Having given reasons for believing that there are business and business-related matters to which ethical reasoning can be applied, it is appropriate to attempt to summarize the kinds of topics that have attracted serious treatment by writers on specifically *business ethics*. It will then be possible to attempt to give a more formal account of the scope and method of the subject, as I see them, and of what sources are available that can indicate what the key issues are (or ought to be).

Topics in Business Ethics

The range of topics in business ethics is potentially very wide, if not limitless. By way of illustration, the following extracts are taken from various lists in papers and collections of articles in the last decade.

In the first essay in a collection of papers published in 1978, Richard T.

De George puts the proposition that "Ethics is concerned with the goods worth seeking in life, and with the rules that ought to govern human behavior and social interaction. . ." Business is ". . . basic to human society", and, "it would be nice to show that moral action is always best for business. But this seems not to be true, especially in the short run: lying, fraud, deception and theft sometimes lead to greater profits than their opposites", hence, "moral judgements sometimes differ from business judgements" (De George and Pichler, 1978, pp. 3–4).

Thus it is not always the case that companies 'do well by doing good'. Whether business should be allowed simply to get on with the business of making profit is the mirror image of the above problem. A view is sometimes expressed that 'the business of business is business', taken to mean that business should not concern itself with moral issues. If it obeys the law and operates as efficiently as possible, it will then maximize the gains accruing to 'society as a whole'. Far from doing well by doing good, business will only do good by doing well, on this view at least. Unfortunately, there are few *sustained* attempts at explaining this view, though some well-known statements of it will be discussed in Part Three.

A European collection of papers, edited by Van Dam and Stallaert, and coincidentally published in the same year as the De George and Pichler collection, puts an opposing view to that which prescribes that business ought not to get involved in ethical matters: the business corporation must play ". . . an increasingly active part as a responsible member" (of modern society) (R. H. Viola, in Van Dam and Stallaert, 1978, p. 95). Viola sees responsibility as going well beyond profit making, providing employment or making products for sale to customers. The corporation ". . . must be in a position to improve the society in which it operates" (loc. cit).

Some of the topics included in the volumes are: whether capitalism is morally justifiable, or is, on a stronger thesis, the embodiment of justice; the notion of justice and the most likely way of meeting it; the treatment of minorities and *positive discrimination* in favour of members of them; the morality of strikes and strike violence (whichever party indulges in it); the ethics of advertising; codes of conduct; the energy heritage; famine; the behaviour of multinational companies (Kansas); standards and values in business; the nature of man; trade unionism and ethics; social responsibility; ethics and the science of decision making (Nijenrode).

The list of issues internal to firms as organizations is limitless. A few examples are: nepotism; scapegoating; excessive secrecy; transference of risk from strong to weak individuais (it is common to justify the position of owners of businesses in terms of risk, but to transfer the risk to employees in terms of redundancy); stereotyping; discrimination on irrelevant grounds; groupthink; and the many forms of 'bureaupathology'; conspiratorial politicking; failure to consult; cooking of figures for internal consumption; manipulation of agenda at meetings; falsifying of records of meetings; individual and group fiddles and rackets; promotion rules not adhered to; bribery; suppression of alternative views; in short, all the features of 'the rat race' and lack of commitment to standards, even low ones.

The range and variety of topics which express values is thus huge. The values discussed so far have been *moral* values, but it should be noted that not all values are *moral* values. Some are technical, as for example, when something is described as 'the appropriate' or 'right' tool for a particular job, or when a mathematical conclusion is judged to be true or false. Indeed, logical appraisal can be two-valued ('true' or 'false' judgments about propositions) or multi-valued: true, false, indeterminate, relevant, skilled, etc. But the use of these non-moral values is apt to raise many moral ones. Examples of the links between techniques and values are provided frequently by technology, for instance in the design of a plant or equipment that satisfies technical criteria, but puts operators or cleaners at considerable risk. A fiscal policy that raises unemployment has identifiable costs to individuals, and thus raises moral problems of distribution, where solutions are not always obvious or technical. It is true that the literature of economics, as well as ministerial statements, contains attempts to show that such effects are inevitable technical consequences of unavoidable action, but this is merely shifting the blame from decisions made by people to impersonal mechanisms such as 'immutable' economic 'laws' or inevitable trade-offs, which, of course, are unable to answer for themselves—convenient, but mute *Dei ex machina*. Occasionally the changes are rung on this theme by regarding the consequences of policy decisions as inevitable results of policies directed towards the greater and agreed good, which also is mute.

In attempting to achieve an orderly account of the interplay of values, techniques and values, it is traditional to distinguish, since Leibniz and Hume wrote in the seventeenth and eighteenth centuries, between *analytical* and *descriptive* or synthetic expressions and ideas. Values fall, if the distinction is taken to be exhaustive, as most philosophers seem to do, on the *analytical* side. They are not descriptive features, of events, states or processes, but are valuations or judgments of the importance (among other things) of the statements (Grice and Strawson, 1956; Hare, 1963). The distinction will prove to be useful as the argument unfolds, but it is important at the present to bear in mind that the most thoroughgoing attempts to describe any observation without using any analytical procedures would be faced with the impossible task of explaining how only some of the infinite number of possible descriptions of any object or 'observable' can be selected without the use of some selection process involving choices. Such choices are always value related. Indeed, the notion of choice without values (moral or non-moral) is incoherent.

By the same token it is logically impossible to offer a meaningful piece of analysis without having some descriptive content: even in 'pure' systems of symbols, the symbols themselves must be descriptively distinguishable, otherwise no argument could be shown even to be consistent. The critical point is that at the present stage of the argument, values (moral and non-moral) and 'facts' or 'theories' cannot logically be considered in complete isolation from each other. However, for logical purposes it is possible to make useful (though not absolute) distinctions between them. This point has rarely been acknowledged in the literature of business or of ethics, but seems to me to be funadamental to systematic discussion (Leibniz, 1765; Hume, 1779; Grice and Strawson, 1956; Hare, 1963).

These distinctions and their limitations should be borne in mind in the following discussions of the literatures of business and of business ethics. Two further distinctions should be noted. (a) Discussions can be of the *first-order issues* themselves, e.g. can high levels of unemployment be morally tolerated? Is the capitalist system the embodiment of justice? Should union membership agreements ('the closed shop') be banned? Should insider share dealing in companies be illegal and punished heavily? Should employees tell lies on their companies' behalf? Or, (b) non-first-order discussions include all discussions of ethical theory or of the meanings of ethical terms and all attempts to evaluate an ethical statement or argument. Non-first-order issues then are variously described as 'critical', 'theoretical' or 'methodological'. This usage is similar to the distinction often made in industrial relations between *substantive* matters (such as pay levels and systems) and *procedural* matters (such as how they may be changed). The distinction is derived from the standard logical terminology, as described in Strawson's *Introduction to Logical Theory* (Strawson, 1952).

As in industrial relations, it will be seen in business ethics that the procedural or higher order issues are the most complex, leading sometimes to the misleading conclusion that values are, for that reason 'subjective' and therefore beyond debate. The review of the literature will concentrate on procedural issues, but the distinction, like all such broad distinctions, is useful only for some purposes. To add further complication, the list of substantive issues is in part determined, for each individual, by the procedural stance taken, and vice versa.

The Literature on Business and on Business Ethics

The literature on business contains, as might be expected, a great deal of technical material that is related to particular business activities, such as the functions of *marketing, finance, business policy/strategy, personnel* or *production*. We are not primarily concerned with these literatures here, but it is important to note that moral issues are being increasingly discussed both in the technical literatures and by professional institutions. These include calls for codes of practice, for aid or support for managers at odds morally with their companies, or for protection of consumers. These add to a considerable pre-existing literature on medical, scientific and legal ethics and codes. These will be discussed in Part Three. It is very rare for books or articles on organizational behaviour or general management to contain any direct references at all to ethical matters. An exception is Elliott and Lawrence, *Introducing Management* (1985). These references are, however, brief, and judging by the fate of 'contingency theory', which has been 'the most promising newcomer' for 40 years (see Luthans, 1985), the absorption rate can be expected to be low until more research is reported in the area.

The literature of *economics* has long contained a great deal of ethical reasoning, but has also been dominated (though never completely) by 'positivist' modes of thought which seek to treat all the subjects in a way that deliberately excludes all analysis of values. This forms the core of Chapter Two, and will not be pursued further at this point except to say that the reabsorption of direct ethical reasoning in economics appears to be making a spirited return (Hahn, 1982; Sen, 1987). The literature on organizational behaviour would appear to be the natural place in which to find detailed discussions of ethical matters, but such discussions are very rare. The reasons for this are matters for speculation. The influence of the 'positivist' tradition, through the formative social scientists such as Max Weber, Durkheim, Talcott Parsons and, perhaps the Marxist schools, should be noted in this context. The historical materialism of the latter School would seem to preclude direct reference to ethics, though the language and concepts do seem to be redolent of it. Whatever the reasons, ethical matters have rarely appeared in the mainstream business literature, and the prohibition of prescription is commonplace in the social sciences. Scientists are by no means unanimous on the matter of the role of prescription. There is, however, a recent sustained expansion in the literature that is self-consciously 'business ethics'. This mostly appears in North America, with some interest in parts of Europe. There is even in Britain a strong tradition of business practice founded on clearly articulated ethical principles, ranging in the nineteenth century from the elder and younger Peel to Robert Owen, the 'Utopian Socialist' (as dubbed by Marx) and early cooperator and cotton mill owner. Included also are the whole school of thought described as 'the Utilitarians', or 'philosophical radicals'.

The Utilitarians were prominent reformers in the nineteenth century, but other prominent reformers, such as Lord Shaftesbury or Charles Kingsley, owed little to them and much to the Anglican church. The

Quaker families, and other 'philanthropists' such as Lord Leverhulme, came from varied traditions. The conclusion is that ethical reasoning and drives are much more strongly represented in business practice than could be learned from the various management literatures. In most cases, the practitioners or their institutions such as the various churches, foundations and societies, do publish regular or occasional materials that have never become absorbed into the management literature. This is also true of American organizations such as the churches, who have also had much to say on business matters. To the positivist trend already noted, we might also add the trend to secularism, including a kind of commitment to scientific ideologies that have been only loosely connected with formal 'positivist' doctrines. Whatever the causes, the general and technical literature of management provides little self-conscious ethical discussion, even though the materials presented therein often have very major ethical implications.

The first point to note in describing and evaluating the literature dedicated to *business ethics* is that of the great variety both of topics covered and of ways of dealing with them, that is the variety extends both to substance and methods. For instance, some treatments include judicial decisions such as those concerning companies, emphasizing external relations, as in Beauchamp and Bowie, *Ethical Theory and Business* (1979), whereas others are more concerned with standards at the personal level, and on decision-making processes, as in Van Dam and Stallaert, in *Trends in Business Ethics* (1978). These are edited volumes, containing the work of many authors, as is the seminal collection by De George and Pichler, *Ethics, Free Enterprise and Public Policy* (1978). The core of issues in all of the texts mentioned above includes the substantive matters of the status of the free market economic system, corporate responsibility, advertising codes, possibilities for industry self-regulation and treatment of minorities. In the April 1987 issue of *The Journal of Business Ethics*, Richard De George offers an account of the *field* of business ethics, drawn from a review of the literature:

> Business ethics is a field to the extent that it deals with a set of interrelated questions to be untangled and addressed within an overarching framework. This framework is not supplied by any ethical theory—Kantian, Utilitarian, or theological—but by the systematic interdependence of the questions, which can be approached from various philosophical, theological or other points of view. (De George, 1987, p. 204.)

He adds:

> as a field of academic investigation its aim is theoretical, even though the product has practical applications. (loc. cit.)

De George identifies in the review article three levels of analysis. The first is on the *macro* level: "the economic system of free enterprise". The second level embraces the role of corporations (and unions) within the free enterprise system. The third level is a more personal focus, and deals with individual relationships.

In terms of procedure, De George identifies five types of analysis: *Development and analysis of cases of immorality in business* (under this heading would, on my account, be included 'bureaupathology'), *empirical study of business practices, clarifying basic terms and uncovering ethical presuppositions in business, metaethical problems*, such as the moral status of corporations and finally, *the untangling of embedded problems*, such as those concerned with the *obligations of multinationals to the underdeveloped countries in which they operate* (loc. cit.).

These three levels and five modes of analysis give a succinct and illuminating account of the scope and methods of business ethics. As a field, it is one of enormous complexity. In De George's view, there is yet a need for some "consensus in determining progress and success in the field". His suggested solution is to use criteria from the relevant disciplines, further revealing of the presuppositions of business practices, study of international issues rather than inward-looking topics, and the replacement of over concern with abuses by 'positive' models of what is possible, and what might be paraphrased as 'educating the educators', i.e. encouraging teachers of business to include ethical teaching or at least to include ethical concepts. Finally, De George puts the view that further progress is most likely to come from research, as opposed to mere analysis of stances already taken.

There is little of De George's review and assessment with which the present author can disagree, and in the presence of the widespread commitment to the civilized values which De George clearly represents, his list would be near enough exhaustive to provide a complete prospectus for business ethics as a discipline and as a practical set of ideas for business. However, the rival doctrines mentioned (and others) are mutually exclusive in some respects. The tolerance of different viewpoints is a moral imperative in its own right, but the various viewpoints do have dramatically differerent implications for practice, and there may yet be major gains to be made from attempts at reconciliation or synthesis of opposing viewpoints. The resistance of other disciplines to ethical reasoning or more generally to philosophical reasoning is strong, even though examples can always be found of work against the trend. In general ethics, as opposed to business ethics, there are still rival schools of thought, and major unresolved controversies. The resistance to the inclusion of ethical reasoning is strong also among practictioners of business (albeit more so in Britain than in North America).

Expositions in general ethics have not reached a definitive account of even how many different kinds of ethical theories exist or of what distinguishes one theory from another. There are in addition cognate literatures, such as those of law, jurisprudence, organizational behaviour, economics, political theory, industrial relations and history, which discuss ethical and methodological issues. By no means all of these seek to show that values cannot be treated systematically. There is, as I see it, a need, if business ethics is to raise and maintain its level of influence, to provide convincing reasons why other disciplines should incorporate some ideas from business ethics in ways analogous to those by which business ethics learns from them.

In sum, other disciplines indulge in prescription (sometimes robustly denying it the while), and have as much to gain from the insights of business ethics as it has from them. Spokespersons for the various disciplines are prone to pronouncing on the proper role of their disciplines; such roles need to be argued for, and should be capable of development. Such justifications often run in terms of what are thought to be definitive accounts of the nature and methods of science alike. It is arguably more the duty of specific sciences to admit it when they are prescribing practice, and indeed to get on with the prescriptions, subject to informed debate, than to evade the issues altogether by appeal to spurious notions such as 'the scientific method', or to moral concepts dressed up as technical ones. Business ethics, as I see it, is entitled to devise its own criteria and proposals for improvement, drawing, where useful, on work already done in the sciences, welfare economics, or the practices in business, organizations and the professions. If this wider view of the scope and role of business ethics is accepted, then the problem of up-to-dateness in the various literatures is more acute than in the case of confining reference only to the self-consciously 'business ethics' literature.

Within the *ethics* literature, some treatments reflect religious impulses, and others are clearly secular. There is little agreement on what theoretical alternatives are, and there is no definitive classification scheme for theories. Rival groups of theorists lay claim to having identified the scope and methods and the proper agenda for the subject. Rival groups, sets, cliques, schools and the like make claims to being 'high fashion', or *sine qua non* for any serious student of the subject. Fortunately, unlike some other disciplines, no set of dogmatists has captured the territory yet. The problem is an age-old one:

> The history of any definite 'school' of philosophical opinion will generally show that its foundation was made possible by personal friendship. So few men devote themselves to continuous thought, that if several think on the same lines for many years it is almost always because they have encouraged each other to proceed. And varieties of opinion and temperament are so infinite that those who accept a new party name, and thereby make them-

selves responsible for each other's utterances, are generally bound by personal loyalty as well as by intellectual agreement. (Wallis, 1898.)

Wallis was here referring to the Benthamite or utilitarian school of 'philosophical radicals' whose influence on the reform movement and legislation in Britain in the nineteenth century was profound, and whose ideas are embedded deeply still in textbook economics in the 'classical' or 'neo-classical' schools. The variety of outlooks and the pretensions of the various *cliques* or schools present students of business ethics with a strategic problem: ideally, the most recent work should be considered alongside the 'classic' statements. On the one hand, academic controversies are often ephemeral, leaving subsequent readers (and many contemporaries) mystified as to why the controversialists thought there was a problem in the first place. The obscure boundary skirmishes of rival groups can safely be ignored, once recognized as such, but to be recognized they have to be read. A conscientious student could spend a lifetime in the libraries without reaching the twentieth century materials. But even if all 'known' groups were consulted and their output assiduously considered, a major piece of work may be in the process of development in some hitherto unsuspected quarter. There are some ethical theorists who would say, with some plausibility, that "there is nothing new under the sun", or that at least, nothing importantly new has been said for several centuries, and that all that is needed is a few timely reminders of the eternal verities. In short, complete up-to-dateness, even if it were possible, is neither necessary nor sufficient for a proper understanding of the state and nature of standards and values in business and industry. What appears to one student to be a gross neglect of an important line of thought can be sensibly seen by another to be a justifiable ignoring of some trivial and ephemeral matter. It is not sufficient that a doctrine is currently fashionable in some quarters to give it prominence. Doctrines can be, according to defensible criteria, fashionable and important, fashionable but not important, novel and trivial, novel and important (a very rare category), of great antiquity and largely resolved (a highly debatable set would go into this category), old and unsettled, long since refuted, but recurring—and much else. In very few cases is it obvious to which category ideas or topics belong, and they may yet be classified as either 'true' or 'false'.

There is thus a difference between being fashionable and being tenable, or important.

To import a term from economic theory, the market for ideas in business and in ethics is highly imperfect. For these reasons, the choice of topics has to be judgmental and argued for. A literature search is not enough. The possibility of missing some important work or of seeing it and not recognizing its importance is not negligible. Such was the fate for a long time of Hume's *Treatise of Human Nature* (1739). Wittgenstein's (1963) *Philosophical Investigations* included, apart from a brief and sketchy reference to Michael Faraday and to Aristotle, no references whatever. (The opposite problem has to be faced, i.e. that a scholar can spend so much time reading everything that has been published in cognate areas that all independent thought evaporates.) Tawney had little to say on Weber's *Protestant Ethic and the Spirit of Capitalism* when he (Tawney) first published *Religion and the Rise of Capitalism* (Weber's English translation was not available until 1930). Tawney's book on the theme was published in 1927. The Hume, Tawney, Wittgenstein and Weber books are all classics.

The literature on business ethics and on ethics generally is vital and growing. It reflects attempts to apply traditional, rival outlooks to an uncertain, but very large range of topics, many of which are claimed to be the proper provinces of other disciplines, such as politics, law, economics and other social sciences, or of 'imperializing' outlooks, such as the idea that there is a (known and definitive) 'scientific method', which lays claim to all worthwhile thinking.

Up-to-dateness is limited both as a virtue and as a possibility. The choice of traditional or contemporary literature with which to illustrate the argument has to be personal. Despite all the foregoing, it is possible and desirable to sample both the antique and contemporary texts, reviews of literature, theses and reports, unpublished and published. In all these matters, it is up to the individual student or scholar to decide on the basis of argument what is important. Fashion and rival cliques of theorists cannot relieve scholars from this responsibility.

Business Ethics: The Key Issues

An *issue* is taken throughout this book to mean any point in question or any important problem or topic for discussion. It implies that there are at least two sides to every issue, and sometimes many more. Clearly, not all issues are of the same urgency or the same level of importance. It will be assumed, for the time being at least, that there is some kind of hierarchy of issues, some being less general or less controversial than others. For instance, whether the free market system of arranging the production and distribution of income and wealth causes the distribution to be more or less unequal than in a centrally planned system is an issue of fact which is likely to have a bearing on most arguments concerning the respective merits of the systems, but it could not be decisive in any choice of system to adopt, because the spokespersons for the two systems argue principally from ideological stances. The evidence, such as it is, can always be reinterpreted (and usually is) to show that like is not really being compared with like, or that equality of income and wealth, though an important aim in some versions of both doctrines, is not the only value, nor yet the most important. In this context, freedom, efficiency, total output, and much else are typically cited.

The ethics literature contains many examples of dilemmas showing that major principles usually held to be moral imperatives can, in some circumstances, be incompatible, and yet apparently required to be acted upon. Here the problem is the particular form of the hierarchy, not the principle itself.

Some issues are such that commitment to one set of values implies commitment to another: for instance, as Hare (1963) points out, 'ought' implies 'can', but what is judged to be possible is influenced by other preferences. The actual issues raised in the literature of business ethics and in business practice, as well as in the literature of general ethics, come in all shapes and sizes. The various levels of organization, from whole economic and political systems via institutions and organizations to individual relationships, suggest one kind of hierarchy of principles. The levels of analysis, in terms of specific principles, 'middle range' and general and philosophical (including religious, theological and metaphysical outlooks), suggest another hierarchy. At one level, we could list a set of values held to be generally agreed, such as keeping promises, telling the truth, not punishing the innocent, treating other people as 'ends' not merely as 'means', and identify the issues as the extent to which these values are put into practice in business. At another level we could argue about the status of the allegedly common values themselves. At a third level, we could debate the status of the kinds of philosophical methods that are appropriate to such arguments; at the most rarified level, we could debate the nature of the absolute logical and metaphysical principles that enable such debate to take place.

(i) The first issue is thus, *Is business ethics possible?* As Gotbaum (1978) seems to imply, the methodological and metaphysical principles governing behaviour on and around the picket line would be likely to give way to tactical matters in the debate when strikers and strike breakers are considering whether to break each others' limbs, or when managers are considering whether or not to give in to what appears to be a system of bribery in obtaining major contracts. We might ask whether business ethics is likely to be influential in such circumstances, or indeed, relevant. My own view is that business ethics is indeed relevant, but the picket line and the board meeting are not always the most promising times and places to introduce it. In the case of particular events it may simply be too late to have any influence, but to say so is not to say that in the two, very common, types of situation mentioned, a range of defensible answers may not be possible. The first of the key issues to be identified follows from the discussion so far: various viewpoints are offered from time to time to show that business ethics as a discipline is not possible, and the various arguments, from special circumstances, from group interests, from technique or from misanthropy, were adduced to demonstrate the existence of this negative view. The absence of sustained arguments for these negative views is taken to be sufficient reason to regard them as non-decisive, even though they are often frequently expressed, and thus influential. They will recur in various forms in subsequent pages.

(ii) *Are values, standards and arguments in business ethics capable of objective analysis?* This is the problem that is discussed in the various literatures as that of 'objectivity versus subjectivity', in others as 'ethical or historical relativism'. In some social science literature it is referred to as 'indexicality'. It crops up in economics as the issue of 'positive' versus 'normative' economics. Lately it has been revived in management as 'the action frame of reference', but was long ago discussed in John Rex's *Key Problems of Sociological Theory*, where Rex traces it back to Max Weber. Ernst Mach and Auguste Comte in the nineteenth century were positivists, Mach being an engineer. Positivism crops up in the debates surrounding positive law ('law as command'), often associated with Thomas Hobbes' work in the seventeenth century. Vigorous statements of a subjectivist nature as well as Plato's own objectivism can be found in *The Republic*. The issue is thus of great antiquity, but some stances are often spoken of as though both newly discovered and obviously true, or false. The problem of objectivity *versus* subjectivity is a key issue because the implications for action are dramatically different between the two sets of outlooks, or at least appear at first sight to be so.

(iii) *Can general ethical principles, such as that of the 'utilitarianism' or the 'Golden Rule' be proved?* The general principles of utilitarianism and the Golden Rule provide the most systematically argued, rival general principles. They are related to, but are not the same issues as those of objectivism and subjectivism. These principles will occupy much of Chapter Four. In the meantime, by way of first approximations, the key to the *utilitarian principle* is here taken to be the idea that certain values, usually 'good' or 'happiness' or 'utility', are what human beings strive for. A good system, or a morally defensible one, or, for that matter, a good act, is one that maximizes good or minimizes 'bad' or 'pain' or some such, or produces a credit balance of 'good' or 'utility' over 'bad' or some analogous act, state, etc. that 'ought' to be avoided.

By contrast, the Golden Rule group of theories is based upon some principle of value reversal, such as 'do as you would be done by'.

Much of the present book is based on a defence of the Golden Rule-type of approach, but this does not imply that there is here held to be no merit in other approaches, or that the Golden Rule is sufficient for analysing current practices or for proposing new ones. Advocacy of the Golden Rule is consistent with the philosophical doctrine of 'pluralism', i.e. that different values, principles, beliefs, institutions, methodological outlooks (and much else) are valuable and can fruitfully coexist even when incompatible in some contexts.

This leads directly to the fourth issue.

(iv) *Can different values or sets of values be reconciled?* This may be paraphrased in terms of whether the practices of one group, nation or period in time can only be evaluated, if at all, by reference to the standards and values specific to time and place. It is often thought that the meanings of particular actions or prohibitions are different in different cultures, and that the factual circumstances and assumptions, once recognized, will make the conclusion inevitable that the practices and prohibitions are inevitable, or not the business of outsiders. There are many sides to this argument. All that needs to be said at the present stage is its truth or falsity is far from obvious.

(v) *Can different theories of ethics be reconciled?* Different ethical theories have different implications for practice (although what they have in common should not be ignored). Rival general theories have coexisted for centuries, if not millennia. None has succeeded in completely refuting the others, though some arguments for some theories have been shown to be untenable. There is no definitive account of how many theories there are, or even of how many types of theories exist in the field. Ethics is by no means unique in this. How the diversity can best be treated must be central to any study of business ethics.

(vi) *How can the boundaries between business ethics and related matters be established?* Business ethics touches upon many other disciplines, such as law, government policy, politics, psychology, economics, logic and language and much else. Drawing the dividing lines involves establishing methodological as well as substantive principles. There are no reasons for thinking that the boundaries between disciplines are fixed and immutable. A dialogue is required between methodological and substantive principles and evidence. This involves getting down to cases. Real world cases are imperative here. On these matters, a suspicion of *casuistry* based on the abuses in the seventeenth and eighteenth centuries has been mooted by Drucker (1981), the popular management writer. Such distaste for such elderly abuses is often well placed, but is not sufficient reason for deciding that business ethics is irrelevant, or must necessarily be a hired mercenary for the purpose of making managerial malpractice acceptable. In particular, one substantive issue that has been widely discussed is that of whether the free enterprise system is the embodiment of justice, or is the best way to ensure individual freedom. Interesting though the question is, there are several reasons for thinking that the matter cannot usefully be regarded as falling within the scope of business ethics. One such argument is that the matter is a political one. There may be reasons drawn from moral and political philosophy for thinking that one politico-economic system is *more* or *less* defensible than others in some respects, but they tend to raise some similar issues and some different ones. The line has to be drawn somewhere, and until the matter of which general system to choose genuinely appears on the agenda (which seems highly unlikely), business ethics could sensibly regard it as a 'brute fact' that the major industrial powers have existing systems. Many questions arise as to the legitimacy of practices within the system, and even more questions arise as to the consistency and coherence of the systems themselves. In short, neither the capitalist, 'free market' system nor any other is capable of yielding to a definitive description, still less a justification. All systems have victims. That some, on the whole, seem to 'do better' than others is not for most people a sufficient reason for advocating them.

To quote from John Hospers, referring to the state as a *leviathan* in the manner of Thomas Hobbes, the seventeenth century English political theorist:

> The free market, whatever its limitations in achieving justice in individual cases is a paragon of justice compared with this monster leviathan. If the state has taught us anything at all about justice, it is by presenting us with its very antithesis. (Hospers in De George and Pichler, 1978, p. 95.)

It would seem, however, that even the more totalitarian states do not oppress everyone, and enterprises in liberal democratic states oppress some people. The general proposition is not much comfort to the victims of either, unless they adhere to the utilitarian principle of 'the greatest happiness of the greatest number', unqualified by John Stuart Mill's scruples, and are prepared to be victims for the greater good. The demarcation problem is then a live issue.

(vii) *How can the 'abstract' principles of business ethics be translated into practice?* (criteria of and procedures for improvement). Each theoretical outlook has implications for practice. Translation into practice can be done using *codes* (legal and self-regulating), education, propaganda methods and channels, but above all, the theoretical outlooks need to be confronted by detailed evidence. How this can be done raises many issues of what is possible or prudent or in conformity with human nature and raises issues on the status and methods of the various kinds of evidence.

The drift of the argument so far is that the key issues of business ethics are methodological (i.e. procedural, critical, meta-ethical, second and higher order) rather than substantive. The final issue listed, the translation into practice, refers to some widely differing views as to the proper role of the discipline. At one end of the spectrum is the idea that the subject should be limited to interpreting what happens, and helping practitioners and clients (for example) to understand it, making the implications of practice clear. At the other end it is possible to see business ethics and its theorists as part of the system in which they live, with a legitimate active role. It could, on the latter view, properly offer help in identifying an agreed agenda for business and industry, and propose ways forward. Although the key issues are methodological rather than substantive or first order, the the way they are answered has profound implications for the evaluation of practices and proposed changes in them. Even though there is no case to be made out for business ethics to become dogma, and that pluralism is a value in its own right, theorists of business ethics are entitled to their own views and to recommend them, just as the theorists of other disciplines do. Theorists of business ethics can set an example by being open about where they stand, rather than sheltering behind an implausible 'scientific detachment'. An open-mindness and a generally tolerant outlook is consistent with having strong substantive views. Tolerance is not the same as believing that any practice or belief will do, or that any one is as good as another. Being non-dogmatic is not the same as being unprincipled, or being incapable of saying what is believed to be right or wrong.

The Language of Ethics and of Business

It is commonplace among linguistic philosophers that language has many uses. They include communication and miscommunication. Language can be used to inform or mislead, to describe, persuade, evade issues, analyse, express emotions, give warnings, amuse, entertain and much else. One person's technical terms are another person's jargon. Most groups have taboo words, and use 'buzz' words, whose purpose includes the signal that the user takes on the values of the group. Some words are often little more than slogans, or rallying cries. Among these can be included, 'democracy', 'freedom', 'the brotherhood of man', 'free enterprise', 'the market', 'maximization', 'optimization', 'science', for example. A minimum vocabulary is needed in order to use the concepts of business and of ethics. There is a vast literature on the nature and uses of definitions. For present purposes, an attempt will be made to adhere to the following principles.

(a) *Definitions* can be reports on the ways in which words have been used ('lexical definitions'). Here the *Concise Oxford Dictionary* has been chosen as a readily available authoritative source. A dictionary is not a philosophical or scientific treatise. Some concepts take on much more than can be indicated in a dictionary. There are whole shelves of books dedicated to explain such words as 'democracy', 'freedom', 'meaning', 'rationality' and many others. Definitions can also be recommendations as to the use of particular words ('prescriptive definitions'). Schools of thought often take control of particular words and word combinations and give them technical meanings which are often fed back into apparently technical advice and applied to situations in which the technical restrictions are forgotten. The economic concept of 'the market' is one case in point; the concept of motivation in organizational behaviour is another. Precise definitions when offered are usually difficut to adhere to, and too often end up with no empirical content. Their use thus ends up as mainly emotive or prescriptive, in which propaganda and ideology dominate what is often presented as rational, and perhaps scientific, enquiry. It is thus advisable, in attempts at conducting unbiased (i.e. objective) enquiry, to take care in the use of words. This often involves drawing out ambiguities in ordinary uses of expressions, and noting when technical and moral values are conflated, or when ideological stances are imported in the guise of technical language. For example, 'the optimum employment/inflation equilibrium' looks technical, but is an ideological statement.

(b) From time to time it is essential to pay close attention to the meanings and uses of particular words, such as those mentioned above, but also including 'moral', 'ethical', 'good', 'bad', 'right', 'wrong', 'analytical', 'descriptive', 'progress', 'improvement', 'efficiency', 'effectiveness' or 'fairness'. Such discussions are sometimes dismissed as 'mere semantics'. But it is clear that such attitudes miss the point. The meanings, connotations and overtones of words and phrases are deployed in inter-group and intra-group conflicts and struggles for supremacy. Words do need to be used with care, even though quick and easy definitions are not always serviceable. The language of management is rich in emotive and ideological content—so much so that one observer referred to one of the major management theories as 'orgies of avuncular pontification'. The evangelical flavour of some management texts is clearly discernible. It is no accident that one of the most common descriptions of managment spokespersons is that of 'bullshitters' and the description is by no means always derogatory, being often used with great admiration, presumably of skills in persuading people to act on information which all concerned know for certain to be both false and against their own major principles and interests.

To return to the general proposition that the key issues of business ethics are methodological in nature: support for the proposition can, I believe, be found quite generally in the management literature, and in the economic literature.

Chapter Two considers an outlook that dominates management, economics and the social sciences, and which is intended to treat business (among other matters) in a way that is policy relevant, but deliberately excludes values. I refer to the set of doctrines under the general heading of 'positivism', usually thought of as representing the 'scientific' as opposed to the unsystematic as well as the value-laden approaches to the world and to business.

CHAPTER TWO

Science, Ethics and Business Growth

The Idea of Growth and the Role of Science

This chapter addresses a set of ideas which, though of great antiquity, recur in various disciplines and schools of thought. This set of ideas is generally placed under the heading of 'positivism'. The label probably dates from the nineteenth century philosopher, Auguste Comte, but the ideas are much older. The doctrine takes many forms, but as a first approximation it can be regarded as any outlook which seeks to explain events, states and processes either in the physical sciences or in human affairs by reference to theoretical 'models' and to 'empirical' observation, excluding all 'metaphysical' or religious theories and ideas, and excluding all values. It is usually contrasted with 'normative' thinking. This last distinction is one much favoured by positivists, but rarely used by others. Different disciplines and schools have different relationships with positivist ideas, ranging from almost apologetic references to a tired old debate in politics, to almost breathless sense of revelation.

The following quotations will perhaps serve to give the flavour of the notion.

According to Charles Taylor:

> A few years ago one heard it frequently said that political philosophy was dead, that it had been killed by the growth of science, the growth of positivism, the end of ideology, or some combination of these forces, but that, wheatever the cause, it was dead. It is not my intention to rake over the coals of this issue once more. (Taylor, 1978, p. 25.)

Taylor continues:

> The view was indeed that political science has come of age in freeing itself from the incubus of political philosophy. No more would its scope be narrowed and its work prejudiced by some value position which operated as an initial weight holding back the whole enterprise. The belief was that political science had freed itself from philosophy in becoming value-free and in adopting the scientific method. These two moves were felt to be closely

connected; indeed, the second contains the first. For scientific method is, if nothing else, a dispassionate study of the facts as they are without metaphysical presuppositions and without value biases. (loc. cit.)

Taylor's own view, expressed in the article, is that the development of normative theory is virtually inevitable, and justifiable, but it helps to try to be aware of one's own values and to make attempts to avoid bias.

Stanley L. Jaki, reflecting as an historian and philosopher of science on textbooks on decision making in business, takes as examples the work of Ackoff (1962) and Churchman (1961):

> The concept of science endorsed by Ackoff and Churchman is essentially that advocated by logical positivists. Both Ackoff and Churchman stress the idea of empirical verifiability and the notion of control over data and processes as the essence of a concept of science underlying the science of decision-making in business. (Jaki, 1978, p. 141.)

In his Inaugural Lecture at the London School of Economics, Harry G. Johnson set out to show that:

> Yet Economics is essentially a *social* science, concerned to further understanding of society by the application of scientific methods of analysis and research to the economic aspects of society's activities, and the great advance of the science that has occurred in the past thirty-odd years has made it more and not less capable of illuminating social questions. (Johnson, 1967.)

According to Johnson there is such a thing as *the* economic approach to social questions, and its method, following Robbins (1935), distinguishes between

> ...an interdependent system, in which the quantities and prices reflect a balancing of opposing forces... In relation to social questions it has two important implications: that things are the way they are for some powerful reason or reasons, which have to be understood if effective social solutions are to be devised; and that any solutions so devised and applied will have repercussions elsewhere, which will have to be faced, and which ought to be taken into account. (loc. cit.)

Further:

> On the normative side, the more generally applicable concepts of economic theory are associated with the distinction between means and ends, and the problem of choice implicit in the concept of allocation of scarce resources.

and

> Much of the work of economists concerned with policy issues is devoted to sorting out the true ends of policy from the means intended to achieve those ends, and to assessing the relevance and relative efficiencies of the various

means proposed—in short, to determining what the problem really is, and attempting to evaluate the various ways of solving it. (loc. cit.)

Johnson recognized the existence, even the legitimacy, of alternative systems of values. In what he saw as a replacement of dogmatism by pragmatism, he saw a legitimate role in recognizing alternative systems of values and making policy prescriptions in terms of them. There was, however, no method of analysis of the values themselves, for instance in terms of their coherence, compatibility or acceptability. The last of these appears by implication to be drawn from claims that the theory of perfect competition has implications, i.e. 'predictions' that are similar to those of imperfect competition, such as that competition will eliminate the inefficient firms. In other words, we are presented with an impersonal system, changes in which can be predicted to some extent. Judgments about the changes are to be made on pragmatic grounds, as opposed to *a priori* grounds, and decisions as to whether a change is for better or worse are to be taken in the light of the individual case (i.e. policy change).

The idea of positivism, then, is best described by what some people call a 'programme', whose main item is to predict and explain the physical, economic, political and social world in a way in which values can be excluded altogether, or can be treated as externally determined policy options, if they are recognized at all; whose implications can be predicted, but not approved of, disapproved of, reconciled, or clarified, although Johnson would allow some limited clarification of their meaning in relation to specific disciplines.

Not all work in business and related disciplines that adopts positivist assumptions is self-conscious about it. In some cases, the work is described simply as 'scientific', 'behavioural science' or 'social science'. From the point of view of analysis of the state and growth of business, industry and the economy in general, it is not vital to show that particular theories or policies of research are positivist, or thus inspired; only that the models in use do not treat values systematically, or seek to ignore them altogether. It is the achievements and limitations of the general outlook that is important at the present stage. The actual influence and theoretical weaknesses (as well as the strengths) of the doctrine can best be seen in relation to its treatment of evidence and of practical matters.

The examples which follow all have an apparent freedom from being contaminated by values. The idea of economic and business growth in general appears, at first sight, to be a sound example of the possibility of treating important matters in a value-free way.

The Industrial Revolution was largely formed, or at least made possible, by the application of scientific and technical knowledge and of improved

methods of industrial organization. Continued economic well-being probably depends on their further development and on their wider application
in industry. This is true, I believe, for those countries which are fortunate
enough to belong to the 'developed' category and to those which are still in
the early stages of attempting to secure sustained economic growth. Such
growth is generally thought to bring choices and opportunities of a
political and moral kind, as when economic and political theorists link
the expansion of choice, the growth of the economy and especially the
'market' economy with welfare.

Following this, there is a widely held belief that economic and business
growth are sufficient conditions, together with *political democracy* for
ensuring the possibility of the expansion of choices, the realization of
values, and in particular of the value of freedom of choice. In economic
terms accounts of the mechanisms of growth always include *investment*,
viewed as the construction and installation of more machinery, and of
more sophisticated machinery, backed by the necessary 'infrastructures',
such as roads, education, other communication networks, and research and
development. Early statements of the relation between investment and
growth are to be found in Colin Clark's *The Conditions of Economic
Progress* (1940). Economic textbooks usually include growth models, in
which the national income is seen as depending for its size and growth
upon investment expenditure, consumption expenditure, productivity,
levels of inflation, exports, imports, levels and rates of change in 'wages'.
For short-term predictions, many institutions exist which are able, with
varying degrees of accuracy, to explain the effects of one variable or
another on the rest (e.g. Ball and Doyle, 1974; Bell and Kristol, 1981).

The links between the growth of scientific and technical knowledge, and
economic or moral and political welfare are far from unproblematic. How
the applications of such knowledge combine to produce 'growth' is
controversial and the question has given rise to rival theories of economic
growth. Both the technical *concept* of growth and the technical mechanisms
operating have given rise to much controversy. Even if we say that
uncertainties as to the concept and mechanism of growth are merely trivia
when set beside the undoubted fact that growth does occur in some
countries on a sustained basis, it is clear that many major unresolved issues
remain.

Examples include the recurrent crises in finance and balance of payments which seem to have been increasing in severity and frequency since
the mid 1960s. Theorists of economic growth have long questioned the
links between 'growth' and welfare. Scientific and economic progress have
also been held to bring with them many consequences that are held by
some people to be undesirable, such as the pollution and destruction of

parts of the environment. Health problems are held to be caused by some food additives and by some household cleaning materials, and many other products. It is one of the contentions of this book that the development of scientific and technical knowledge (including economic and organizational knowledge) can be seen to have had its application to industry to generate growth, in a way that has been unwarrantedly separated from the systematic treatment of values. This separation has left problems that can only be partially relieved by the application of further scientific and technical knowledge and research. The rival technical doctrines (in relation to growth, inflation and international payments, or environmental pollution, for example) continue to coexist at least in part because the issues are not only technical but also inevitably moral. Such problems can be partially relieved (even when predicted) by using only scientific and technical modes of thought. The technologies that led to attempts to stabilize the trade cycle in the 1950s and 1960s on a world-wide scale eventually led to recognition of 'trade-offs' between employment and inflation (for example), especially in those countries in which the techniques of growth were held to create choices. These choices in turn were restricted by what came to be known as 'monetarism' (a new label for an old doctrine). The application of the insecticide DDT in the late 1940s is but one of the more well-known instances of unforeseen consequences of the application of technology, as the recognition of its effects on wildlife and the food chain took many years to be accepted. In the case of inflation, attempts to treat it as technical, for instance as requiring 'incomes policy' restraints on pay, or monetary contraction as methods of changing what were thought to be 'inflationary expectations' all belong to the scientific and technical tradition, and in most cases have been quietly abandoned after considerable expense and ingenuity have been applied. The common features, such as late recognition of consequences, after much enthusiasm and conviction, together with much effort and application of resources, are sure signs that the problems are at least in part problems of *value*, rather than merely of technique. It will not be claimed in this book that scientific and technical modes of thought have not been helpful, or that there could be any philosophical, metaphysical or theological system of thought that can replace the scientific tradition. The claim will be that the systematic handling of values in relation to industrial and economic growth and management has potentially much to contribute in identifying and helping to achieve the values ('ends') that the scientific and technical modes of thought have generally regarded as unproblematic, or someone else's problem, or as incapable of analytical treatment, or recognized too late.

In sum, the processes which produce economic and business growth without considering the value implications are inevitably unable to recognize the crises and value consequences because the ideologies attached to the techniques forbid it. Such ideologies make it imperative to ignore the dissenting voices which almost always appear along with the techniques and ideologies themselves. Economic growth has always had its critics. Some of these have, no doubt, been idiosyncratic, or even eccentric, but not all have been so.

For example, scientific successes have been convincingly shown, by Koestler in the late 1950s and by Burtt in the 1920s, to have led to an overconfidence that has in turn been encouraged by such convenient, but highly problematic, doctrines as positivism. The causes are not even wholly confined to the 'sleepwalking' and the overconfidence of some scientists and writers on their behalf.

Business ethics has been underdeveloped because philosophers and other ethical theorists have been separated, perhaps by their own choice in part, from business. It would seem that business people have preferred the philosophers to remain in their 'ivory towers' whilst philosophers appear to have thought of business as capable of providing only lists of practices containing little scope for theoretical development. The evidence on how representative such attitudes are, admittedly, is hard to come by, but the evidence for the separation is overwhelming. One indicator is the difficulty in finding business research done by philosophers or in finding systematic treatment of values by practical business people, or by teachers or researchers on management. The fact is that business ethics is under-developed.

The trend in the economic literature that has sought to show that the ends that are thought to be universally required will be automatically produced by economic growth and scientific progress has only rarely been analysed with much depth. Establishing the links between the varying opinions of economists and business and industrial growth is a notoriously difficult undertaking. It is not that anyone would seriously deny that there are such links, but rather that any specification of their nature is likely to offend at least one school of thought, and not please any. Winch describes some of the difficulties in his historical study of the relationship between economics and policy: speaking of differences of opinion as to what constitutes both problem and solution, and on the possibilities of politicians acting on bad advice or not acting on good advice, he notes:

> The moral of this for a study of this kind is the need to accept a certain amount of untidiness and eclecticism. Economic advisers are only one of the influences that must be considered alongside others of a more overt political nature as helping to shape economic policy. Interpreted in a different way, Keynes' dictum concerning the power of ideas contains an element of truth which supports this appraoch. Policies that appear to have no conscious basis

in economic knowledge may nonetheless contain an implicit rationale which is important to distil. In addition to the technocratic application of economic ideas, the connection between economics, political decisions, party alignments, and the broad sweep of ideology must be taken into consideration. (Winch, 1972.)

Despite this circumspect view, a great deal of circumstantial evidence points to the pervasiveness of positivist dogma from the popularity of economic textbooks which claim positivism as the guiding principle, and choose for their content a standard mixture of topics ranging from atomistic consumers and firms operating in a standard variety of competitive conditions to the explanation of the determinants of employment, incomes and much else that belong to an earlier, though non-self-conscious mixture of positivism and Benthamism.

Early writers on economic policy, such as Adam Smith, were well aware of the ethical importance of the issues that they discussed. As Sen points out, Adam Smith's doctrine of the 'hidden hand' had a much more defensibly limited application than could be learned from twentieth century applications of his ideas (Sen, 1987). It is not difficult to find widely used texts which saw the economic system, in its growth phase of the 1950s and early 1960s as having delivered all that could be desired in terms of the principal determinants of welfare—employment, food, shelter, health provision and consumer durables.

Such optimistic views have never been universal, but the circumstantial evidence as seen in the 'growth' debates of the 1950s and 1960s suggest that they were then dominant. The links between growth and welfare that appeared to justify the exclusion of explicit and systematic handling of values and value-related matters have been questioned anew in recent years but cogently argued doubts had always been available:

> Underlying the notions of continued economic growth is the assumption of a dwindling role for Government. The public services are increasingly seen, as Galbraith says, as an incubus; an unnecessary, doctrinaire burden on private enterprise. The act of affirmation, the positive political decision about equality and its correlate, freedom, becomes harder to make, as the majority of voters (and not just the top 10 per cent) grow richer. Negatively, they assume—in so far as they are helped to think about these matters at all—that the unseen mechanisms of a more prosperous market will automatically solve the problems of the poverty of dependency, the slums of obsolescence, the growth of irresponsible power and all the contradictions that flow from undirected or misdirected social policies. (Titmuss, 1960.)

Titmuss was here referring to Galbraith's *The Affluent Society* (Galbraith, 1958).

In *The Costs of Economic Growth* Mishan puts a similar point:

> While his father thought himself fortunate to be decently employed, the European worker today expresses resentment if his attention is drawn to any lag of his earnings behind those of other occupations. If, before the war, the nation was thankful for a prosperous year, today we are urged to chafe and fret on discovering that other nations have done perhaps better yet. Indeed, with the establishment of the National Economic Development Council in 1962 economic growth has become an official feature of the establishment. To be *with* growth is manifestly to be "with it", and, like speed itself, the faster the better. (Mishan, 1967.)

Twenty years on, even these critics appear remarkably sanguine about the ability of the positivist-minded economic technocracies to retain even the growth whose costs were being identified, as the trade cycle (thought in the 1960s to have yielded to Keynesianism and the computer) has reappeared. It has brought with it high levels of unemployment associated with even higher levels of inflation than were experienced during most of the 1950s and 1960s in America and most of Western Europe, including Britain. Whether the 'post-Keynesian' policies and techniques have prepared the ground for a sustained revival (or recrudescence, depending on what clues are adopted) of growth remains to be seen.

It is far from obvious that technical economic skills, understanding of the growth process and political will have yet been applied in a sufficient combination to recreate even the problems of affluence of the 1960s, of which at least some people now have cause to be envious. In the meantime, there are indications that scepticism about the mechanisms of the economic system and the links between growth and welfare is giving way to some more constructive approaches, at least in some quarters, to the problems of the balance between techniques and ethical understanding:

> The predominant conclusion must be that we are quite uncertain of what really is the case. The pretence that it is otherwise comes under the heading of religion or magic. Once the uncertainty is recognised it will greatly affect the set of rational or reasonable actions. Traditional theory is quite powerful on the question of the control of systems which are imperfectly understood. It suggests that, exceptional and near catastrophic circumstances apart, it will not in general be wise to put all your eggs in one basket or to give harsh pulls on levers. That is unless you are what economists call a risk-lover. That is unless you are willing to pay much more than the actuarial value of a bet. But risk-loving itself is unreasonable. In any case these are the reasons why. . . the wishy-washy, step-by-step, case by case approach seems to me to be the only reasonable one in economic policy. (Hahn, 1982.)

Here, Hahn was mainly referring to the technical arguments relating to whether or not the economic system can usefully be seen as an automatic mechanism for identifying people's values and meeting them *to the extent that they can be traded*. His conclusion, that the notion of the economic system as an automatic mechanism is useful but often given exaggerated importance, does seem to me to be consistent with the scepticism that the performance of policies based on such doctrines warrants. In my terms, the doctrines themselves are value-laden, and will improve only when the value matters and technical matters are taken together.

According to Sen, the automatic link between atomistic economic agents, pursuing narrowly defined 'rational' means to well-ordered ends, is both logically flawed and a distorted version of the beliefs of the formative economist, Adam Smith, which are often used to justify the exclusion of values from economic analysis:

> Indeed, it is precisely the narrowing of the broad Smithian view of human beings, in modern economies, that can be seen as one of the major deficiencies of contemporary economic theory. This improvement is closely related to the distancing of economics from ethics. (Sen, 1987, p. 28.)

and speaking of welfare economics, he adds:

> Contact with the outside world has been mainly in the form of a one-way relationship by which the findings of predictive economics are allowed to influence welfare economic analysis, but welfare economic ideas are not allowed to influence predictive economics, since actual human action is taken to be based on self-interest only, without any impact of ethical considerations or of welfare economic judgements. For example, ideas about the response of labour to wage incentives are brought into welfare economic analysis of, say, wages policy or optimum taxation, but welfare economic ideas are not permitted to affect the behaviour of workers and thus influence the incentive problem itself. Welfare economics has been something like an economic equivalent of the 'black hole'—things can get into it, but nothing can escape from it. (Sen, 1987, p. 29.)

Sen argues for more willingness to inform ethical issues with technical ideas and for the ethical ideas to inform and to make more self-conscious the technical approaches to the issues of allocation and growth, and the relation between the economic system and sets of ethical values. It may be that economics has already gone too far down the technical path to make any return to its ethical roots much more than cosmetic, given the enormous technical complexity of the procedures and conclusions based on the currently popular, highly simplified assumptions it uses. If it does succeed, a transformation, rather than a grafting process will be evident.

It is worth adding that, according to press reports, some scientists are considering the possibility that science (not just 'economic science') may have reached its own limits to growth. However unlikely such a possibility may be, the danger of it being believed has moved at least one businessman to write:

> However, in today's world, stagnation can only lead to oblivion. It is now generally accepted that science and technology are essential to the growth of the economic and social welfare of a nation. Robert Solow recently won the Nobel Prize for economics for making the link absolutely clear. (Braben, 1989.)

Returning to the economic literature, it is clear that that part of it which has sought to deal with values, under the title of 'Welfare Economics', seems to have become discredited with the apparent failure of attempts to produce mathematical formulae which would represent and allow to be measured, some notion of 'total welfare' in the 'social welfare function'. Similar attempts to find mathematical criteria for improvement associated, for example, with Scitovsky, Samuelson and others in the 1950s and 1960s, were abandoned. In virtually all of the cases cited above, there has been an assumption that values are all of one kind, that is, that they are *moral* values. It has long been pointed out that there are several distinct kinds of values. Immanuel Kant, for example, regarded all values as *rules* and distinguished between *rules of skill, counsels of prudence* and *the categorical imperative*. In modern terminology these would be called *technical norms* or *technical values**, *constraints*, and *policy objectives* to be assumed, or assumed away. Thus there are different kinds of values, just as there are different kinds of techniques. As Sen and Hahn point out in the works referred to above, the technical, positivist-minded achievements are real enough. Their exaggeration and their limitations are genuine causes for concern.

My own list of the achievements of the positivist outlook in economics would include the production of growth-encouraging economic models, the attempts at detachment in conducting economic arguments in cause-and-effect terms (even when cause–effect terminologies are denied), and a recognition of Hume's distinction between 'relations of ideas and matters of fact'. This has undoubtedly helped towards the conduct of detached analysis. The weaknesses, in economics at least, have included the logical mistake that the differences in the modes of thought imply that they are not connected at all, that facts can and *should* be discussed in isolation from values. The distinction is valid for some purposes, but not others. The practical weaknesses include the obvious difficulties that even in its own terms, 'positive economics' has had no solution to the faltering growth and continuing problems of inflation and financial crises at the international level. The illegal behaviour in an increasing number of cases that have

---

* The word 'values' would be thought of in a mathematical, and not ethical sense.

come to light in the sectors of industry that should be the greatest achievements of the techniques ought to be cause for theoretical as well as practical concern. Scientific detachment and value freedom seem to produce a moral vacuum, and we should not be surprised at that. In terms of the other business-related disciplines, the legacy of attempts at value freedom can be identified by reference to less grand considerations that necessarily have to be introduced in discussing matters of economic growth and its relation to positivism. It is to these that we now turn.

Reference was made in Chapter One to the idea that there is a clearly identifiable role for 'social science', i.e. to describe, analyse and explain but not to evaluate. Unfortunately, all of these expressions are ambiguous. Description and analysis are logical distinctions that have many grey areas and many ambiguous cases. W. V. O. Quine (the philosopher) referred to the distinction as one of the "dogmas of empiricism" (1953). The qualified defence by the philosophers Grice and Strawson (1956) recognized that the distinction can occasionally break down—often enough to be used with caution. Hare (1963) points out the close links in logic between *analytical* and *value* ('prescriptive') concepts. Evaluation can involve finding the amount of a thing or process, finding numerical expressions for, appraising and assessing, including the reliability of evidence. Again, the problem seems to come back to a widespread lack of awareness among scientists of the proposition that values are not all of one kind, and are not all moral values, but even if they were, the proposition that scientists should not consider values is itself a value position, and would seem to be quite self-defeating. In this context it will not do to amend the proposition to the effect that scientists are not really scientists unless they eschew moral or normative ideas. This is only to put the prescriptive, i.e. value-laden reasoning back to the methodological stage by prescribing a role for science at that level.

Perhaps the natural place to find analysis of values would be in the literature and practice that seeks to explain and teach the principles of organizational behaviour. It is, in fact, very rare to find much reference at all to value issues in the organizational behaviour literature. An outsider might reasonably think that the discipline should give as much prominence to the analysis of values and standards as is given to the descriptive and causal 'models'. Here, the use of 'analysis' is in the context of providing explanatory principles which explain the observed behaviours. Standards rarely get a mention at all in the literature, except by implication at the level of skilled operation in pursuit of 'goals', which are taken as 'brute facts'. Organizational behaviour is a relative newcomer to management education and training. Although there is not much evidence that it much affects what managers do, it is generally considered in the business schools and in professional management courses as essential. It is probably the nearest to a general management discipline of all the scholarly efforts. It is generally regarded as a multi-disciplinary subject. This reflects the origins of the subject. It incorporates the work of the pioneers of systematic management and organizational thought in the early twentieth century such as Frederick Taylor, the American engineer. Taylor had many patents to his credit, and some spectacular successes in raising labour productivity. His work gave rise to the development of time and motion study, or more generally, work study. His achievements were much praised by Lenin, who saw Taylor's work as capitalism's supreme achievement (Taylor, 1947; Sofer, 1972).

Other formative influences include the French mining engineer, Henri Fayol, who is credited with being one of the first writers to articulate general principles of management. He wrote in the period from the late nineteenth century to the early twentieth.

A third writer, the German polymath Max Weber, is usually regarded as the contributor who completes the set of early advice for running organizations. Weber wrote from the 1880s to the 1920s. (Characteristic extracts from the work of these authors can be found in the collection of readings edited by D. S. Pugh (1971/1987).) Taylor's work can be regarded as setting the scene for providing management-led methods of improving productivity on a continuous basis. Some critics would see the work as, in effect, more specifically that of acclimatizing raw work forces to Taylor's own inventions. This view does make the point that Taylor's work was developed under specific conditions which may not apply, but even that point is the subject of debate in organization theory. Neither Taylor nor Fayol was self-consciously positivist, but they both avoided with care the analysis of values. Taylor insisted that his system was 'scientific', and was at some pains to convince a Congressional Committee of Enquiry of the scientific nature of his work. Along with Fayol, Taylor also insisted that his system was *fair* and was designed to enable all concerned to satisfy their values. For instance, Taylor spoke of the great burden of planning that managers take upon themselves, and tried to show that it was the equivalent of the burden of work undertaken by manual employees. Fayol speaks of 'esprit de corps', and of fair remuneration, as well as subordination of individual interest to group interests. In saying that these contributors avoided the analysis of values I do not mean to imply that they were unaware of values. This is clearly not so: they were well aware of the importance of showing that their prescriptions *had to be* in everyone's interest, since without continued prosperity, people would be unable to achieve the continuing rise in standards that they were assumed to want. It is not, then, that Taylor and Fayol were unaware of the need to come to terms with values, but rather that they wanted to make sure that theirs brooked no interference. The following extracts illustrate the point:

> The first great advantage which scientific management has over the management of initiative and incentive is that under scientific management the initiative of the workmen—that is, their hard work, their good will, their ingenuity—is obtained practically with absolute regularity, while even under the best of the older type of management this initiative is only obtained spasmodically and somewhat irregularly. This obtaining, however, of the initiative of the workmen is the lesser of the two great causes which make scientific management better for both sides than the older type of management. By far the greater gain under scientific managment comes from the new, the very great and extraordinary burdens and duties which are voluntarily assumed by those on management's side. (Taylor, 1912, reprinted in Pugh, 1984.)

and from Fayol, Taylor's contemporary:

> Surprise might be expressed at the outset that the eternal moral principles, the laws of the Decalogue and Commandments of the Church are not sufficient guide for the manager, and that a special code is needed. The explanation is this: the higher laws of religious or moral order envisage the individuals only, or else interests which are not of this world, whereas management principles aim at the success of associations of individuals and at the satisfying of economic interests. Given that the aim is different, it is not surprising that the means are not the same. There is no identity, so there is no contradiction. Without principles, one is in darkness and chaos; interest, experience and proportion are still very handicapped, even with the best principles. The principle is the lighthouse fixing the bearings but it can only serve those who already know the way into port. (H. Fayol, reprinted in Pugh, 1984.)

In some respects, the above quotations demonstrate that Taylor and Fayol were more advanced in their thinking than those of their successors who, for whatever reason, ignore values altogether. The extracts show them to operate in the scientific rather than the philosophical tradition. The third of the trio of formative influences, Max Weber, belonged to the newer outlook of 'social science'. Although, like Taylor and Fayol, Weber saw himself as offering scientific contributions to the economic and industrial system, he differed in that he was quite self-consciously a methodologist. He, too, recognized that values were important, but saw them as beyond rational analysis, except in terms of means–ends relationships. He saw himself as offering an objective analysis of industrial and social processes.

According to MacRae:

> To Weber all history and every sociology is relative, but necessarily and

properly so: the realm of values does not guarantee objectivity, but, having chosen his interest and thus asserted his value-position, the historian or sociologist is committed to such objectivity and truth as can, painfully, be attained. Every diagnosis involves, after all, standards and value-judgements, as to the proper working of the patient. (MacRae, 1974.)

This approach can be properly regarded as positivist, in that values are seen as not fit for systematic analysis. Weber's work, in making extensive use of 'ideal types', used them in much the same way as economists use the 'perfect competition' theory of the firm and industry. The general idea is that the theory (or the ideal type) is a device that describes without recourse to values, a mechanism or system, so that analyses and predictions can be made in as near as possible a mechanistic way. The theory of the firm is supposed to tell us what will happen, say, if a tax is levied on an industry. The Weberian theory of bureaucracy is supposed to tell us what it is in that form of organization that keeps it going despite the quirks and values of the individuals involved. Indeed, Weber's bureaucracy can be seen as a very ingenious way of squaring the circle of values and facts: his bureaucracy survives because it is 'the most efficient form of organization possible'. It is acceptable because at all levels, officials have prescribed and limited powers, and their rules and commands are acceptable by virtue of that, and by virtue of the fact (supposedly) that managerial authority in bureaucracies is attained by merit, and is open to all who acquire the necessary qualifications and skills. There is a fascinating literature on the problems of bureaucracy, often under the heading of 'bureau-pathology'. Many writers have pointed out the lack of juridical process inherent in Weber's ideal-type bureaucracy (e.g. Bennis, 1972). Some authors have seen the comical effects of and causes of bureaucratic growth (Parkinson, 1981; Peter 1986). Some have provided many illustrations of the great difficulties that most bureaucracies have in dealing with, or even recognizing the need for change (Bennis). Other faults identified are the ambiguities raised by what appear to be several distinct kinds of bureaucracy. Gouldner (1954), in *Patterns of Industrial Bureaucracy*, identifies 'punishment-centred', 'mock' and 'representative' bureaucracies. Burns and Stalker (1961) identify three main 'pathological forms' of bureaucracy, exhibited when faced with turbulent economic and industrial environments: the mechanistic jungle, the ambiguous figure system and the superperson, or committee. They see these forms as inextricably bound up with the career structure and the political process in bureaucracies.

Speaking of the general mode of thought represented by Taylor, Weber and Fayol, and in particular to the uses to which the ideas have been put in modern management, Argyris (1971) sees the result as putting the needs of mature individuals inevitably at odds with the formal systems and structures and their demands: generating frustration, conflict and pathological behaviour.

The model of management in almost universal use is derived from the outlooks represented by the authors discussed above. It is often referred to as the 'planning, organizing and controlling' model. In addition to the frustrations generated and low ability to change, the lack of juridical processes and endemic conflict, there are many problems related to its efficiency at transforming inputs into outputs with the minimum of waste. There are even suggestions (Woodward, 1965) that the operation of the principles described extends only to a superficial resemblance. Woodward's study and those of Gouldner would give some support to the contention. If these contributors are right, then the 'official' systems of management and organization are not typically the ones that are in fact used. In partial recognition of this, a whole school of thought developed in America from the 1920s onwards. Their main inspiration is generally given as the seminal Hawthorne studies and experiments, at the Western Electric Company, a supply organization for the Bell Telephone Company. The studies, apart from the productivity experiments, included a massive interview programme, which generated very rich data on employee attitudes. Readers unfamiliar with the studies are referred to the original publications by Roethlisberger and Dickson (1939a,b). Many descriptions and discussions of them followed.

The result was what came to be known as 'the human relations movement'. Exponents include Elton Mayo, who was actively involved in the studies after the first experiments. Mayo, unusually among management theorists, was very familiar with the literature of political theory and political philosophy, and was well aware of the destructive possibilities of industrial conflict. He set out to eliminate it in a campaign to persuade all participants that organizations are 'essentially cooperative entities' (Mayo, 1949). As with Taylor, Weber and Fayol, and for that matter, with the positive economists and the welfare economists, Mayo was sure that he knew what values were in fact desired by mankind. For him, these were derived from the universal needs, which could be discovered, and which could be met in organizations by means of supportive supervision, and permission to fulfil social needs in the work setting. Recognizing and meeting people's needs became an article of faith to the human relationists, and spun off a large number of techniques or ideas to be incorporated into 'management' courses. These included the hierarchy of needs (Maslow, reprinted in Pugh, 1984), developing interpersonal competence (Argyris, 1971, 1974), the motivator-hygiene theory (Herzberg, 1966), the 'theory Y' assumptions about the nature of mankind and its motivations to work (MacGregor, 1960).

What the 'planning, organizing and controlling' theorists and the human relationists have in common often goes unrecognized. It is rarely questioned that they all purport to be scientific, but the main difference is typically held to be that the earlier model was less sophisticated in understanding human needs and motivations. That is to say that the science of the earlier model was held to be defective *qua* science. Subsequent theories in the organizational behaviour field seem typically to be striving to replace what is thought to be defective science with more circumspect science. This takes two main forms: the social science branch, as represented by, for example, the contingency theorists, such as Lawrence and Lorsch (1969) in America, and the researchers from the Tavistock Institute of Human Relations such as Miller and Rice (1967); the second branch is what has come to be known as 'behavioural science' (some theorists acknowledge membership of both, e.g. see Luthans, 1985).

It is not suggested here that the scientific approaches to the understanding of organizations have had no successes. The Hawthorne studies referred to above and the case studies of bureaucracy by Gouldner, Lupton's *On the Shop Floor* (1964), the Burns and Stalker (1961) studies on *The Management of Innovation*, Crozier's *The Bureaucratic Phenomenon*, Aargyris' *Behind the Front Page* (1974), and a host of case material in case collections such as that of Harvard in the United States, or Cranfield in Britain, and many experiments have provided a great deal of understanding of the processes of management and the problems of conflict, efficiency, organizational change and much else. The work has shown rather modest rates of absorption into management which still seems to be dominated by custom and practice, and by the elusive search for the special managers Taylor sought to free industry from. The concept of the 'effort bargain' and that of 'overcontrol', or of 'system', 'structure', and detailed studies of leadership, and obedience are of seminal importance. And yet the impact on management thinking has been small. These scientific techniques have been developed alongside a major recession, destruction of whole industries, some of which have been at the forefront of technical sophistication, continued major conflicts, persistent poverty and an almost (apparently) unchangeable income structure (Donaldson and Philby, 1985).

What is suggested is that the scientific urge, in economics and in management generally, whether self-consciously positivist or not, has allowed an accumulation of issues and conditions to occur which can only be recognized and treated by the explicit inclusion of systematic analysis of values, or more specifically, of business ethics. What is being suggested is not a claim that somehow, by accident, value issues have not appealed to economists and management theorists as fit subjects for systematic study.

The more specific thesis is that the positivist tradition has influenced notions of what it is to be *scientific* to the extent that the notions in current use are too narrow to be able to achieve the sort of skilled control, understanding and prediction of industrial and business practices being sought. There is a 'missing link', i.e. the systematic treatment of values, and that the link is missing because positivist outlook, which is pervasive, has some serious flaws, many of which are well known, but strangely ignored. Identification and analysis of the flaws in the complex of positivistic scientific outlooks will, I believe, provide better explanations for the inability of the relevant management disciplines to recognize and deal with the issues than failures of communication between managers and scholars, greed of trade unions pushing policy measures off course, or human weakness, or the possibility that the scientific knowledge required is not yet available, but will become so in due course.

Some Critiques of Positivism

Positivism is sometimes thought of as though it were invented by Robbins in 1935 (Johnson, 1967) or by the logical positivists of the Vienna Circle, such as Schlick, Carnap or Waismann, but, as many supporters would acknowledge, the idea is very much older. A major influence on the Vienna Circle itself was the engineer, Ernst Mach, sometime professor of the philosophy of the physical sciences at Vienna, whose work ranges in scope from *The Science of Mechanics* (1893) to *Analysis of Sensations* (1886). Positivist ideas were well represented in the early nineteenth century, for example in Auguste Comte's *Cours de Philosophie Positive*, written as early as 1830. Comte's positivist outlook included in particular the notion that all knowledge "consists in a description of the coexistence and succession of phenomena" (Passmore, 1957, p. 14), and that human development proceeded in stages, from the theological, in which man tries to explain nature in terms of gods and devils, the metaphysical in which philosophical abstractions begin to replace the theological explanations, and finally, the *positive*, or *scientific* stage, which finds truth through experiment and observation. Naturally enough, modern positivists seem to have selected various elements of the Comtian view which suit their outlook or programme, in much the same way as the development of management theory starts, according to the textbooks, with Taylor's *Principles of Scientific Management* in 1910. The parallel continues. The contributions to industrial and management theory and practice of such nineteenth century writers, practitioners and campaigners as Robert Owen, Lord Shaftesbury, the elder and younger Sir Robert Peel, the philanthropist Salt, constructor of the village of Saltaire in Yorkshire, the Quaker cocoa families, rarely figure in the management literature, and never prominently. Nor will it do to explain this by reference to the undoubted fact that since much of the management literature has been inspired by American authors, researchers and practitioners, these British contributors were unknown. America also had its share of contributors to systematic thinking about industrial organization long before Taylor wrote, including mass production pioneers such as Samuel Colt, the gunmaker. Many examples of the same process can be identified, for instance, the selective reading of Adam Smith to give the impression of founding the 'market' theory of economics in which the private interests of individuals, relentlessly pursued, will necessarily and always generate the welfare of all, has been shown to be seriously misleading (e.g. Routh, 1982; Sen, 1987). Having traced positivism back to Comte in the nineteenth century, it is worth noting that the idea is much older still, and can be traced back to the Enlightenment and the separation of science from religion. Burtt identifies it in Newton, Boyle and Galileo (Burtt, 1924/59). A critique of positivism, as of any other important doctrine, must include a sympathetic account of what it tries to do. This is important if the 'straw man' effect is to be avoided, i.e. presenting a caricature of the doctrine under discussion in order to recommend or condemn it.

The statements from Robbins, Johnson and Comte above give something of the flavour of the doctrine. To these can be added contributions from Popper (1957), Ayer (1936), Harré (1974), Winch (1972), Mackenzie (1967), MacRae (1974), Rex (1961), Friedman (1953) and Lipsey (1963).

The doctrine is self-consciously *scientific* in outlook. Comte saw it as descriptive of the objective analysis of all phenomena and experience. Not only were values to be excluded, but much of philosophy, especially metaphysics, and religion also. In some hands the notion becomes a way of drawing the boundaries between disciplines, so that, for example, the policy issues raised by, and consequences of acting on the information provided by, the scientific investigators cannot be traced back to them. The responsibility is posted elsewhere.

Turning to critiques of positivism, it is important to note, by way of preface, that it is a *range* of doctrines, rather than a single body of acknowledged principles. For eighteenth century positivisits it was a convenient method of escaping from the dogmas which pronounced on the nature of the universe from first principles, often (but not always) without careful investigation. Burtt (1924) notes the close connection between the positivists' concept of reality and the urge to measure. For Comte in the nineteenth century it was a way of applying the successes in the physical sciences, through adopting their methods, to human affairs, with a strong notion of the progress of knowledge and of mankind. Comte even developed an alternative religion of positivism, with rituals and all. The Vienna Circle in the twentieth century continued earlier distastes for religion and metaphysics, and added all values to their proscribed list, characterizing them as no more than expressions of emotion, worth little more analysis than, for example, that accorded to grunts. Their doctrine of logical positivism added considerable formal logical and philosophical sophistication, and the emphasis changed to accepting only two kinds of statements as valid: *analytical statements*, validated (i.e. verified) by reference to the meanings of words, and *synthetic* statements, verified by scientific observation. The analytic/synthetic distinction was not invented by the logical positivists, being clearly articulated by Hume, Leibniz and Kant in the seventeenth and eighteenth centuries. The doctrine became identified with the second-order problem of the method of verification of statements. In Popper's version, 'falsification' replaces 'verification'. This latter version has been highly attractive to management sciences and social sciences, providing a *rationale* for an emphasis on technique, particularly of the mathematical and statistical kinds. Such emphasis does not prevent the common use of such expressions as 'scientific progress', or 'advancement', or 'economic growth', 'economic development', and the like. Some ingenuity has been shown in presenting such terms as technical ones, as, for example, when 'perfect competition' in economic theory is described as an impersonal mechanism, whose behaviour can be predicted from theoretical assumptions. The strengths of the positivist outlook merit some emphasis.

First, the distinction between *values* and *facts* is an important one, and the logical gulf between the two first articulated by the Scottish Enlightenment philosopher and historian David Hume (1739), has never been bridged. 'Facts' do not imply and cannot be deduced from values and vice versa. Second, the deep concern expressed for 'empirical' knowledge (i.e. evidence) is clearly a mark of high scholarly standards (at least when genuinely followed). And third, positivist suspicion of high-flown and imprecise language and of generalizations without evidence seems, on the face of it, to be a major requirement of scholarship.

The achievements in the business context include a whole range of useful techniques and ways of thinking, such as statistical and econometric analysis, and prediction, the concept of *system* in management, the analysis of group formation in organizations, and of group behaviour, description of syndromes such as those of frustration behaviour, stress, or the dynamics of conflict.

The above strengths and achievements do need to be set against the limitations, ambiguities, points of incoherence and gaps between aspiration and achievement, and omissions. The weaknesses are the other side of the coin faced by their strengths; that is they necessarily go together.

It is important to note that positivism, like most other metaphysical doctrines, is not a single clear set of theorems, but is a 'family' of related ideas and aspirations. The fact that in some versions it is explicitly anti-metaphysical should not be taken to prove that it is not a metaphysical doctrine in itself, or does not have major metaphysical assumptions or presuppositions. A strength or weakness of one particular version need not apply with equal force to all others.

The first criticism to be noted here is central to the doctrine, and to the theme of this book, and concerns the ability of the outlook to provide convincing ways of avoiding the systematic analysis and handling of values; as Mackenzie puts it:

> For some time there has been a dispute among social scientists concerning whether or not they ought to keep their works value-free. The whole dispute rests, however, on the assumption that they could keep their works value-free if they wanted to. . . In this paper I hope to show that the assumption that it is always possible to cleanse value loaded statements of their value content is essentially mistaken. Value is fused into many statements about social life and can only be removed at the expense of radically changing their meaning and rendering them useless for those who study social life. (Mackenzie, 1967.)

Mackenzie's argument was based on hypothetical examples, and took the form of analysis of the statement that someone was the president of a club. According to Mackenzie, the acceptance of the individual as president implies acceptance that, for example, the claimant is not an imposter, and that the rules were properly obeyed in the election to the presidency, and without the existence of certain rights implicit in the concept of president, no sensible ascription can be made. An implication of Mackenzie's argument as I read it is that it is possible to find values that are not in dispute, and that arguments within that framework can have an acceptably low content in terms of possible value controversies, but that value concepts are not reducible to factual ones. This, as it happens, is also an implication of the Humean distinction between facts and values, or 'ought' and 'is'. The implication is also that the reasons why people regard topics as *important* or *interesting*, is that they are vehicles for values, 'important' and 'interesting' being values themselves.

The second point is that to say that enquiry *ought* to be value free is in itself expressing a value. The presence of 'ought' is a clear give-away. At this point it could be objected that not all 'oughts' are moral or ethical. This is so, but the *fact* that they are not moral values does not imply that they are not values at all. Some values are aptly described as non-moral values, such as the ascription of logical truth values (the claim that something is true), and norms of accuracy, appropriateness or relevance. The proposition that enquiry *ought* to be value free is self defeating. Furthermore, it is not surprising that positivist theorists tend to be silent on the treatment of non-moral values, tending to ignore them. The reason is that all the problems attached to the presence and pervasiveness of moral values that positivism was invented to avoid are present in equal measure in non-moral values. It has to be so simply because they are *values*. Science is a value system in its own right, as, indeed, is positivism itself.

Science, Ethics and Business Growth: Conclusions

That there are links between science (even on the narrow conception of it that has been discussed in this chapter) and business and economic growth cannot be sensibly doubted. This narrow, positivist account of science can itself be seen to be deeply flawed, value laden, and with little to offer towards the alleviation of the ethical issues of management and industry that have mushroomed in the present century and in particular in the last decade. Indeed, it can be said that the complacency with regard to values implicit and often explicit in positivist thought has contributed to the growth of the issues, by omission at the least.

Analysis of values and of value issues has been carried out for a couple of millennia by moral philosophers. Chapter Three examines the extent to which their legacy has been or could be helpfully applied to business and industry.

CHAPTER THREE

Critical Business Ethics

The Nature of Ethical Argument in Business

The discussion so far has sought to show that the relative neglect of the systematic handling of values in business has been self-conscious, and that the consequences of the neglect can be seen both in anxiety about industrial performance in the West and a rise of concern about moral or 'ethical' issues. The patchy awareness of the problem is to be seen in the sporadic nature of attempts of business and governments to regulate industry, as in the Financial Services Legislation in Britain in the 1980s and in the continued growth of *ad hoc* codes of practice in these and other areas.

The successive reworking, again, especially in Britain, of legislation on such matters as restrictive trade and labour practices, control of fraud or of incomes and pay systems provides further examples. At the theoretical level, attempts to return economic thinking to its early, moral, roots tend to be restricted to a specialized, 'normative' branch (as it is usually called). Movement towards such a return is more advanced in the specialized literature of business ethics, but De George's proposition (De George, 1987) that so far developments in the subject have often been restricted to placing side by side some summarized accounts of a few of the more well-known rival ethical theories and some details of case studies, is a fair summary of a necessary and valuable developmental stage.

This chapter addresses the idea that the rival outlooks can throw some light on the nature of the practical issues, and offers clues towards ways forward, that is, they provide relatively stable frameworks within which to make critical assessments of business, union, group and governmental practices and of the ways in which they are protected, for example by institutional arrangements, or by styles of arguments, applied to facts or pseudo-facts, logic and pseudo-logic, propaganda and information management.

It can be taken for granted that there is a series of connections between

59

economic growth, increased sophistication of management techniques and rising standards in some areas. The nature of the connections is troublesome both on technical and philosophical levels. Before the connection can be discussed in terms of prospects for sustained development of rising standards with reduced side-effects, there are some prior matters.

The *first* of these is the extent to which the various rival approaches to the systematic handling of value and value-related matters can shed light on the nature of the ethical issues in and arising from the activities of business and industry and related institutions. Attempts to show that the approaches can do so need to have regard to several strands that tend to get entangled in discussions, both theoretical and practical. The method of exposition and argument used in this chapter is first to list a number of problem areas which need to be addressed by any outlook that promises to shed light on the systematic handling of values and of value-related matters in business and industry.

Second, having in mind that ethical theories have a history which goes back for at least a couple of millennia, it is important to know which theories are serious rivals in the field of business ethics, how many of them there are and whether they can be classified in such a way as to identify the *critical* or *key* issues that divide them.

Third, we need to know how rival views can be reconciled and to what extent. What practical inference can be drawn from areas in which they arise and from the remaining incompatibilities?

Fourth, can a critical ethics be established that does not seek to instil a particular code on others?

In terms of method, two dangers (at least) need to be avoided. Discussions in terms of principles can become excessively abstract, with genuine application and practical consequences hard to find. Here resort is often made to the expedient of inventing a hypothetical example to illustrate what attitude would have to be adopted if this or that theoretical principle were to be espoused. This method usually shows a conflict of principles. It is a weak method, which rarely sheds helpful light on the matters at hand. Hypothetical cases are not real cases, and reducing their complexity in order to make a theoretical point denatures them.

At another extreme, a long list of cases or a particular case described with all its ramifications tends to dilute the principles to the extent that consistency is lost. It is true that some outlooks do not see the latter as a disadvantage at all, preferring to treat each case as unique. This *existentialist* outlook has never been articulated with much clarity, and it is doubtful whether it ever could be (Warnock, M., 1967). In any case it does not seem to hold much promise in the field of business ethics. With these considerations in mind, the procedure will be to use the four kinds of areas already referred to in Chapter Two as sources of evidence and illustration in relation to the rival theoretical outlooks. These are: (1) *regulations of financial services*, especially control of fraud, investor protection and the identification of the legitimate role of financial services; (2) *restrictive trade and labour practices* and consumer protection; (3) *control of inflation*; (4) *dangerous processes and products*. All of these are treated in some detail in Part Two, whose purpose is to attempt to establish whether the conclusions (i.e. the ground rules) arrived at in Part One, on the basis of abbreviated treatments of the four areas of practice, still hold for more detailed investigations.

The argument of the chapter will, I believe, show why the *key* issues in business ethics are methodological in nature, even though the substantive issues are legion and widespread and include matters of perennial and major concern.

Methods of Analysis: Some Problem Areas

An examination of the general literature on business ethics leaves little room for doubt that ethical issues pervade the whole range of business activity, and extend to what may be called 'business support systems', including the governmental policies towards businesses, the law, the institutional framework and opinion-forming agencies, including the academic disciplines which seek to explain, train for or provide advice to business and management. There is no business practice, action, statement or omission that cannot have an ethical dimension. This being so, it is worthwhile attempting in a book whose aim is to identify *key* issues in business ethics, to propose some practical dimensions: it is grandiose to suggest that such a thing as 'the purpose' or function of business 'in society' could be identified, although attempts to do so have been made from time to time. It does make sense to think of business as serving a variety of purposes for different people, so that as a necessary condition, business activities are *justifiable* only in so far as they can be shown to meet the legitimate requirements of people. These requirements can be, and often are, in conflict between people and can change over time. In the nature of things the requirements are highly problematic when it comes to identifying them and even more so when it comes to reconciling them. These requirements are often seen as 'interests', but can be shown to be a good deal wider than that, extending to what are variously called 'principles', 'ideals', or 'moral values'. If a restriction of ethics to the requirements of people is accepted, it rules out the legitimacy of firms or organizations gaining primacy over individuals. Business is a means, not an end, and it is a means for satisfying the requirements of all who have a legitimate claim. It is not sufficient for managers to lay formal claim to caring for the interests of shareholders and employees alike. There is ample evidence that sometimes no such concern for either group is visible, as witnessed by the rising tide of financial scandals, frauds and mismanagements reported daily in the press. Of course, other combinations of interest groups are possible, as when managers and unions collude to gain at the expense of shareholders, public, or other members of unions. There is evidence of that too. These coalitions of interest groups are not simple outcomes of inevitable process or 'micropolitics' within firms. They are such products, but they are not simple ones. Nor are they only processes of micropolitical bargaining: they are moral matters, and not inevitable. They raise ethical matters as well as matters of calculation of whose interests are promoted and whose are suppressed.

If the restriction is allowed, then it rules out both the possibility of what Silverman (1970) called "reifying" organizations, but which is better seen as a process of personification. Organizations are things, but not people. They 'have' characteristics (in the sense that characteristics can sensibly be ascribed to them), but they are not people and cannot claim to be treated as though they were, even if they can be usefully treated in law as 'legal persons'. In law, the practice is a useful expedient that is, of course, termed a 'legal fiction'. If business activities or omissions are to be justified or criticized only insofar as they affect the requirements of people, then any claims on behalf of animals (e.g. in relation to factory farming), or the 'ecosystem' will be ignored. The argument of this book excludes them only because the issues are quite complicated enough when they concern people. The arguments for moral rights of animals and ecosystems are far from cut and dried, and not very different from arguments relating to people.

In pursuing the idea that rival and even inconsistent outlooks can shed light on the nature of the practical issues, the complexity of the issues emerges at every stage. Restricting the issues to those that affect only people is one way towards making the matters treatable. Another line, at first sight promising, needs to be considered, but eventually abandoned. That is the idea that there might be a difference between 'ethics' and 'morals'. One argument for this view is that 'morality' is a personal matter, but 'ethics' is a matter for business or professional codes of conduct 'when on duty' in business or the professions. The problem is that even if a consistent recommendation could be made for distinguishing between the words, it could at best only operate as a specialized, technical distinction. But such a recommendation would be at odds with a long tradition of usage. Instances are:

From Frankena's *Ethics* (page xi):

My aim in this book is not just to introduce the problems and positions of moral philosophers, but also to do moral philosophy. (Frankena, 1963.)

From Singer's *Applied Ethics* (page 1):

This book is about ethics or morals—I use the words interchangeably. (Singer, 1986.)

From Nowell-Smith's *Ethics*:

The words "morals" and "ethics" are derived from words meaning "customs" or "behaviour"... (Nowell-Smith, 1954.)

Similar usages can be found in Warnock's *Contemporary Moral Philosophy* (1967), in Grayeff (1980), *A Short Treatise on Ethics*, and in the *Concise Oxford Dictionary*. The practice of using the words interchangeably is thus well established, and less confusing than attempting to force a distinction.

There are few ways of reducing the complexity of moral issues. If it is accepted that any act, decision, structure, practice, procedure, process, claim or omission that affects other people is potentially a moral or ethical issue, this identifies an extremely wide area. The standard way in which to reduce the complexities is to formulate an ethical theory, or moral philosophy. With the possible exception of existentialist theories, the various rivals in the field attempt to identify rules or principles or categories to which actual or potential behaviour can be ascribed. Once a category has been established, then any topic or act which is a member of that category falls under the rule. Thus, to use the utilitarian principles described in Chapter Two, if, for example, the control of incomes can be shown to be capable of producing a balance of good (reduced inflation which benefits everyone) over the costs (or pains or inconveniences), then incomes control would be justified simply by reference to the principle, rather than by starting a whole philosophical debate from the beginning. The principle, if accepted, is a time- and effort-saving device. Debate among utilitarians could then appear only in relation to whether, in fact, incomes control could work in the way expected, and whether the distribution of goods or benefits would satisfy the utilitarian principle. How the matter is to be resolved depends upon which branch of utilitarianism is accepted. The overwhelming evidence is that it does not. (Donaldson, 1974, 1978).

The first outcome, or rather, one of the first outcomes of formulating ethical theories is that, as expected, the number of issues is dramatically reduced: a decision for one member of a category stands for any other member of the same category. But the problems, though reduced in number are intensified in difficulty. For example, even if some theoretical position could be reached in which, in the incomes control case, reduction of inflation could be proved, the distributional effects can only be dealt with in one of two ways: the first is a system of recording such that everyone affected were to be fully aware of the issues. Agreed weights would be attached to the costs and benefits for everyone. If this then produced an agreed improvement according to pre-established principles—and the new, post incomes control distributions were, according to pre-agreed principles, an improvement for everyone, then those who were worse-off financially than they would otherwise have been could agree that they ought to be so. The second way would be to deny that the issues are ethical in the first place, perhaps on the grounds that the issues are all at the level of mere interests, not of moral principles. Now, incomes control proponents have never attempted to show that there has been a sophisticated and knowledgeable agreement, as described above, nor have they been willing to abandon the administrative weapon of supporting the decision by moral appeals. The conclusion is that the moral sense of people is a useful tool for control, as governments world-wide were aware as they pursued the policies with great vigour through the 1940s to the 1970s. None of this argues against the control of incomes, only that using moral theories to justify policies reduces the number of issues, at the expense of increasing their intensity and complexity.

Apart from the general issues of economic control, growth and progress, the substantive matters have only appeared in the arguments so far as items on lists. The general reason for this is because at least someone has thought the events, decisions, states, practices, processes or omissions to be preventing the realization of at least someone's presumed legitimate interest, ideal or expectation, or more generally, to be against someone's *values*. The presumption is easier to defend in some cases than in others. For instance, Velasquez (1988) describes in considerable detail the events leading up to and following the emission of lethal gas at the Union Carbide plant at Bhopal in India in 1984. The gas in fact killed thousands of people and injured many thousands of others, which was (we may safely presume) against their interests even though they were unable to articulate their interests in not having an emission of gas before the event. The dead, of course, were unable to articulate their interests at all. But there was no question in the Bhopal case of the company claiming a right to emit the gas. The leak was then regarded as an accident. There is no doubt in Velasquez' account that an element of neglect or complacency contributed to the disaster, which would have produced fewer injuries if squatters had not taken up residence close to the plant. The problem in the Bhopal case is one of deciding where negligent or imprudent behaviour by several parties including the operators of the plant amounts to unethical behaviour. Whichever it was, the outcome was serious damage to the unmistakable interests of people. For it to be an ethical matter, there would need to be an element of intention or wilful negligence. Would the events leading to the disaster be justifiable or excusable in terms of the 'legitimate interests' criterion? If the disaster resulted from lack of skill or lack of prudence or both on the part of various people, then some ethical theories would hesitate to regard it by itself as unethical. Whether the event could have been foreseen clearly has a strong bearing, but on Velasquez' account, no laws seem to have been broken, except by some of the victims, i.e. the squatters. The suggestion here is there would have to be an intention (including possibly the intention to take unreasonable risks through imprudence) or lack of skill before the events could properly be described as unethical. By February 1989 the company agreed to an order by the Indian Supreme Court for a final settlement of $470 million. The company denied responsibility, putting the blame on sabotage (Bose, 1989). But breaking the law is not necessarily unethical, even though it is, by definition, illegal. Conversely, there are many cases in which obeying the law conflicts with major ethical imperatives, a point well explored in the moral and political theory literature, for instance in the Devlin/Hart discussions of the 1960s (Mitchell, 1967).

In attempting to establish criteria for recognizing ethical issues, two principles seem, at first sight, to emerge from the discussion. The first relates to *identifying legitimate interests, ideals or aspirations* and the second relates to *intention*. But we have not yet identified how the principles themselves have been established, other than by saying that at least someone has claimed that there is an ethical issue to be considered. For the present it is sufficient to note that they *are* made. If we now move to more general cases of continuing practices, (rather than particular dramatic events) such as the problems of control in 'the City', or of particular trade or labour practices, or pay and inflation control, it may be possible to shed light on the matters at issue.

Restrictive Trade and Labour Market Practices
The problem here is not that events suddenly catch up on people, or that people are not able to articulate their interests, for example because they have been killed, as in the Bhopal Case, but that some people carefully articulate a claim that some practices are proper or improper, though not always using the expression 'unethical' or 'immoral'. Examples are common in relation to restrictive trade and labour practices and inflation control.

Taking trade practices first. The original aim of this chapter was to identify *substantive ethical issues* in terms of claimed ability or failure to meet (prescribed or expressed) interests or ideals or legitimate expectations.

If the Bhopal case illustrates difficulties in distinguishing issues of prudence or skill from ethical ones, discussions on restrictive trade and labour practices illustrate difficulties in distinguishing *issues of substance from issues of method* and of *technique*. For instance, governments sometimes declare themselves to be anxious to keep unemployment down. They sometimes allow it to rise, claiming that (a) it is not their fault or (b) it is a necessary transitional phase or (c) it is not really much of a rise anyway. Opponents do charge them with complacency, inconsistency or with manipulating the figures (which governments control anyway). Opponents can be, and are, accused of being unrealistic and irresponsible. The problem here is a continuing argument, with both sides, apparently, holding *the values* or *principles* that unemployment *should be low*, that the *system* should be *competently* analysed or understood, that figures should be truthfully collated or presented, and that *honest* conclusions should be drawn from them. The 'sides' differ in their assessment of their opponents' ability and intentions. The substantive issues then turn on the interpretation of intentions, of motivation, skill, competence, prudence and consistency. The values and the evidence are typically entangled.

According to one observer:

> An important sector of the information industry has grown up around official economic statistics—predicting, analysing and disputing them. Financial analysts and traders in the City can add on or wipe off billions of pounds from the value of shares and currencies by their reaction to these economic indicators. Politicians attempt to interpret them so as to favour government or opposition, particularly in the run up to elections. Employers and trade unions fasten upon such key numbers as the inflation rate as an essential input into pay negotiations. (Johnson, 1988.)

Johnson quotes the Treasury Select Committee of the British House of Commons as showing concern that judgments about the state of the economy are seriously hampered by the unsatisfactory state of official statistics, commenting that the government's competence and motives are in question, but leaves open the question whether the deficiencies in the figures themselves and their availability are due to lack of coordination skills in official circles, or to disreputable intent.

Similarly, Kellner, in contemplating the apparent fall in unemployment in Britain between 1986 and 1988, concludes:

> What we can say with certainty is that the much-publicised two-year fall of 800,000 in the unemployment figures is a statistical illusion. There is no consistent definition of the phenomenon that yields those figures. On the other hand, an increasing number of people have jobs; a decreasing number of people want work but cannot find it. An honest figure would look less

dramatic than the distorted impressionist painting we are offered each month, but would still look tolerably bright. (Kellner, 1988.)

Turning specifically to trade union activities, the claim is often made that pay rises are inflationary and ought to be moderated. We need to decide whether, and on what grounds, it is wrong to make 'inflationary pay claims'. The assumption that trade union pay claims are main causes of inflation has been long doubted, for cogent reasons (Jackson *et al.*, 1975) but for the purposes of the present argument it can be assumed that they are among the causes.

The answer is usually that such claims make illegitimate redistributions of pay from the weak bargainers to the stronger ones, appealing to a value of *equity* in making claims. The principle of equity is usually met by counter claims by unions that the pay demands are necessary to restore their present, inequitable, position to a former, slightly less inequitable one. Trade unions typically organize the people who inhabit the lower half of the pay distribution, thus demonstrating their relative weakness. For the present, this chapter does not seek to offer a judgment as to whether the unions or their critics are in the right, or who is more in the right. The aim is to show that the argument is typically a mixture of moral, prudential, technical and factual claims, counter claims, distortions and evasions. The argument against the trade unions proceeds on the lines that other people's interests or the national interest are being damaged, through having to pay higher prices, which reduce exports and raise imports, causing balance-of-payments difficulties and requiring crisis action by governments, which in turn can have the effect of an arbitrary imposition of costs or difficulties upon innocent individuals. The argument proceeds to say that the unions' action is irrational because one of the effects of the crisis measures is unemployment among the members themselves of the unions which are held to initiate the inflationary spiral. However, this sequence cannot be proved, because as has been seen, the statistical sources are of uncertain reliability. A further difficulty is that the very sophisticated econometric studies of wages and inflation have yielded no definitive causal sequences, partly because of the unreliability of the figures, partly because of the considerable methodological difficulties, and partly because the econometric methods are predicated upon the theoretical idea that the sequence is more or less as described above. But the theory is in question, because of its entanglement of value, factual and theoretical issues.

Objections to trade union activities extend well beyond direct matters of financial interests. Part of the case against unions is that they are accused of destroying such widely held moral imperatives as *freedom*. In particular, the operation of some British unions and employers in operating the 'closed shop' has come under continuous criticism. Under the closed shop, an employee is obliged, in order to retain (and in some cases, to obtain) a job, to be a member of a (usually specified) union. In the 1980s the closed shop has been the object of much legislation, aimed at limiting, and as far as possible, dismantling it. It was described by one of the participants in one of the *causes célèbres* of the 1970s as 'that ultimate affront to human dignity' (Ward, 1977). For the present this raises a large number of value issues, ranging from contractual obligation, low pay and high pay, minimum standards, individual freedom of employers and employees, the existence or otherwise of collective rights, 'corporatism', managerial pre-rogatives and control at work, union democracy and industrial democracy.

The values cited by unions tended to be the same ones as used by their critics: democracy, freedom, rights, contractual obligation, equity. In addition, the idea of collective rights is often held to be implicit in union attitudes and expectations, and these relate to minimum standards of pay and safety at work, and freedom from arbitrary treatment by employers.

At the other end of the scale from the arguments surrounding low pay, union membership agreements and the processes of inflation are matters to do with the behaviour at what have been called 'the commanding heights of industry', or, more generally, 'the top'. In the late 1980s a series of inquiries, investigations, frauds and collapses has appeared in many manufacturing countries in industry and the financial sector. They have ranged from individual frauds to collapses of major banks, massive over-charging on defence contracts, major bribery accusations, prevention of professional 'watchdogs' such as auditors from performing their duties. Anxieties that professional bodies are often unable to support individuals, such as senior managers when faced with the knowledge of malpractices, are raised from time to time (Kenny, 1976; Velasquez, 1988; Irvine, 1988).

Now, most of the examples discussed so far raise a variety of demar-cation problems: how far, for example, are they technical matters to be dealt with in economics, political science, law, collective bargaining or engineering safety standards? Should we say that, for example, the law seeks to enforce moral codes or principles and that so long as proper procedures exist for amending the law when it is mistaken, or when circumstances or standards change, it should be obeyed? One noticeable feature, comparing the closed shop and city fraud, is that no one doubts that the fraud is both immoral and illegal. Union practices are sometimes illegal, but their ethical correctness is debated. A second feature is that, as already noted, the law and morality are different, though they overlap in places. If law and morality are different, then major issues arise, as for example in the case of public sector strikes in America, or 'sympathetic' strikes in Britain. Should companies have only one 'objective' to make profit and obey the law? Or is this two principles, and if only two, why are there not more? In the Bhopal case, no law was thought to be broken, in the original discussions. The allegations of sabotage came later. Since no law was broken, are there no causes for concern? The problem of specifying the relation between law and morals is a very old one, and it has by no means been resolved. It will be a recurring theme in subsequent pages, together with that most pervasive form of business organization and management and generator of ethical issues in its own right, bureaucracy.

What is evident in view of the above considerations is that the ethical (moral, and other value) issues arising from the activities of unions and companies are endless in number and complexity. When the evidence is not clear-cut, as is usual in the case of fraud, a very large number of values is appealed to in argument. The facts are typically in dispute, as are motivations, consequences and principles. They become more deeply entangled as the debate continues. If a change, action or policy cannot be justified by appeals to restore conditions to some former, preferred state of affairs, or by appeal to convincing criteria for improvement, then the parties remain reluctant to abandon moral tones. This can only be because appeal to moral principle can be effective, whether done honestly or cynically.

The entanglement of values and evidence and the uncertainties of both are not the worst of the problem. Attempts to cut the knot by offering pragmatic criteria often make things worse. The sheer variety of the values appealed to make it seem attractive to propose a hierarchy of values: is the redistributional effect (in terms of income) worse than the redistributional effect of institutional arrangements that allow anomalies to develop, as for instance when groups who were overdue for pay rises were prevented from having them in the 'incomes policies' of the 1950s to 1970s? Remaining with what I earlier called 'business support systems', such as the institutions that gather and present statistics and process them, opinion-forming media, quasi-governmental institutions and trade unions, the problems of 'knot-cutting' can be explored.

It may seem strange to some readers to classify unions as 'business support systems', as they are often seen as hostile to business. Their opposition is to what they see as bad decisions or managerial malpractice. At the company level, it is as easy to see the unions as part of the control system—a point often made by industrial relations specialists (see Fox, *Man Mismanagement*, 1974).

Anti-monopoly measures feature in most major 'capitalist', 'free enterprise', or 'market' economies. Often other restrictive trade practices are covered, to bring into the net collusive arrangements between firms. In such legislation, there is an implicit or explicit appeal to the 'public interest', the 'national interest' or some similar expression. The ideal that appears in great detail in virtually all the textbooks of economics is that of a perfectly competitive market, in which no company has any market power (which is technically described in terms of relationships between costs and revenues, but less technically in terms of power to trade on more than equal terms than those applicable to competitors).

At the other extreme from the 'ideal' or perfectly competitive market is the notion of monopoly. Literally a single seller in a defined market, there are major difficulties in identifying a pure monopoly, partly because the boundaries between one market and another are usually far from clear, and partly because markets can be dominated by a large firm which tolerates some locally based, small ones. There are many other theoretical issues in defining markets, but the above are sufficient to explain the pragmatic solution that is offered to legislators who wish to control monopoly, even though they cannot identify or recognize any pure cases. The usual pragmatic solution is to make an arbitrary cut-off point, which is usually around the 30% level, i.e. that if a firm 'controls', or sells to an estimated third of the market in the product line under review, then the firm is regarded as a monopoly. This monopoly is not usually seen as necessarily acting against the 'public interest', but may be regarded, *prima facie* as doing so. 'The public interest' is, broadly, viewed as the right of the public to buy at prices that reflect the level that a free market would produce, if there were one. The technical economic requirements need not detain us, but the notion of 'the public interest' requires a comment. In terms of the main issue at hand, is the notion of 'the public interest' a technical economic concept, or is the relevant technical economic concept that of the 'free market'? Can we say that the concept of the free market serves to provide a procedure by which the public interest can be identified? It looks as though the technical economic concept would be pointless without a prior notion of the public interest which requires it. It cannot therefore logically be used to clinch an argument that a practice is in the public interest to say that it is what we would have had if the market had been free. Logically, if we want to make the point, we have to say that *if* we accept that it is defined as the kind of relationship of price to cost structures *for the existing distribution of income* (and ignoring the complications of 'second best' considerations) that we would have in a completely free market, and all other things being equal, then the practice is in the public interest, unless other things are not equal, but are unequal in the direction that is judged to be favourable to the public. In other words, a monopoly practice may give a more expensive, but safer product, and some administrators are empowered to decide on behalf of the public whether the safety aspects outweigh the cost. The notion of the public interest is central, but it cannot be defined in technical terms: the terms serve only to provide a criterion once the notion has been decided on value grounds. The public interest begins to look very much like a 'collective right' claimed by (and usually denied to) unions.

One of the many ambiguities on this matter is that the grounds for believing in 'the public interest' but not in collective rights for groups or subgroups of the public arises from the fiction that the state is a unity, to which subgroups cannot claim preferential treatment; but on the other hand the denial of collective rights arises from real difficulties in identifying collective rights in a legal system that recognizes (and sometimes invents) persons, but not collectivities. Now the dilemma should be clear: if a subgroup is too complicated an invention to be able to ascribe collective rights to it, then the very much vaguer and more disparate 'public interest' has to be infinitely more complex.

In the above example the substantive issue of price fixing cannot be separated from the methodological issue of why it is regarded as an issue at all, and how the public interest can be explained, as they are all bound up with some highly technical arguments about price determination. It is not claimed here that the notions are useless, or that the technical and value issues cannot be disentangled. It is claimed that the major underlying concept, that of the public interest, is value laden and cannot be justified by appeal to technical economic arguments, which become relevant and potent only when the values implicit in the notion of the public interest have been justified in context. The value is logically prior to the technical concept. It would seem to be the case that much of the historical argument about monopolies and restrictive practices has fallen into the trap of logical circularity: by trying to treat value matters as technical economic ones. Much the same can be said of anti-strike legislation, in which the diverse value judgments (no doubt for pragmatic reasons) of different members of the public are ignored in favour of technically based notions of the public interest with regard to strikes. Again, the legitimacy of the value position is not in question here. What is in question is the ability of legislators and administrators to avoid the trap of attempting to justify value positions on technical grounds. Once the value issues are settled, the technical ones become relevant, but not before then. There is an unbridgeable logical gulf between values and technical concepts, as Hume pointed out in the eighteenth century:

> In every system of morality, which I have hitherto met with, I have always remark'd that the author proceeds for some time in the ordinary way of reasoning, and establishes the being of a God, or makes observations concerning human affairs when of a sudden I am surpris'd to find, that instead of the usual copulations of propositions, *is* and *is not*, I meet with no

proposition that is not connected with an *ought* or *ought not*. This change is imperceptible; but it is, however, of the last consequence. For as this *ought* or *ought not*, expresses some new relation or affirmation, 'tis necessary that it shou'd be observ'd and explain'd; and at the same time that a reason should be given for what reasons altogether inconceivable, how this relation can be a deduction from others, which are entirely different from it. But as authors do not commonly use this precaution, I shall presume to recommend it to the readers; and I am persuaded, that this small attention would subvert all the vulgar systems of morality, and let us see, that the distinction of vice and virtue is not founded merely on the relationships of objects, nor is perceived by reason. (Hume, 1739/1965, pp. 469–470).

Hume's distinction has proved to be impeccable, and though many attempts have been made to derive 'ought' from 'is', none has been free from fatal flaws. Just how the relevant value issues can be identified and settled is a matter for Part Three, below. For the present, the argument against monopoly tends to be couched in terms of departures from technical efficiency, with a nod, occasionally, to unexamined notions of choice and maximization. Whether consumers want the kinds of choice and maxima theoretically on offer is not open to discussion, apparently, and consumers are not asked, their preferences being inferred from within the technical arguments, or as assumptions. We may justifiably call the latter 'presumptions', since there is no direct or unproblematic way of telling what the 'public' wants, or would want if in possession of all the relevant arguments. The public is not in possession because the arguments are esoteric, and mostly beyond reach.

The Role of Theory in Ethics: Reducing the Complexities

Whether the major ethical issues are or are not entangled with technical ones in either case, the problem arises of how to reduce the great variety of issues to a manageable number. The long lists that appear in the business ethics texts, of which samples have already been given, appear to include matters ranging from vitally important to fairly trivial: are there any substantive issues that are in any way 'keys' to the rest? There are several common ways of making the reduction to manageable proportions: (a) classification of issues according to the moral principle involved, using a hierarchy of principles; (b) taking a step back to a more general level, and attempting to establish a single principle or small set that will enable a ruling to be made on any issue, old or new, as it crops up.

As with the entanglement of substantive, technical and methodological matters, the tendency in the literature has been to involve some mix of these two procedures irrespective of the starting point adopted. For instance, Ross (1939), in attempting to identify moral duties, reduces them to a small number; having, rightly, eliminated the possibility of there being only one, single, ground of 'rightness'.

> After all, there is no more justification for expecting a single ground of rightness, than for expecting a single ground of goodness... (1939, p. 83.)

and

> It is, to my mind, a mistake in principle to think that there is any presumption in favour of the truth of a monistic against a pluralistic theory in morals, or, for that matter in metaphysics either. When we are faced with two or more ostensible grounds of rightness, it is proper to examine them to find whether they have a single character in common; but if we cannot find one we have no reason to assume that our failure is due to the weakness of our thought and not to the nature of the facts (*ibid.*)

and further

> But it may be argued that the plurality of moral intuitions is disproved by the fact that the supposed intuitions in practice contradict each other; that we often cannot obey one without disobeying the other; that sometimes we cannot obey the principle of telling the truth without disobeying the principle of not causing needless pain, or the principle of keeping promises without disobeying the principles of producing the maximum goods (*ibid.*, p. 84)

and

> Moral intuitions are not principles by the immediate application of which our duty in particular circumstances can be deduced. They state what I have elsewhere called *prima facie* obligations (loc. cit.).

These *prima facie* obligatory acts or prohibitions, according to Ross, become obligatory or forbidden only when all the ethically relevant features are taken into account. Ross does not speculate on exactly how many *prima facie* duties there are, but solves the problem (pp. 170ff) by holding that people have managed to recognize 'right' acts before any general principles had been formulated by ethical theorists, so that the principles, or *prima facie* duties are inferred from consideration of judgments as to what are or are not 'right' acts, not the other way round. On this reading, the question of how many ethical principles or moral duties there are would be as pointless as asking how many scientific laws there are. Nevertheless, Ross is driven by the logic of his arguments to produce a single principle by which primacy can be established in a particular case, and by which *prima facie* duties can be recognized. That principle is intuition, and the *prima facie* duties repeatedly reduce in Ross's work to keeping promises, not doing harm or causing needless pain, and telling the truth.

Ross's answers are now unfashionable, but the problem remains: if there is a single principle of ethics or morality, what is it and how can it be established, and if there are more than one, what are they, and how many are there, and how can they be reconciled or placed in priority order?

Before attempting to offer a solution to this problem it will be useful to review the problem from a different angle. We began by considering a criterion for identifying ethical issues, namely that based on people's legitimate interests, ideals or aspirations. What were to be regarded as candidates for legitimacy in these respects depended upon the possibility of articulating a claim. The first problem with this criterion was that it could not deal with the problems of intention that do crop up in moral arguments. A second was that it could not deal with issues of skill, negligence or prudence. When intentions are to be added, we see a rapid multiplication of value issues, such as those related to honesty, truth, accuracy, equity, 'public interest', consistency and many others. In the case of restrictive practices, the moral, technical theoretical and pragmatic issues become easily entangled in a circularity which, though possibly of some pragmatic value, obscures the value issues in relation to restrictive practices, and seems in public discussion to attempt to derive values from facts, apparently ignoring the Humean gulf.

Multiplicity of Theories
If the main role of theories is to reduce the complexity and number of principles and to reduce their even more complex interrelations with matters of fact, prudence and the like, then the problem raised by Ross does require an answer. The trouble here is that there are rival accounts of how many basic principles there are, and what they are. The problem is compounded when we consider the matter of how we can justify a claim to knowledge of what the principles are. The continued existence, over millennia in some cases, centuries in others, of rival ethical theories is testimony to their (albeit limited) success at reducing the issues to a small number of principles. These principles are usually, though not always, mainly procedural or methodological, or, which amounts to the same thing, operate at the second-order or higher-order level. These rival theories or outlooks view a similar range of issues and evidence differently. They seem to be necessary, incompatible and at the same time, incomplete, taken either together or separately. They continue to exist because they do have a wide coverage, and individually are often able to give convincing interpretations of matters which their rivals are unable to do. To illustrate the argument, utilitarians, such as Bentham (quoted in Chapter Two above), seem to be committed to the generally unpalatable conclusion that in pursuing the greatest happiness of the greatest number, it is legitimate

to use scapegoats, thus, as their critics sometimes say, 'punishing the innocent for the public good'; whereas deontologists , such as Kant, who base their arguments on notions of duty or moral laws, would emphatically exclude that possibility, but would themselves be open to the charge that they would countenance harsh consequences if the intentions of those who instigate or call up the moral law were good, as for instance in the controversial case in which offenders against the law are held to will their own punishment, or have a right to it, since it affirms their status as moral agents.

Similarly, deontologists such as Rousseau (1762) can talk of "forcing people to be free". Allowing the majority to gain at the expense of the minority is always a danger in using utilitarian arguments. A recent example is from a newspaper article referring to the stringent financial policies in Britain in the 1980s: headed 'Shock Treatment for the Economy May Have Hurt, But It Has Worked', the article proceeded to show reasons for believing that the policies had rid the economy of many restrictive attitudes and practices which were preventing growth of the economy. Given that one of the key features of the treatment was a high level of unemployment and bankruptcies, there remains the problem that those for whom the shock treatment worked and those who received the shock treatment were, largely different groups of people. In utilitarian terms (assuming that the policies actually have generated growth) the end justified the means. Now a deontological interpretation might consistently say that if the economy is riddled with restrictive practices and lazy management and union or workforce attitudes, then only those who have been lazy or complacent or guilty of deplorable industrial practice should pay the costs, just as only the virtuous should reap the rewards. A problem is that no administrator could tell the guilty from the victims, or devise an instrument that could discriminate. Both theories are problematic when it comes to who is to decide whether an act is beneficial (utilitarian) or right (deontologists), but both outlooks are persuasive, up to a point. Economic theory has little to tell us here, but may help in assessing whether or not the 'treatment worked'. One principle from economics is that 'those who benefit should pay'—a moral principle, but an empty one when there are no criteria for telling one from another. Of course, the 'do nothing alternative' might be canvassed, but then there is no principle which can tell us that 'benign neglect' would produce a result that, for example, does not leave the authorities open to a charge of culpable irresponsibility.

Some Rival Ethical Theories and Classification Schemes
There are many lucid accounts of the main (i.e. most widely discussed) ethical theories or moral philosophies. Readers who are not familiar with

them would find a selection from a number of texts helpful. Examples are: Frankena's *Ethics* (1963/1973); Foot's edited volume, *Theories of Ethics* (1967); Grayeff's *A Short Treatise on Ethics* (1980); Warnock's *Contemporary Moral Philosophy* (1967); Hare's *Moral Thinking: Its Levels, Method and Point* (1987); or Finnis's *Fundamentals of Ethics* (1983). General accounts appear also in texts dedicated to business ethics, such as Velasquez *Business Ethics: Concepts and Cases* (second edition, 1988) and Beauchamp and Bowie (Editors), *Ethical Theory and Business* (third edition, 1988).

My claim that the main rival theories are necessary, incompatible and incomplete would, however, not be intelligible without some indication of what I take their main messages to be. This will be explained in context of particular issues by means of some characteristic ideas of some of the influential historical authorities, such as Kant, Bentham, Rousseau, Hobbes, Hume, Mill, Moore and Ross, together with some ideas from influential contemporary authors. Because there are so many theories, with differing emphasis on substantive and methodological issues, it is common practice to use classification schemes (sometimes called taxonomies). These have the advantages of pointing out some principles by which the theories are differentiated. They also give readers an orientation which helps to explain what otherwise might appear to be obscure points made by particular authors. Thus, when, for example, Kant tells us that criminals will their own punishment, the proposition is more understandable when it can be shown to have been inferred from Kant's standpoint as a deontologist: that people are under an obligation to show reverence for the moral law as such, and should be treated as responsible individuals, responsible for their own actions.

The argument appears to many modern people to be odd and harsh, but whether or not it is so, the argument is not intelligible except in relation to the deontological theory from which it is derived. There seems often to be an unstated assumption that for a given set of problems (in our case, those of business ethics), when all approaches towards general solutions that are known to be serious and appear to have survived despite general criticism, the reader can be assured that no relevant and important information has been omitted by the author. Where the author stands is not always made immediately clear, but insofar as the reader accepts the drift of the author's argument as to the importance of the issues, the reader can then choose whether to accept the choice of theories, to choose one (or more), and proceed to a conclusion on the basis of any factual evidence provided, or known by the reader. Many other possibilities occur, but the main case for classification schemes appears to rest on having made a conscious effort to avoid one-sided, narrow-minded interpretations of the case in hand. This is an admirable principle in its own right, but it is not without difficulties.

For example, there seem to be as many classification schemes for ethical theories as there are authors on the subject, and it does not require much stretching of the imagination to conclude that the objective of the classification schemes—usually to illustrate absence of bias, or objectivity (in one important sense of the word)—is lost unless all serious theories are considered. On the other hand, the simplicity and ease of understanding is lost if all known outlooks are considered, and given an equal voice. A further problem is that unless the basis of the classification scheme is explained, the choice appears to be arbitrary. One solution is to present a group of theories on the grounds that they are the common ones. A useful strategy for argument is then to invite the reader to apply the theories in turn to some problems, and then decide what conclusion appears to fit the problem.

As a way of introducing the subject of business ethics, the above strategy has much to commend it, and few serious criticisms. At a more general level of discourse there is a reasonable presumption that rival and incomplete explanations ought not to be left with a non-committal handing over to others. Some attempt at reconciliation may be reasonably expected of writers on business ethics. A further, superficially attractive, solution is to insist that all the rival theories are no more than relative to a particular age or set of circumstances. This is a version of the doctrine referred to earlier under various aliases, such as 'relativism', 'historical relativism', 'ethical relativism', or 'indexicality'. I will suggest that the idea is flawed for a variety of reasons. The first of these is that on its own principles the doctrine is to be regarded as necessarily historically relative. A number of grounds have been suggested for a relativist view, that people can adopt different attitudes and values in relation to the same facts, or that particular practices only have meaning to the actors in their own time, place, class, sect or group, or that faced with different practices or values, it seems to be possible to show that the costs are very high of a particular practice, but still value it, and insist on its continuation:

> It is not contrary to reason to prefer the destruction of the world to the scratching of my finger (Hume).

Now, if all moral theories are historically relative, then the doctrine that they are relative, being a higher order moral doctrine, must be relative. If it is so, then presumably it reflects the values of an age. But the values of an age vary from person to person, so which values, and more importantly, whose value does the doctrine of relativism (historical or other) express? Should we say, with Thrasymachus in Plato's *Republic*, that justice (or morality) is the interest of the stronger? Is relativism no more than an excuse for letting powerful people and institutions off the duty of adjusting to the legitimate interests and expectations of others? The 'Vicar of Bray' implications of relativism ought to be worrying.

But if the doctrine that moral doctrines are relative is not relative, then we need to know on what grounds the particular rival in the context for ethical 'rightness' makes exception to the rule in its own cause. So far as I can make out, the only reply that has been offered to this objection is to challenge the holders of other doctrines to show some of their prescriptions that are universally held or practised. The difficulty with that particular method of challenge is that acts performed by everyone could still be unethical on some principles, and acts that no one manages to perform could still be duties, in some theories. As Hume says, we cannot derive values from facts, or vice versa. Another approach might be to say that relativism is not a moral doctrine at all, but a logical one. There is, however, no known logical principle from which the statement can be derived, and relativism, in all its forms, remains one of the rival ethical doctrines. Before the arguments for the rival doctrines can be treated at length, it is worth while spelling out what seems to me to be a more tenable solution: different theories of ethics emphasize different insights. This explains their longevity, but the comfortable solution that they add up, between them, to a reasonably complete treatment of the problems of value is not available. This is because at some levels the doctrines are rivals: if some of the insights, say of utilitarianism, are true, then some of the deontological doctrines must be false, and vice versa. The doctrines taken together would still be incomplete even if they were compatible. Evidence of this combined incompleteness is to be found in the lack of compelling and agreed answers to the perennial question, 'why should anyone be moral (act ethically) in practice?' The answers are necessarily contingent, i.e. they depend upon prior commitments, of the form: if you believe proposition A (e.g. 'human happiness is important'), or is the supreme 'end', then you are committed to an action that tends towards it, unless some other action is more efficient in meeting the objective or 'end'. But there are no compelling reasons why people should be committed to a happiness principle in the first place. Either they are so committed or they are not. The freedom of choice of fundamental principles ensures that, at least. Ethical arguments always have elements of preaching to the converted. At the same time, at least some ethical commitments seem to be necessary to orderly conduct. If people were not required to give consideration to 'right behaviour', there would be no ethics, and as Hobbes rightly pointed out, there would be no civilization either (Hobbes, 1651/1962).

Commitment to a 'greatest happiness of the greatest number' (GHGN) principle, without a sense of duty (for example a duty to be truthful and consistent, as well as the duty to provide for the GHGN) would be precarious, even whimsical, and certainly withdrawable by anyone at anytime. A sense of duty to 'the moral law' would be inexplicable without some notion of what the moral law is. The substance of the moral law is then problematic: why should GHGN or some principle of benevolence or of selfishness be chosen? Can intuition, revelation, or the customs and practices of nation, state, class, tribe, group or sect relieve individuals of the responsibility for choosing what principles to live by? (Hare, 1963). Can we say with assurance that individuals have the responsibility in the first place? It does not help to call the principles 'axioms', since that is no more than putting a new label on the problem. The conclusion is by no means original or surprising that there is no compelling reason other than individuals' own convictions for adopting any of the moral principles offered by the various schools of thought. As implied in the Hume quotation above, it would be irrational to deny that the achievements of modern science and technology are not based on important mathematical and physical principles (even though their own status seems to change over time); but it is not irrational to choose eccentric values, merely unconventional.

Given that some ethical principles seem to be necessary for human survival, there do not appear, on the face of it, to be any compelling reasons for choosing any particular set of values. The actual choices made by people tend to be made on grounds of revelation, convention, prudence, habit, and much else. But knowledge of why people actually do choose particular principles provides no compelling reasons for explaining why they ought to do so. The reasons, if they exist, appear as the deontologists maintain, to need an important methodological element. The principles of the main established schools of thought seem to some degree to be necessary, incomplete, and incompatible. Solutions to the problem that deny the possibility of systematic treatment of moral problems, such as espoused by the positivists, are logically problematic, and, as has been seen, have led to an explosion of untreated (or inadequately treated) value issues in business and in business-support systems—difficulties of their own making.

It is possible to construct some ground rules from these difficulties. The complexities and uncertainties of the grounds for moral outlooks and principles do provide possibilities for integrative principles, but before these are offered, there are other elements to be dealt with. Classification schemes are helpful in this respect because they provide a synoptic view of the field, as an aid to understanding, and point to contrasts between rival doctrines, providing common frameworks for discussion, and much else. It should be clear from inspection of the different schemes that none is definitive, in that different ones suit different analytical purposes, and, as we found in the case of attempting to justify restrictive trade practices legislation in terms of positive economic theory, the first-order and methodological issues quickly become entangled with an apparently infinite variety of values, both moral and non-moral.

Some Classification Schemes

The entanglement of substantive and methodological matters is well illustrated in classification schemes: in the preface to his book *Ethics*, Frankena (op. cit.) explains his intentions as:

> ... both to present some of the standard material of ethics that beginners and others should know

and, because there is not a substantial body of agreement among experts in the field,

> to do moral philosophy.

As he explains it, it is not feasible to expect an exposition of ethical arguments to get readers to mirror his opinions:

> Their coming to disagree clearly and on carefully reasoned grounds will serve the purpose . . . . as well. (loc. cit.)

In fact, Frankena uses more than one classification scheme (for what to my mind are highly defensible and helpful reasons): *normative ethics* (in which people identify right or obligatory behaviour and give their grounds for believing it so); *analytical* or *critical* (meta-ethical) thinking (which in this book is called 'higher-order' reasoning)—the nature and validity of the kinds of arguments deployed, for example; and *descriptive thinking*, including scientific evidence relating to the normative matters. In terms of the first-order ethical (normative) theory, Frankena distinguishes:

(1) *Teleological theories*: these assert that the basic criterion is some non-moral value to be brought into being. Examples are happiness, pleasure, avoidance of pain, power or knowledge.

(2) *Deontological theories* (of various kinds) whose basis is found in rules expressive of duties, such as truth-telling or promise-keeping.

(3) *Egoism* (of various kinds), in which the ethical persons are seen as promoting what is good for themselves (which could be other people's happiness, for example).

Frankena identifies two basic and independent principles of morality (recognizing that there may be other basic principles); those of beneficence (or utility, in Bentham's terms), and that of justice. Combining the two basic principles produces a mixed deontological theory. Thus, Frankena offers at least seven categories, or three categories with some subcategories, depending on how the argument is viewed.

Grayeff (1980) uses a compound categorization, making a major division between *classical* and *modern* ethics, the former category including the ancient Greeks, the Renaissance and the eighteenth century thinkers, and the modern category includes four subdivisions: (a) *a priori ethics*, which, in brief, seeks to find principles that precede (in a logical sense), practices or issues; (b) *intuitionist ethics*, as expounded for example by G. E. Moore (1903) who thought that 'good' is a 'non-natural property' of objects, states, processes (either they had the property or they did not), recognizable by intuition, or 'straight off'; (c) *ethical relativism*, in which the moral judgments are held to be valid for whoever makes the judgment, being dependent upon time and place; and (d) *moral scepticism*, interpreted as the view that those judgments that purport to be moral are really something else such as expressions of emotions. (This view was eloquently expressed by A. J. Ayer in *Language, Truth and Logic* (1936). Ayer's book ran to three editions and many impressions, and was a major statement of the 'logical positivist' outlook—a brisk form of positivism.)

Grayeff's account includes the ideas of R. M. Hare (1963, 1981) whose twin principles are the methodological ones that all moral statements are rules, and are, logically, prescriptions made by individuals (the first principle), and are valid if only applied 'universally', i.e. rules prescribed for the behaviour of others must also prescribe one's own behaviour in relevantly similar circumstances. It is not clear where Hare's ideas fit into Grayeff's scheme, and they would appear to cut across the main categories used.

P. D. Marsh (1980) uses the four categories of *hedonism, utilitarianism, Kantian* and *prescriptivism* (p. 43), adopting, oddly, perhaps a major different principle of the use of *subjectivism* as the main ethical insight.

In his review article in the *Journal of Business Ethics* De George's (1987) main categories are expressed thus:

> Business ethics is a field to the extent that it deals with a set of interrelated questions to be untangled and addressed within an overarching framework. The framework is not supplied by any ethical theory—Kantian, utilitarian or theological—but by the systematic interdependence of the questions, which can be approached from various philosophical, theological or other points of view. (p. 204.)

Mary Warnock identifies *intuitionism, emotivism, prescriptivism, naturalism* and, almost as a separate category, '*the content of morals*' (Warnock, M., 1967); Beauchamp and Bowie (1979/1988) in their theoretical first chapter distinguish between *act* and *rule utilitarianism*, and *deontological* theory, with the notion of *justice* related in various ways to the others to form a third category.

Finnis (1983) uses, as a set of categories, *utilitarianism, consequentialism, teleological ethics*, and *proportionalism*, with the caveat that

> Those whose opinions I criticise often reply that theirs is not a utilitarianism, but a consequentialism; or not a consequentialism, but a proportionalism; or not a proportionalism but a teleological ethics ... or is simply not to be labelled at all. So we must take each opinion without using any of these labels. But we are entitled to stipulate how we use such-and-such a label in our own critique. The label we stipulate should approximate to its ordinary uses. (p. 80.)

Several conclusions should be clear from the variety of classification schemes, of which the above sources are but a few; *first*, the categories overlap and do not appear to be amenable to articulation in any definitive set; *second*, that the set of categories used by each author is specific to the line of argument to be adopted; *third*, that recurring themes are those that relate to a distinction between first-order theories of what ethical acts, states of processes, or 'goods' actually are, and the methodological theories of how such claims can be made, known or justified; and *fourth*, that the differing views are variations on a small number of major themes.

Chapter Four will discuss four representative and widely used categories in more detail. These are utilitarianism, deontology, objectivism and subjectivism. Some ways will be suggested in which a partial reconciliation can be attempted for the rival doctrines in relation to some of the cases and institutions already discussed: monopoly control, the Bhopal case, trade unions in relation to inflation. Discussions of further cases and institutions will be introduced. There are, in the nature of things, limitations to the extent to which reconciliation is possible, for reasons outlined earlier: the doctrines are incomplete, partially incompatible, and in some cases, necessary. At the practical level it will be seen that the inability of any of the various doctrines to refute any of the others is a healthy and positive state of affairs, which can be profitably transferred to practice, or, for that matter, to other disciplines. When one or other becomes a dominant dogma, the result is always baleful: 'The sleep of reason brings forth monsters'.

CHAPTER FOUR

Rival Theories and Methods

There is no action or inaction, decision, structure, state, process, relationship, institution, procedure, rule or attitude that cannot have an ethical dimension. Attempts to exclude ethics from business and business-related activities tend to consign the issues away from the mainstream of thought, where they accumulate, often to crisis point, as has been the case for example with the mushrooming 'City' irregularities, deterioration of product and service quality, and decreased responsiveness of bureaucratic organizations (public or private) to all but an influential few of their constituents. The huge number and variety of ethical issues in industry, and their complex interrelationships, were indicated in the previous chapters. Although scientific and technical advance have undoubtedly been major causes of business growth and of improvements in standards (where they have occurred) there is much in the self-image of science and scientists that precludes systematic treatment of the value issues that science and technology generate, when applied. This has long been noted by such authors as Koestler (1959), Burtt (1924) and Mishan (1967). In these respects, the more developed field of medical ethics is a special case, with a unique history. The presence of rival explanatory frameworks and the uncertainty as to how many rivals there are in the field is no more serious a problem in business ethics than it is in other disciplines, such as mathematics, economics, industrial relations, organization theory or law, for example. In Chapter Three, the view was offered that the main rival outlooks seem to be incomplete and incompatible in some respects. Some of them seem, at the same time, necessary for a plausible-looking account of business ethics.

The practical matters identified or sketched in the earlier chapters appear to be capable of analysis from differing standpoints. We can agree with Hare (1981) that there has been much ambiguity and some confusion in the debate between the advocates of 'objectivism' and 'subjectivism (relativism)' in ethics, and that many of the disagreements can be reconciled by analysis of the meanings of the various key terms:

Moral philosophers of the present time, with a few honourable exceptions all seem to think that they have to take sides on the question of whether "objectivism" or "subjectivism" is the correct account of the status of moral judgements. Most of them have the ambition to establish their objectivity, that being the more respectable side to be on; but quite a number are attracted by subjectivism (sometimes, without any clear distinction of meaning, called "relativism") as being more go-ahead and free thinking. Hardly any of them give any clear idea of how they are using the terms "objective" and "subjective"; and almost none realises that, in the most natural senses of the words, moral judgements are neither objective nor subjective, and the belief that they have to be one or the other is the result of a fundamental error (viz. descriptivism) which both objectivists and subjectivists, in one of the senses of those words, commit... (Hare, 1981, p. 206.)

Some basic incompatibilities remain after the linguistic puzzle dissolving has been completed. Hare himself takes the defensible view that the notion of *rationality* is much more promising than that of objectivism or subjectivism:

It has been my aim to find a system of moral reasoning which we can use when faced with a moral question. If such a system can be found which is rational, then the question of the objectivity of its results can be left to look after itself.

The problem of objectivism *versus* subjectivism, though it occupies much of the time of contemporary moral philosophers, is very old. Hare's synthesis, which looks towards rationality, does look promising. The controversy itself approaches the problem from a methodological direction, where the concern is with how first-order statements in ethics can be validated, or confirmed, refuted, or rendered clear and accessible. The debate has much in common with other 'great divides', for instance between utilitarianism and duty-based theories (deontology), and between 'determinism' (the idea that all events are caused by some kind of scientific or historical laws) and libertarianism (the idea that people have free will and therefore are responsible for their actions). This fourfold distinction, between objectivism, subjectivism, utilitarianism and deontology, will be used in the present chapter to provide examples of the reasons why incompatible approaches survive, without any one vanquishing another. But it is too easy to become sidetracked into the abstractions of modern philosophical debate, and to lose contact with the pressing issues of contemporary business. Would objectivism or subjectivism offer a set of criteria by which people who have to do with industry could judge contemporary practices and attitudes, and would utilitarianism or deontology provide a means by which the decision rules could be validated? More problematically, would business owners, managers, employees, customers or suppliers, trade unionists, governments or administrators be willing to reduce the roles of self interest, expediency, prudence and hierarchy? A preliminary answer may be offered: people who have to do with business and industry already do use ethical language and concepts to justify their actions. Appeals by managers to realism and to efficiency, competitiveness and so on, express values and are highly charged with moral overtones. Business language is replete with ethical concepts. Trade union claims are not announced as anything other than wholly 'justifiable': the language of collective bargaining is a mixture of self-interest, moral obligation, appeals to loyalty, solidarity, public interest prudence, justice, fairness, appeals to honour the spirit of agreements, freedom, standards, honesty and much else. Company chairmen's speeches are redolent of appeals to recognition of the full discharge of the onerous responsibilities of office, wisdom of policies, and much else. It will not do to dismiss all of these statements as empty rhetoric: although some undoubtedly are, we cannot know them all to be empty either from evidence (because the evidence tends to be mainly circumstantial and well hidden) or arising from non-moral first principles.

Nor will it do to claim that as a matter of fact, everyone knows that people are motivated by self-interest alone, and therefore appeals to fairness or moral principles could not possibly work: if notions of fairness, truth and honest dealing were always 'phoney' and known to be so, then they could serve no purpose whatever. People can only be deceived into thinking that a 'phoney' action, state, process, structure, etc. is an honest one if people have honest examples for comparison. So if no one ever acted honestly, no one could ever be taken in by a phoney claim to honesty.

Standards of conduct in and towards business have generally risen on a number of dimensions, described in Chapter One. The rise has not been uniform, universal, or without serious reversals. It is as naively optimistic to believe that these hesitant improvements have only arisen from advancing scientific knowledge and application of management skill, as it is to claim that they are due to an overriding beneficence on the part of the owners and managers of industry, governments, trade unions or the instititutions that support and train them, such as universities and professional bodies, though it is probable that principled, ethical, behaviour has played a much more significant part than is usually admitted.

Such progress as is observable cannot be plausibly explained in terms of the application of coherent ethical theories, except in a few cases, any more than it can be explained in terms of the applications of science (physical and social); but the insistent ignoring of methods for the systematic handling of values by the dominant scientific culture has inevitably led to the growth of new forms of ethical issues, or at least new contexts, as seen in the burgeoning City frauds, manipulation of government statistics in many areas, or the frequent total abandonment of other-regarding principles that trade unions used to pride themselves on. We saw in Chapter Three that the ethical theories (as well as the issues) are legion, and cannot be reduced to an agreed order by means of any widely accepted classification scheme (taxonomy); but they are reducible, for purposes of analysis, to a few, traditionally rival outlooks, which can be made to stand for the rest in that they illustrate the propositions that rival ethical theories refer to as partial, inconsistent though often necessary, insights. The next stage of the argument is to answer the 'key issue': *can rival ethical theories be reconciled?* My contention will be that a partial reconciliation is possible, using the traditional 'Golden Rule' as a major element in the basis for criteria for improvement in business and in industrial standards of behaviour. That any attempt at reconciliation will still leave the main theories fundamentally at odds in some respects need be no more of a handicap to the development of a practical business ethics than it has been in the case of, say, mathematics, economics or industrial relations, for example.

Does it Matter which Theory is Dominant?

The language of business and of business-related academic disciplines is primarily a language of persuasion and of setting, establishing and reinforcing values. Sometimes this is fully intentional and fully recognized, as can be seen, for example, in the defence of scientific management before the House of Representatives by F. W. Taylor quoted in Chapter Two.

Here, Taylor was candidly setting out what, in his view, were the benefits to everyone of the use of his management methods. Consumers would get cheaper products because the goods were more efficiently produced, the distribution of effort and reward between managers and workers would be equitable, and production would be taken out of the realm of custom and practice, to become scientific (on his understanding of what it meant to be scientific). In economic theory, the notion of efficiency is a value, albeit a non-moral one, as are the notions of profit, growth, consumer sovereignty, maximum and minimum, welfare, optimum (the best), utility and many others. They are values in the mathematical sense that a number or symbol can be used in terms of these ideas, in evaluating observations (or, more often, in evaluating explanations of observations). In doing so, a common standard, or norm is set on the basis of assumptions, or other technical norms, such as statistical tests and the like. But a maximum or a chi-squared number is a judgment, made within laid-down, argued-for standards in relation to empirical observations, rather than empirical observations 'straight off'. You can put money in a till, but you cannot put a chi-squared, a maximum and an assumption, or a rule determining what assumptions *ought* to be made, in with the money. The most that could be done is to put some kind of symbolic representation in. Now, several further points emerge at this stage: the treatment in the technical economic literature is often and rightly held to provide 'good', or 'exemplary' standards of rigour in analysis. These judgments are, of course, values in their own right. There is no argument in existence, to my knowledge, that attempts to show that these non-moral values exhibit a different logic from moral ones, or from prudential ones, for that matter. If we say, "such and such a set of assumptions forms *the* assumptions of 'economic theory' ", we are open to the question, on whose authority are these *the* assumptions? From the usual answer, they are the assumptions of 'standard' economic theory, but we need to show the source of the standard setting. Some writers, wisely, trace this back to the mature judgments of the leaders of the profession. In other words, the notions of profit, maximization, 'standard' theory and the rest are norms that set other, lower-order technical norms, but they have an arbitrary, or apparently 'subjective' element that is crucial, and is not logically different from moral values. Professional standards also require honesty in argument, truthfulness in empirical claims, and much more. This 'requirement' is not a formal requirement to be found in textbooks, but can be assumed to be taken for granted. I know of no business or economics text that declares honesty, accuracy, skill, etc. to be irrelevant or undesirable.

From Taylor and Mayo, and from 'standard' 'economic theory' we can gain the idea that there are technical skills which, when applied, lead to the furtherance of the interests of all participants. There are indications also that not only interests in the sense of material gain are on offer, but that welfare at a prudential level is also available within the enterprise system. Some would go further and see the free enterprise system as the embodiment of justice, echoing the older debates about 'the economic theory of democracy' (Hospers, 1978; Macpherson, 1978, 1987).

Given then, that the language of business and of business-related disciplines is primarily a language of persuasion and of value setting, the next problem is to ascertain whether it matters which set of values is chosen. On the substantive matter, in the theory of the firm, the assumptions are clearly chosen on the basis of the values of 'free markets', consumer sovereignty, and private ownership. Once these values are accepted, the lower order values are amenable to more technical treatments, using technical values. But technical values are still values. There is a fascinating literature on the extent to which the theory is true, useful, predictive, amenable to quantification, testable, and much else. It will not be pursued here. The main point is that the business system based on the values listed dominates much of the world, and is a fact of life. It should now be clear that the positivist accounts criticized in Chapter Two are less problematic, and more useful when seen as operating within a value framework that is explicit and open to rational amendment. The positivist accounts are baleful only when they become ideologies that claim to convert the guiding values themselves into techniques or push the responsibility for values elsewhere.

The value assumptions, their origin and validity in such well-established disciplines as economics can be seen to be problematic. The view is sometimes expressed that revisions of 'standard' theories may only be proposed from within the academic disciplines by individuals who have furnished sufficient proof of their loyalty to the discipline by making acclaimed contributions within the theory (Machlup, 1974).

This belief seems to be implicit in many academic attitudes, and may be fairly described as 'the argument from gerontological hierarchy'. It may well be that the argument is functional, giving order and incremental progress in scholarly research, but the origins and justification of economic and business practice, in terms of their ethical content, are central to business ethics, and thus may not be dismissed without discussion. The theory of the firm in economics is broadly utilitarian in outlook. The dominant form of business organization, i.e. bureaucracy, seems to offer a utilitarian element in that in principle there is equality of opportunity in bureaucracy, allowing people to use it for career purposes, in return for limited services. But bureaucracy also offers justice, in the sense used in Weber's 'pure' form of bureaucracy (Pugh, 1984, Ch. 1) where conduct is governed by rules and contractual obligation. But the notion of obligation is a deontological one. The problem now arises that the dominant forms of business in Western economies, i.e. bureaucracies, in a market-led environment seem to rest on incompatible foundations: a utilitarianism and a deontology. Once the assumptions and values of these systems are accepted, then the 'positivist' trends have made some headway in explaining the behaviour of the systems, but the values and assumptions themselves are not generated by either utilitarianism or deontology. These are theories by which actions, states, processes or institutions can be evaluated or justified. There is nothing in deontological theory that implies bureaucracy. The particular values chosen within the systems can be thought of as arriving from a variety of sources. The traditional way of describing these is in terms of either the general outlook that sees values as generally irrational or non-rational, arising from custom and practice or individual taste, or the general outlook which sees values as emerging from logical considerations of 'the nature of things'. The former is the subjectivist or relativist tradition already referred to, and the latter is the objectivist tradition.

Historically, deontologists have tended to be objectivists. Utilitarians and positivists have tended to be both relativists and subjectivists. As the quotation above from Hare shows, it is not necessary to take sides on the various matters, but to see part of the problem as arising from linguistic confusions. It is the remaining, non-linguistic matters that occupy the next section.

The Practical Issue of Autonomy

The four examples, of utilitarianism, deontology, objectivism and subjectivism, are chosen because they are so widespread, and because they can be made to stand for all the competing theories, both 'standard' and otherwise.

The practical differences that the adoption of any one or any combination of the doctrines would make are best illustrated by applying them for the purposes of interpretation to various kinds of evidence. Different kinds of data are essential because in studying business practice and its results, the many different methods have characteristic uses and limitations and can be contradictory. A synthesis that is consistent with all four ethical approaches and supported by several kinds of evidence would be too much to hope for, but an attempt to find one might be instructive.

As a methodological aside, it is useful at this point to forestall one potential criticism. It might be said that according to Hume's principle, values cannot imply facts and vice versa, and therefore no amount of evidence could or disprove the theoretical and value positions under discussion: although an empirical hypothesis can be refuted or disproved, it takes a theory to kill a theory. There is some truth in this, but a theory that has no application is at least empirically worthless, and one that is empirically radically ambiguous needs some strong *prima facie* support.

The practical issue that is chosen is whether or not individuals when faced with conflicts of belief, principle and/or interests can and do act according to their own beliefs about what ought to be done. This will be set against a characteristic answer that would be offered by the two substantive theories, utilitarianism and deontology, and the two methodological theories, subjectivism and objectivism.

Presumably the possibility of holding out against pressures to break with one's own beliefs will be accepted as one form of conduct that will be accepted as a characteristically ethical issue. There are many behavioural possibilities. People can, for example, merely pretend to conform, but still disapprove, or can conform and disapprove, change beliefs to match those 'required', conform only so long as the pressures remain, protest, verbally or physically, withdraw from the situation, or seek advice or help. It seems well-enough established that such pressures exist: according to Gellerman (1986), of the top 500 American companies or corporations, two-thirds have been involved in ethical or legal transgressions. Gellerman also quotes an older study in the *Harvard Business Review* to the effect that, from a survey 75% of the managers studied "felt a conflict between profit considerations and ethical conduct" (Baumhart, 1961, p. 163). A study in *The Hong Kong Manager* in 1987 gives a figure of 92% of Hong Kong managers and just over 40% of American managers in a survey expressed affirmation of the proposition, "I find that sometimes I must compromise my personal principles to conform to my organization's expectations" (Dolecheck and Dolecheck, 1987, p. 33). One of the most widely discussed conflicts between an individual and the corporation that employed him shows little direct conflict (rather, a different outlook) until after the employee had taken steps to inform the authorities of suspected price-rigging, having already left the corporation (Adams, 1985). Instead, a whole tangle of legal and moral issues emerged, on an international scale, leading to tragedy (Adams, op. cit.; Newbiggin, 1984). Experimental evidence raises the possibility that values are often not deeply held, or if they are, then they may be easily pushed aside. For instance, in the famous Milgram experiments (Milgram, 1965) people would deliver what they had reason to believe were electric shocks to 'subjects' in a 'learning experiment'. It appeared that the members of the public invited to do so would be more likely to deliver the (supposed) shocks if they were asked to by respectable-looking 'scientists', and less likely to do so if asked by less respectable-looking ones. They were more likely to deliver if paid than otherwise, or if encouraged by the experimenter. This appears to challenge general assumptions about the autonomy and beneficence of individuals.

The matter of the strength of the autonomy of individual belief and action raised a new crop of issues whose treatment by the four representative rival ethical theories may now be considered.

A Utilitarian Interpretation

A utilitarian view is likely to hold that interpretation of the above evidence could be made on the following lines: admittedly, businesses do not always conform to the law, or to codes of ethical conduct. Individuals vary in what they believe and in the strength of their beliefs. The questions that we must answer are whether the business practices will provide greatest benefit by being allowed to continue than they will if, for example, all such practices were to be stamped out. Would it not be preferable to reconize that the individual values that are in conflict with those of companies are unrealistic, perhaps a luxury? This would depend on several matters. Are the individuals whose values are at odds with their company trying to uphold the law, or are they expressing idiosyncratic beliefs? The matter can be resolved in many ways. Surveys will tell us whether the individual's values are or are not idiosyncratic. Social science will tell us whether enforcing the legal or (supposed) ethical requirements on firms would be counterproductive. For instance, enforcement of compliance on companies may need to be so severe as to offend other social values. The decision, in the end, is to be based on how effective control would be, and how we value the benefits from business practice as it now is. There is no merit in forcing compliance if the social costs outweigh the benefits. If, however, the contrary can be shown, then the compliance should be forced. Individuals should be forced to accept the tensions between their values and those of the company if it can be shown that the social benefits of doing so outweigh the costs. Further, it should be remembered that in the event of a clash of company and individual values, where there is no case of law breaking, it should not be assumed that the company is wrong just because it is more powerful than an individual. The decision in that case is a straightforward calculation of the costs and benefits of individual conformity, changing the company's practices, or the individual leaving to seek a better trade-off between personal and group values elsewhere. The purpose of the company and of the individual's involvement is to secure, if not maximize, mutual gains. Values that do not do that are irrelevant.

This is not the only line that a utilitarian could follow, but it is a characteristic one. An exhaustive account of all possible utilitarian interpretations would be never-ending—a point whose main significance will become plainer as the argument proceeds.

A Deontological Interpretation

Deontology has to do with duty. It differs from utilitariansim not because notions of duty have no place in utilitarianism—they do have a place—but in that some notion of duty provides the overriding reason for justifying or requiring an action of a particular kind. It would be to miss the point to suggest that because the two theories have some notions in common, they are not importantly different. For the utilitarian it may be a duty to maximize economic growth, or profit or utility, but only because they are thought to be the ends of moral action in the first place. Similarly, consequences do matter to deontologists, but the consequences are of a moral and logical nature, such as the duty to count every individual as one, and not more or less than one, or not to use scapegoats, even if the benefits grossly outweigh the costs of doing so. 'Who benefits should pay' is a deontological principle. The notion that those more able to pay should subsidize the individuals who are less able to pay if the 'social welfare' would be higher is a utilitarian principle. For utilitarians, ends can justify means, or as many deontologists would say, utilitarians cannot avoid the accusation that unethical means may be used if the outcome is to everyone's benefit. Deontologists would forego beneficial ends if they could only be obtained by improper means. One way or proceeding from here would be to invent a hypothetical situation in which the rival principles would make someone who holds them uncomfortable. But hypothetical cases are not substitutes for real cases, and there are more than enough real cases to go round.

A deontologist could interpret the evidence in question by regarding it as illustrative of several propositions: *first*, that admittedly, people sometimes do not spell out, even to themselves, what rules they live by. Sometimes people are easily influenced not to live by such rules as they hold even if they do spell them out, but no amount of evidence can mask the imperative nature of duties. Whatever the social costs and benefits, and whatever the facts are in relation to people's weaknesses or inconsistencies, or lack of positive commitment to duties, the duties still demand compliance. Ross (1939), in the passage from which quotations have already been taken, points to the *prima facie* duties of telling the truth, keeping promises, avoiding doing harm to others. But why are they duties? Here the deontologists are divided. Some, as for example Hobbes (1651), see the duties as arising in the end from prudence, or self-interest, although he sometimes speaks of contractual obligations as though they were sacrosanct. It is true that readers of Hobbes need to solve the puzzle as to what he thought the source of obligation to be. What does seem to be unavoidable is that the 'laws of nature' oblige people to keep 'compacts' because of the nature of people, who, as we might now say, are programmed to need to do so. For the implication of this is that if people had been different, the 'moral laws of nature' would be different. Much more is at stake than the rational calculation of specific gains and losses which might accrue to any act. That people sometimes make an estimate of gains that impels them to break the law does not absolve them of the duty to obey the law, except in the special case in which their life itself is threatened, on the Hobbesian view.

For Ross, obligation is towards what he considers to be *prima facie* duties (Ross, 1939, p. 313), which are intuitively known. One of these is to produce as much good as we can. Others are to tell the truth and to keep promises. These duties can conflict, but understanding of the circumstances in which the conflict between the rules occurs leads to a decision in favour of whichever rule produces the most fitting answer. This is not a question-begging device, but a statement of what would now be called 'contingency' theory. Like Kant, Ross based the status of the *prima facie* duties in logic. He saw them as axioms, neither needing nor capable of proof:

There are many plain men who already know as well as any moral philosopher could tell them, how they ought to behave. Not only do they see their concrete duty in the different situations of life with admirable clearness and correctness, but they have principles of a certain degree of generality on which no moral philosophers can improve—tell the truth, keep your promises, aim at the happiness of those around you, and so on. (Ross, 1939/63/, pp. 311–312.)

Returning to the evidence of the Milgram experiments, the surveys and the case studies, a deontological outlook in the style of Ross implies a claim that, taking into account all the relevant and known circumstances, the proper ascription of duties and moral condemnations to particular acts is possible with the aid of the *prima facie* duties incumbent upon all relevant parties described in the cases, experiments and surveys. The duties arise on this view because they fall under the authority of the moral axioms, and the fact, if it is a fact, that people are prepared to set aside their general moral duties in order to conform to their company's requirements does not make them any less imperative. Ross does not go as far as to say that the doctrine is to be obeyed even if everyone would be worse off, but implies that utilitarianism requires that if everyone were to be better off in terms of receiving more good, then the duties may be laid aside. Ross avoids the conflict of methodological principle at this stage by making the duty to do good to those around us one of the *prima facie* duties. It may be observed that most people cannot be regarded as holding that view, even if they agreed on what it means to do good: casual observation at least would suggest that many people see the primary duty as being to self and immediate family, and that many have a strong view about what is desirable that people should do, even if it is clearly not for any identifiable good of their own, but rather for the good of 'country' or of some other similar abstraction. We might as well promote the value that people should not deviate from the general norms, but throughout history, moral progress has come from deviants from customary ways of doing things.

Incompatibilities at the Substantive Level
The argument between the deontologists on the lines of Ross's argument and the utilitarians on the lines sketched out above could clearly proceed a good deal further: one side could clarify what it takes to be a caricature or a misunderstanding on the part of its opponent. Some amendment of the various standpoints could be made, different 'facts', evidence, arguments could be adduced. To an extent, Ross makes the utilitarian requirement to 'produce good' one of the axioms, thus incorporating a utilitarian element. There are other forms of duty-based argument that can escape some, but not all of the counter-points made by utilitarians, and vice versa. Neither school can *establish* its basic principles, but can only state them. If we ask

of a utilitarian why, for example, we should maximize 'good' or happiness (or why a firm should maximize profits) we would get the (dusty) answer that this is the whole basis of ethical conduct, and if we cannot see it, then all that can be done is to wait until we do see it. If we ask a deontologist why we should trust the *prima facie* principles we will get one of two groups of answers: that we have or are capable of developing a moral sense that enables us to recognize the *prima facie* duties, and once recognized, their justification is beside the point; or that the principles have stood the test of time. We know, for example, that it may sometimes be to our advantage to lie, but we also know that it is plain wrong, unless a powerful duty outranks it in a particular case. Clearly, there is no possible basis on which the rival intuitions of the utilitarians and the deontologists could be reconciled, or on which one could vanquish the other. The long-running ethical argument between determinists who hold that moral thinking is irrelevant to action because what we do is determined by history, our psychological make-up, physical or genetic laws, conditioning, manipulation by an inevitable political process based in the nature of people, the environment, and much else, and the libertarians who hold that actions are guided by free choices, is in the same category as the arguments between utilitarians and deontologists. As it happens, some ways of thinking seem to incorporate incompatible elements of all of these. For example, standard economic theory, as described in the earlier chapters, is utilitarian to the extent that it sees individuals as maximizing utilities (under various names), firms as maximizing profits, and the whole system as maximizing total output, welfare and even freedom. This is a combined utilitarianism and deontology, but the incompatibilities are masked by the technical intermediary of the 'standard' diagrams and equations which are the *required* vehicles for critical appraisal. Thus, being a professional in the area requires a *duty* to take a *utilitarian* and *technical* viewpoint as a condition of acceptance.

As has often been pointed out (Ross, 1939; Flew, 1984) major ethical outlooks such as these have a hydra-headedness, such that refutation of one form of an argument seems to generate new forms, and leave at least some old forms unscathed. Thus the major ethical standpoints, in their first-order form are radically unprovable, and radically irrefutable. They may be reconciled to some extent, but in the end it is not logically possible to provide conclusive grounds for being a thoroughgoing utilitarian, deontologist, libertarian or determinist. At best, some weak mixture can survive for practical purposes. For example, there is no radical inconsistency in assenting to a principle that a balance needs to be maintained between encouraging the growth of output (a generally utilitarian stance) and maintaining an acceptable distribution of income. This could be argued for on the principle that even if everyone were to gain from 'growth', equitable distribution is a value in its own right—a deontological, 'natural rights' standpoint. In these circumstances, it will not do to speak of 'maximizing' growth, subject to the constraint of an equitable distribution of income, or of achieving an equitable distribution of income, subject to the need to achieve sustained growth. The notions of 'growth', 'constraint', and 'equitable' are no more than weasel words in this context. 'Economic growth' itself is an elusive enough concept, but to talk of maximizing it is to destroy its meaning. We cannot know whether a distribution is equitable until some principles of equity are established, and we cannot know whether 'growth' is capable of producing improvement until we know what the conditions under which the growth occurs are, and how acceptable they are to the participants and to others affected by it. This is neither a counsel of perfection nor a radical scepticism about the possibility about economic growth. What it does mean is that the ethics of the matter cannot be derived from utilitarianism, deontology or some eclectic mixture of the two with, perhaps, notions of justice or egoism added.

Objectivism and Subjectivism

Ethical theories are constructed, among other reasons, in order to reduce the huge variety of issues so that they can be classified under a small and manageable number of principles. Because the rival insights into ethical behaviour and principles of conduct cannot be reconciled at the first-order level, it is usual to attempt to justify them at the second-order (sometimes called the 'meta-ethical') level. Here, the main issues are: *how* can particular ethical theories be justified or refuted? How can we establish the status and validity of first-order assertions or claims? In this context, the 'great divide' is between 'objectivists' and 'subjectivists'. Although, as the above question from Hare shows, it is possible to reject the debate as irrelevant to the constructive development of ethics in general, the debate is old enough, and currently widespread enough to warrant some discussion.

Even this debate has many forms, and exhibits the hydra-headedness of the first-order arguments. The status of ethical propositions, arguments and principles has been variously seen as, for example, arising from their essential character as intuitions (Moore, 1903; Ross, 1939), as expressive emotion (Stevenson, 1938; Ayer, 1939), as axioms (Ross), as logically basic, but recognized by a kind of intuition that can only be made and understood with a great deal of careful thought (Kant, 1785), as prescriptions, freely made (Hare, 1963), as 'social norms' (most social scientists) or as expressive of solutions to the general problems of an age (MacIntyre, 1985). They are also seen as commands of deities (on this, see Frankena (1973) and Hume (1777))—the list is endless.

As might be expected, the argument between the objectivists and the subjectivists is true to form in that like the utilitarians and the deontologists (or for that matter, the economic theory of the firm) there is no definitive statement of the content and implications. Instead we find many similar versions, such that criticisms of any one version do not apply wholly to all others. Some examples of *subjectivism* (also known as, or related to *relativism*, or *historical relativism, historicism, cultural relativism, indexicality*, for example) will be discussed below, but by way of introduction, Flew's *Dictionary of Philosophy* is helpful, in providing a neutral account of both doctrines that would probably be accepted by the various partisans:

> *Subjectivism.* In its simplest form the position held by someone who believes that all moral attitudes are merely a matter of personal taste. "Eating people is wrong", for example, and its contradictory become not true or false, but simply expressions of the dietary preferences of the speaker.

> *Objectivism.* The belief that there are certain moral truths that would remain true whatever anyone or everyone thought or desired. For instance, "no one should ever deliberately inflict pain on another, simply to take pleasure in his suffering" might be thought of as a plausible example. Even in a world of Sadists, who all rejected it, the contention remains true, just as $5 + 7 = 12$ remains correct even if there is no one left to count. (Flew, 1984.)

Some examples of subjectivist stances are:

> Within the broad limits of the welfare of all nature, the choice of specific criteria on which to base any moral evaluation is necessarily subjective: there is no given set of objective values discoverable by reason. (Marsh, 1980, p. 55.)

In the classic *Language, Truth and Logic*, Ayer (1936) describes the key element in subjectivism (which he rejects, linking it with utilitarianism) as beyond rational argument, referring to:

> ... those ethical philosophers who are commonly called subjectivists and those who are known as utilitarians, for the utilitarian defines the rightness of actions in terms of the pleasure or happiness or satisfaction to which they give rise; the subjectivist in terms of feelings of approval which a certain person or group of people, has towards them. (p. 109.)

Ayer's own view as expressed in *Language, Truth and Logic* was described as emotivism which held that ethical judgments cannot be validated by either subjective or objective propositions:

They are unverifiable for the same reason as a cry of pain or a word of command is unverifiable—because they do not express genuine propositions. (loc. cit.)

Insofar as subjectivists up to the mid-1930s thought that ethical statements were descriptive, Ayer's distancing his views from theirs did make a defensible distinction, but in a perfectly normal sense of 'subjective', i.e. as belonging to, or of the consciousness or feelings of a thinking or perceiving subject, as opposed to external things, Ayer's emotivism was a different kind of subjectivism. Emotivism itself enjoyed a vogue in the 1940s and 1950s, but will not be discussed here, as it can reasonably be seen from the viewpoint of the 1980s as a passing fad, whose valuable legacy includes Stevenson's (1938) notion of 'persuasive definitions'. (A balanced critique of emotivism can be found in Warnock, M. (1960) and Warnock, G. (1967.)

Characteristic objectivist stances are provided by Finnis (1983):

For everything that I have been saying supposed that the judgments about human good(s) and the truly worthwhile objects of human existence are objective judgments capable of being true regardless of our decisions or the conventions of our language or the customs of our communities (pp. 22–23)

and from De George:

First, despite the difference in many customs and moral practices from society to society and age to age, there is and has been basic agreement on a large number of central issues. The most basic agreement, though completely formal is that good should be done and evil avoided. Substantively there are moral requirements that the members of any society must follow if it is to survive. These include among others, respect for the lives of its members, respect for the truth (without which it would be impossible to communicate and carry on social life); and respect for cooperation and helpfulness. (De George and Pichler, 1978, p. 4.)

Returning to the evidence from the surveys, cases and experiments discussed above, the lines of debate on the interpretation by objectivists and subjectivists are clear enough. Subjectivists could claim that because the values of individual and company imply different behaviour, the company has the right to demand compliance with the company itself in going about its legitimate business (e.g. in pursuing profit maximization within the law). The subordination of individual to group values is an inevitable part of the political process, indeed, it could not be otherwise if values were mere expressions of will, emotion, preference or custom.

The standard problem for subjectivists is that moral beliefs do change, and if morals are really only expressions of will, emotion, etc., then no subjectivist explanation can be offered as to why they should ever be persuasive. No explanation can be offered as to why people hold the view that they do, other than regarding them as data, given, but not explained. There is a logical problem: if the proposition that moral statements are subjective is itself subjective, then it has validity only for those who believe in it, and *ex hypothesi* can have no persuasive force for anyone else. If, on the other hand, it is held to be verifiable (i.e. objectively true, provable, compelling), then it is to evidence or established logical principle that we might look for support.

But this brings it perilously close to an objectivist stance. There seems to be no logical principle that establishes subjectivism. Subjectivists need to prove that differences in preferences expressed are equally valid or invalid. For example, even if it is true that people do, as a matter of fact, express widely different preferences on moral matters, subjectivists need to be able to show that any expression is as good as another, being of the same logical status. This no doubt explains why subjectivists tend to support their stance by pointing to evidence that customs do vary over time and between different communities. The quotation from De George above shows one line on which the subjectivist account can be criticized: the variations in moral belief can be held to reflect differences in circumstances and in factual beliefs. The principles are discoverable by means of reasoned argument and could still be universal. The applications and genesis of moral ideas are always necessarily contingent, i.e. depending on circum- stances—a point that Ross had made in the 1930s.

The standard problem for objectivists is how to *prove* the rules that they hold to be universal, or to *show* that the values and conclusions are unavoidable, because of the way things are, or because they are logically *implied* by some principle that is not in doubt. In the case of the companies which enforce employees' compliance with company norms, an objectivist can claim that the company is right when the norms are lawful, because employees are under a contractual obligation to serve the legitimate interests of employers insofar as it bears on their work, but that employees are entitled to refuse to obey unlawful demands by the employer, or the employer's agent, or even that there is an absolute duty to report company law-breaking to the proper authorities, usually the law-enforcement agen- cies. As against this it can be objected that the obligation to obey the law is merely prudential: as with Plato's example of the Ring of Gyges, quoted in Chapter One, people often do not obey if they think that they can get away, or if they do so they are being unnecessarily timid or prissy. The standard objectivist response is that if all apparently altruistic behaviour were no more than a form of prudence, even the (allegedly mistaken) belief that people sometimes do things because it is right to do so could never have arisen: people may be deluded into believing that, for example, a confi- dence trickster is guiding them properly if they mistake the trickster's advice for proper advice, but they could only mistake it for the real thing if they already know what the real thing is, i.e. in this case, what form proper advice would take. They might be mistaken in thinking that they observe it in a particular case when it is not present. If there were no real cases there could not be bogus ones. This is not merely a linguistic conclusion, it is a matter of the way things are. We can get the concept of morality or ethical rightness from a variety of sources, but we accept or reject particular rules or decisions on rational grounds, which involve commitments, argument, estimates of consequences (including logical consequences) and much else in ethical reasoning.

It should be clear that the bases of subjectivism and objectivism are no more secure than those of utilitarianism or deontology. On this, the position has changed little since Hume wrote in the eighteenth century:

> There is an inconvenience which attends all abstract reasoning, that is, it may silence without convincing an antagonist, and requires the same intense study to make us sensible of its force, that was at first requisite for its invention. When we leave our closet, and engage in the common affairs of life, its conclusions seem to vanish, like the phantoms of the night, on the appearance of the morning, and 'tis difficult for us to retain even that conviction that we had attained with difficulty. (Hume, 1739/1965, p. 455.)

Further, according to Hume:

> It is not contrary to reason to prefer the destruction of the world to the scratching of my finger. (Hume, 1739.)

In saying so Hume was endorsing the idea that moral commitments come from within, and are the responsibility of individuals, not the state or church. In the terms of this book's main themes, they are not the responsibility of companies, classes, peer groups, professional bodies or occupational groups. He sought a physical cause for preferences.

The rest of this book will present arguments for an account of business ethics that is based in part on a degree of scepticism with regard to the more uncompromising outlooks that claim exclusive sight of the truth. There is some element of utilitariansim, deontology, subjectivism, objectivism that can contribute to solutions to the issues of business ethics. Other outlooks have contributions to make. But this does not argue for an eclecticism that accepts something from every outlook. My own view is that subjectivists are right in thinking that if anyone were to produce an idiosyncratic but consistent set of moral principles and were at the same time willing to defend the set at all costs, it would be impossible to prove them wrong, but that subjectivist accounts are typically too ready to give up the argument in the face of variety of practices, or of robust declarations of contrary principle. It follows from this that the traditional objectivists have by far the stronger case on a 'balance of argument' basis. A version of this view will be explained in more detail at a later stage, when it will be offered as one of the ground rules that emerge, in my view from a discussion of the first few 'key issues in business eithics', i.e. that business ethics is possible, and can be defended against non-ethical interpretations of business behaviour, that values can be handled systematically, and that at least a partial reconciliation of some rival viewpoints can be achieved. The eclecticism that sees some good in every event and some truth in every statement has little to offer. It is important sometimes to dismount from the fence. Some views are just wrong, in many senses of the word, and some are right.

Historical Relativism

One other doctrine can be introduced at this stage. It is one which is very popular among social scientists, and has had a robust exposition in recent years by Alasdair MacIntyre (1985). This doctrine, a close relative of subjectivism, is variously known as relativism, historical relativism, or historicism.

Relativism, along with positivism, has dominated scientific thinking and especially that of the social sciences for a long time, under various aliases such as 'indexicality', 'action theory', contingency or is simply assumed in discussion of variety of 'norms', practices, cultures and much else. We can add cultural relativism, giving a contemporary flavour to historical relativism.

MacIntyre's argument in *After Virtue* can be summarized as having a negative thesis, a positive thesis (which is not to be confused with a self-consciously positivist outlook), and a methodological thesis: MacIntyre seems, on the face of it, to be offering three main, interconnected propositions. The first, which I shall refer to as 'the negative thesis', or view, states that philosophers have not been able to agree on a 'once-for-all' morality, i.e. that philosophers have not agreed on a specific *code* of morals, valid for all time, and that they have not been able to agree on the *general grounds* for holding *any* moral position, i.e. neither the codes nor the moral/ethical grounds for holding them have been agreed.

The Positive Thesis

This is the assertion that moral codes and theories are specific to particular times and places; with no 'morality as such', only that of, for example ancient Athens, seventeenth century Western Europe, or mediaeval Spain.

> Morality which is no particular society's morality is to be found nowhere. There was the morality-of-fourth-century-Athens, there were the-morali-

ties-of-thirteenth-century-Western Europe, there are numerous such moralities, but wherever was or is morality-as-such? (p. 265)

and,

For what the progress of analytic philosophy has succeeded in establishing is that there are *no* grounds for believing in universal necessary principles—outside purely formal enquiries except relative to some set of assumptions (p. 267.)

On p. 267 he claims to be a 'historicist'. However, in an unexplained passage, he also seems to deny that he is a historical relativist (p. 272).

Robert Wachbroit has suggested that one implication of that account . . . (i.e. an earlier account by MacIntyre) is that some version of relativism is inescapable.

The Methodological Thesis

MacIntyre tells us that morality can only be understood in relation to time and place, in relation to their cultural milieu. Again, this *appears* to be historical relativism. A subsidiary part of the methodological thesis is that the academic boundaries between history, philosophy and perhaps the social sciences have not been sensibly drawn, and perhaps that they should not be drawn at all. The methodological thesis also involves a distaste for 'armchair theorizing'. Thus, in the Preface (p. ix).

The notion that the moral philosopher can study *the* concepts of morality by reflecting, Oxford armchair style on what he or she and those around him or her say and do is barren.

MacIntyre's negative thesis is not wholly plausible: even if he is right in that philosophers have disagreed over specific codes and over general grounds for observing them, it does not follow that they are all wrong, and still less does it follow that they can *only* be understood in their historical context, intellectual *milieu*, etc. The latter thesis is one of the set of disagreeing doctrines, and has the same logical status as they do. It is worth noting that John Locke in the seventeenth century, pointed out that "universal assent proves nothing true". Nor does universal condemnation prove a doctrine false. The logic of the argument is the only force that can do that. Philosophers cannot, it is true, always agree what the logic of the argument is. It does not follow that when they disagree it is because they always make different assumptions. It may be because the implications are not clear. In any case, even if they do make different assumptions, it does not follow that they are all equally true, or false. The agreement, approval or disapproval of one's coterie is simply irrelevant.

The proposition that particular historical and environmental conditions incline people to identify and solve problems in a particular way is a sensible one. They incline, without necessitating. The idea has been worked out with some elegance by many organization theorists—Lawrence and Lorsch in America (*Organisation and Environment*), by Joan Woodward in the U.K. (*Industrial Organisation—Theory and Practice*). This work was done in the 1960s and follows the 1950s work of Burns and Stalker in Scotland, and of the Tavistock (e.g. Trist and Bamforth) in the 1940s. This work has been developed with great skill by 'contingency theorists' in Britain and America in the 1970s and 1980s (Lupton, 1971). All this work is based on detailed case studies, involving much field work.

Now, however much influence the economic and political environment have on a particular code or theory, the code or theory is still capable of being criticized on moral and rational grounds. In fact, particular codes do have critics: if the environment determines a particular code or theory, what are we to say of its critics? That their criticisms are likewise environmentally determined—same cause, opposite effect? What is more probable is that the environment (political, economic, scientific) does pose problems, but does not determine the solution. Again, if several moralities exist in the same *milieu*, which one should be taken to be the authentic one? This is different from the questions of conflicting codes discussed by MacIntyre and his critics. Indeed, the final chapter of the second edition makes it clear that the particular historicist thesis is not anything more than an *intention* to prove a thesis, merely to be seen as work in progress.

MacIntyre is correct in his claim that the current discipline boundaries are untenable. He seems willing to demolish the philosophy/history boundary fence. But why stop there? Ethics and business ethics require knowledge of, and arguments in the light of economic, industrial relations, legal, managerial and psychological developments, and knowledge of current trends in these areas is readily available in the range of literature.

The proposition that particular historical conditions incline people to characterize and solve problems in a particular way is itself a plausible one. As Sabine put it:

> This history of political theory is written in the light of the hypothesis that theories of politics are themselves part of politics. In other words they do not refer to an external reality, but are produced as a normal part of the social *milieu* in which politics itself has its being. (Sabine, 1937, Preface.)

Sabine is careful to describe the proposition as a hypothesis, rather than as an inevitable conclusion. It should be said that if theories of politics are part of politics, then so might be theories about theories of politics. To the considerable extent that ethics has a political content, then it applies also to ethics. The insight is sound and instructive, but it does not preclude the possibility of true or false claims, or restrict critiques to matters of consistency within the theories. The theories themselves can be criticized or defended, and often are. The grounds for these criticisms when they occur are varied. Socrates rightly claimed that many of his contemporaries supported unsupportable myths. MacIntyre puts the point that:

> There are no grounds for believing in universally necessary principles—outside purely formal enquiries—except in relation to a set of assumptions. (MacIntyre, 1985, p. 267.)

This sceptical argument is tenable, but it clearly applies to the formal enquiries as well, as was shown in Chapter Two. The problem of identifying a 'morality-as-such' is of the same form as those of some other disciplines. Berkeley showed in the *Principles of Human Understanding* that when we consider the notion of a triangle, we must consider, at least on an image theory of thinking, a particular form of triangle, large or small, equilateral or scalene, and not a triangle-as-such. Similarly we can, in considering motor cars, rightly claim that there is no 'motor car-as-such' but only a number of Fords, Chryslers, Bugattis and Stanley Steamers of a particular model, year, size or colour. We can legitimately claim that we cannot criticize any particular one for not being something else, or for not being fit for some purpose other than intended, or for failing to incorporate knowledge that was not available when the particular vehicle was built.

Nor are the principles of the internal combustion engine anything other than relative to some set of assumptions, and the principles of the expansion of gases are not to be regarded, at least according to some accounts of science, as other than hypotheses, and thus not universally necessary principles. In this way, ethical theories, codes and rules can be seen as vehicles for identifying and meeting the legitimate requirements of those people who are affected by them. A code that does not do so, or which imposes the view of a limited section on the rest, can be legitimately regarded as an incomplete, primitive, degenerate, or simply bad code.

In conclusion, the explosive growth of issues in business ethics has arisen in part from their neglect, stemming from undue enthusiasm for current views on the nature and method of science, and the apparent belief in business that science is sufficient. The natural place to look for guidance towards resolution of the issues is to the theories of ethics. There are many rival theories, both of substance and of methods of analysis. None of these seems to be able to assert dominance over others. All seem to be necessary in that some of their insights are compelling, even though not all are. People can and do pursue idiosyncratic values, and can stick to them, if they are willing to adjust their beliefs about nature to fit. Most ethical arguments involve some techniques of protection of ethical from inconvenient factual beliefs, and stances are typically taken without the full benefit of the relevant evidence, sometimes with good grounds and sometimes not. Progress in ethical reasoning often comes from acceptance that some factual beliefs are false. As Hare says, 'ought' implies 'can'. Scientific progress and changes in people's factual beliefs are not the only grounds for criticism and change of codes. Ideas come from many sources, and frequently come from rediscovery of what was said long ago. It is, of course, possible that the old beliefs or views meant something different, but the idea that what it meant must have been determined wholly by the cultural *milieu* is both implausible and untestable.

This suggests that it might be possible to develop criteria for improvement that are compatible with the main rival doctrines. Chapter Five is an attempt to identify such criteria.

CHAPTER FIVE

The Role of Business Ethics: Towards Some Ground Rules

The argument so far may be summarized: rising standards of conduct in business and industry can be clearly identified in a number of areas, such as health and safety, employment regulation, consumer protection, levels of sophistication in skills and application of codes of practice. For this the fashionable nineteenth century word 'progress' has been replaced by the fashionable twentieth century word 'growth' and other superficially value-free expressions, such as 'advancement of knowledge' or just plain 'scientific developments'. The rise has been uncertain as to continuity and causes, and of limited coverage, as, for example, when traditionally low-paid occupations have shared little in the growth and its benefits. Whether the unevenness of the share is due to inexorable forces or to differential effort and merit is and has been a live issue. The positivist outlook that has dominated the discussions of such matters for so long is being increasingly questioned, but it is fair to say that no authoritative alternative has yet emerged. The narrow vision engendered by positivism has permitted the growth, in some areas, such as 'the City' to crisis proportions, of value-related issues, which have been untreatable because unrecognized by the dominant outlooks.

If these outlooks cannot treat the issues, then it is natural to turn to the formal theories of ethics for guidance. These traditional outlooks, however, do not, and are unable to, provide unequivocal guidance on advice to the owners and managers of business, or of the economy, or more generally to those who have to do with business and industry, such as trade unionists. This is because, separately and together, the theories can provide no guarantees of the correctness or otherwise of moral beliefs. This uncertainty is healthy in that throughout history, when and where bigots have held sway, the results have never been other than baleful: witch hunts, purges, pogroms and inquisitions are far from rare. The relativist insight that has attracted so many scientists (including social scientists) and moral philosophers, that values and ethical theories all express no more than answers to dilemmas posed by particular (usually scientific) beliefs and practices, turns out to be no more conclusive or capable of direct refutation than any other: if what is thought by deontologists (for example) to be the ultimate ground for obedience to the moral law is no more than an expression of 'enlightenment' outlooks, then we have the problem that there have been many, flatly contradictory 'enlightenment' outlooks, and relativism in its various forms can give no clear account of why we should take a particular set of values or beliefs as the sole authentic expressions of an age or place. The problem is not solved by taking the espoused values of whichever group, tribe, set, caste, class or clan happens to be dominant. This Vicar of Bray solution is far from novel or insightful—it was effectively discredited when expressed by Thrasymachus in Plato's *Republic* well over two thousand years ago. If ethical theories are relative to an age, and thus not compelling, then so is relativism itself, unless its supporters wish to make exception in their own cause—a move which has also been condemned as immoral for millennia and rightly so.

This chapter proceeds from the proposition that in ethics and metaethics there are some propositions that are true, false, indeterminate, defensible or indefensible irrespective of when and where and by whom they are expressed. Indefensible ones include, for example, the notion that in conducting moral arguments, speakers, writers and practitioners do not need to be honest or consistent. Winning arguments by verbal trickery or falsifying evidence is not made right by the fact, if it is a fact, that some isolated tribes value trickery. If they exist, then they can rightly be accused of moral confusion, and they will not be alone in that category. A correct insight of the intuitionists is that this proposition must be grasped before anyone can have the concept of *ethical*.

Towards Some Ground Rules

At a seminar in King's College, University of London on the Teaching of Business Ethics, in the Spring of 1988, four aims for such teaching were expressed, without dissent:

(i)   not to prescribe a particular ethical code;
(ii)   to provide the recipients of the teaching with the tools for the analysis of business ethics, and a method based on the various ethical theories;
(iii) to raise awareness of ethical issues in business and management;
(iv)   to counter over-deterministic or fatalistic views that management does not have any options, and to reflect on the possibility of moral development: the 'only doing my job' response is not the only option.

As one who subscribed to the above propositions at the Seminar, I take the view that only the first of the aims requires supplementation. Motives for taking an interest in business ethics are very varied, and to propose seriously that the subject be taught to managers, administrators, or trade unionists could suggest, for example, that current standards are unsatisfactory. As De George (1987) points out, much of business ethics concentrates on drawing attention to the malpractices that are thought to be common. It could also suggest an attempt to justify current practices and much else. Teaching business ethics, or advocating such teaching is to make a commitment, when the alternative of using positivism to stand aside is always available. The principle that a particular ethical code ought not to be taught is an ethical principle in its own right. The first proposition does not prescribe that teachers of business ethics are not entitled to have a code of their own, or that they should not advocate principles. Particular codes and theories can be evaluated in a principled way. There is no reason why individuals should not advocate their own codes, both at the substantive and procedural levels. And such advocacy is unavoidably prescriptive, in the logical sense in which Hare uses the term, in *Freedom and Reason* (1963). This logical prescriptiveness and advocacy is highly defensible when used within the ground rules of ethical debate, once agreed, and subject to some contents of the ground rules that provide for advocacy without brainwashing, indoctrination, or browbeating. Here the old insight is useful: in discussion of values, 'objectivity', i.e. honest attempts to be free from bias is a value in its own right. Speakers and writers have a *duty* to attempt to make their own values clear so that the audience can discount the biases, as they see them. There is always room for point and counter-point in discussions of ethics. We are least able to recognize some of our own biases. There are others that are defensible, such as a preference for one or another kind of research method, distaste for pretentiousness or bigotry. The prescribing of some of these is highly defensible. The difficult cases are those that involve holding to tolerance in the face of intolerance, or to scholarly values in the face of robust declarations of others. I believe that it is possible to suggest a code, or a set of principles, such that, though they cross the boundaries between recommending practices, selecting theoretical instances and awareness of the merits of rival theories, are consistent with some widely held and defensible contemporary beliefs. I hope to show that they should present no serious difficulties for theorists of a relativist or an objectivist stamp, but at the same time suggest criteria for improvement. These criteria should neither offer a blanket condemnation nor a sycophantic endorsement of current *mores* or power structures anywhere—both *errors* are often enough seen in the literature of management, and in business.

The proposed ground rules are: (1) pluralism, based on scepticism (of a sort); (2) the traditional Golden Rule; (3) the development and encouragement of individual autonomy in matters of value. These are explained in turn.

Pluralism

The first thing to note is that all of these ideas are of great antiquity. Pluralism, generally, is the philosophical idea that there may be more than one 'ultimate principle', or that members of minority groups (or of different groups) are entitled to maintain different values. Its opposite is totalitarianism or, more generally, monism. Basing pluralism on scepticism arises from the constitutional inability, explained in detail in Chapter Four, of all the theoretical standpoints to provide the means for decisive refutation of their rivals. In this way, scepticism remains as it always was, one of the hallmarks of scholarly thought, and is far from inconsistent with commitment.

Pluralism can take the form of tolerance, such that people assent to a principle that even views that they believe to be profoundly wrong have a right to exist, or that individuals have a right to express them. Alternatively, it might be thought that all moral principles have the same status, and thus that there are no grounds for discriminating among them, or it might take the form that since there is a gap between ideal and real, principles should be paid lip service, but not put into practice, perhaps on the ground that they cannot be realized. It is clear that the outcome of these views can be an unprincipled attitude of *laissez-faire*. This would be inevitable if the principle of pluralism were to be seen as standing alone.

It takes a different character when linked with autonomy, the idea that people are entitled to decide for themselves what they think to be right, wrong, required or forbidden. The idea would be empty without the means, including the intellectual means, to make their own mind up. This has implications not only for the educational system, but the design of value-setting institutions, such as professional bodies, bureaucracy and other methods of controlling and channelling information by individuals and groups. Such groups go to great lengths to ensure conformity to their 'norms' and values, and have a great range of sanctions and techniques available to them for persuasion and enforcement. The techniques and processes are well described in the literature on groups and group dynamics, and are recorded in many case studies and experiments, examples of which have already been discussed in Chapter Four.

This is another version of the old problem in moral and political theory, of reconciling freedom and order. A pluralism that encourages the extinguishing of autonomy is necessarily a limited pluralism, and raises the question of how pluralist moral and ethical arrangements may become without being self-defeating. It also raised the equally old issue of whether and in what ways ethical principles may be enforced, on the assumption that some enforcement is necessary. In the famous controversy between Lord Devlin and Professor Hart, in the 1960s, no basis was established for drawing the line between those matters which may be enforced by law, and those which may be enforced by other means (Hart, 1963; Devlin, 1965). One clue was that the limits of tolerance by the public tend to shift from time to time, but what, as a matter of fact, *is* tolerable, or required, cannot determine what ought to be so. Further, one person's autonomy may be developed at the cost of someone else's as, for example, when limited resources appear to require selectivity in the provision of higher education, or in the possibility of 'positional goods'—those things that are valued only because they are denied to others, such as the top jobs in a company, or exclusive rights to land or to other privileges. Clearly, the two principles of autonomy and pluralism could give rise to many of the institutions and practices that are widely held to be, if not unethical, then at least problematic, and if they do not give rise to the practices, then the two principles would not be sufficient to prevent or justify them.

The third ground rule offered here is the traditional Golden Rule. Flew (1984) refers to it as a 'fundamental moral rule', and cites Confucius as describing it as 'reciprocity', summarizing the true way. Like the principles of autonomy and pluralism, the Golden Rule does not enjoin or forbid any particular act, rule, institution or practice. It provides a criterion by which any of these can be judged. Hobbes expresses the Golden rule as follows:

> Do not that unto another which thou wouldst not have done to thyself (Hobbes, 1651, Ch. XV.)

Kant's version is

> I ought never to act except in such a way that I can also will that my maxim should become a universal law (Kant, 1785, in Paton, 1965, p. 70.)

It is, of course, the injunction from the Sermon on the Mount,

> Thou shalt love thy neighbour as thyself (St. Matthew, 22.39).

Donaldson and Waller (1980) offered a more prosaic version:

> The legitimacy of administrative acts and organizational codes is related in specific ways to the values of the persons concerned with them and to the arrangements for ensuring that these values are taken seriously and are given due consideration. At its simplest the argument is that the ethical legitimacy

of the behavioural relationships between A (an administrator) and B (a person subject to A's administrative rules and decisions) in a case of an issue that affects only them can be tested by a role-reversal method. The legitimacy of the relationship does not depend on A's imagining himself in B's position with A's own values; it does depend on A's imagining himself in B's position with B's values. We transfer B's values to A and *vice versa*. (p. 50.)

The Golden Rule implies that people are to be regarded as 'ends' in their own right, and not as means. Each person should count as neither more nor less than one. It implies that people have a duty to self as well as to others—a notion which would seem in part redundant to egoists and to utilitarians, but disallows martyrs and masochists. To seek to be exploited has no more merit on the Golden Rule criterion than to seek to exploit. This conflicts with non-pluralist ideologies on management, which assume that management both is and ought to be founded upon the treatment of others as means to organizational ends—whether those others are subordinates, consumers, or passers-by.

Taken together, the three proposed ground rules can, as will be seen subsequently, be used as criteria for judging acts, codes, laws, practices, institutions and events. The first principle of pluralism, it was argued, is rooted in scepticism, in turn derived from the radical inability of the rival ethical doctrines to refute each other or to establish themselves, and the apparent necessity of at least some insights from several doctrines.

We now need to establish the status of the principle of autonomy and of the Golden Rule. The idea of autonomy recurs in the history of moral and political theory, of which theories of business are branches. Hobbes sought the solution in a combination of radical individualism, the destructive nature of people and the logical need for an imposed order. Rousseau offered the modifications that people are less destructive than Hobbes thought, but easily subverted by improper institutions. Mill (1861) took individual liberty as an obvious ideal and produced penetrating analysis as to how its limitations are achieved, offering the notion of self-regarding and other-regarding actions as a way of solving the problem of freedom and order. The problem remains: why should *individuals* be the basic units for a theory of ethics in general, and business ethics in particular? The reason is plain enough: although it is possible to speak of 'the state', or of a profession, group or company as acting, and of a company as 'having' a culture that is separate from individuals, or of characteristics that remain through complete changes of personnel, a company, group, state or profession is not a person. All of these may legitimately be regarded as 'things', thus accepting charges of 'reification' in the analysis. All may be regarded, using 'legal fictions', as persons in law, but they are not capable of making or responding to moral claims, except through the actions of individual representatives. The individual is the basic ethical unit because without individuals there could be no ethics, even if ethics meant only the codes and values that are on offer or are existent. A world of companies, states, professions and cultures is logically impossible without people. A world of people with no ethical issues between them is conceivable, but it would be a world without individuals, or rather without individualism. It exists only in the science fiction literature. I conclude that the notion of autonomy is basic, in that it is a defining feature of individuals. Appeals to individuals, or techniques for persuading them, could not work unless a degree of autonomy were present. The ethical issue of substance is how can autonomy be ensured and justified. As Finnis (1980) points out, autonomy is not derivable from a description of human nature, but is a moral concept in its own right (Finnis, 1980, p. 124).

The notion of individual autonomy is essential to any legal system or institution that applies sanctions to individuals who are treated as guilty of breaking the rules. Without the concept, the application of sanctions can have no moral force, however much it is surrounded by the trappings. A system which applies sanctions against individuals requires autonomy, but autonomous individuals may not accept all the rules. The strength of the case for democracy in institutions at all levels is derived from the idea that it can provide a means to ensuring that individuals can initiate changes in rules, and expect due consideration. The weakness is that the concept and institutionalisation of democracy are both complex and controversial.

The Nature of the Golden Rule

The idea that the Golden Rule is a 'fundamental moral principle' needs some explanation. It is connected with a tangle of issues or questions, such as, why should anyone behave ethically? Why should the Golden Rule be followed? Is it really possible that people can act out of altruism, and if they do, is it not really a form of self-preservation, or perhaps, of instinctive species preservation? The Golden Rule is fundamental in the same way as the logical 'law of contradiction' is fundamental. To ask, 'why should I be moral? is like asking, 'why should I be prudent' (or self-interested)? Ideas such as the essential selfishness of people, or of the instinct for preservation of the species, tend to be regarded as fundamental in the sense that they are thought to be insights into behaviour and its causes that require no further explanation, because they are the grounds on which all behaviour is to be explained. To the question, why do people seek pleasure and avoid pain (to a Benthamite), or seek personal gain (to a textbook economist), or behave aggressively as a permanent trait, are held to be so obvious that even to ask the question leads to suspicions as to the seriousness of the enquirer. If we ask why people are motivated for personal gain we are likely to be told that we are programmed thus, or challenged to examine our own motives, when we will see that every act can be interpreted as selfish. Some economists side-step the issue by claiming that the psychology of economic atomized selfishness is merely a model for predicting behaviour, and is to be treated and assessed only on its predictive abilities. This is another form of positivism in which little effort is made to do sustained comparisons, but in any case trades upon a very idiosyncratic notion of 'explanation', assimilating it to 'prediction'. A detailed analysis and critique of this outlook is provided in Dray's *Laws and Explanation in History* (Dray, 1957/1979).

The main point is that even if such models consistently out-predicted more reflective models of behaviour (which they do not), the reasons would remain mystical until the processes were exhibited. As a pluralist, it seems equally clear to me that people act out of a variety of motives for a variety of reasons, and often act without serious thought, out of habit, misunderstanding, or generally from a mixture of rational and non-rational motives. This can be seen from many case studies in industry, and from major surveys, experiments and interview programmes, such as those discussed in Chapter Four. People may believe that the Golden Rule ought to be applied because people are programmed to obey it, or because those who have a moral sense can see intuitively that the Golden Rule must be used, or that the Golden Rule is a command of the Deity. These are sufficient grounds, but the Golden Rule can be sustained and be seen to be valid even for those who do not accept the above grounds. The logical claim for the Golden Rule can afford to be much more modest than the claims to ground universal selfishness in human nature or in the species. The more modest claim for the Golden Rule would be that whatever the actual source of ethical, moral or rule-making beliefs in individuals, the ethical validity of the beliefs depends on their satisfying the test implied by the Golden Rule—the value reversal test. Thus people's motives are irrelevant to the Golden Rule on my interpretation of it, since it is a criterion for judging actions, not motives. The question, why should I behave ethically? can be answered: the Golden Rule cannot compel compliance or persuade people to comply, but if people claim rights, duties, propriety, conformity from others or fair treatment from others, then the claim, if justified, will satisfy the Golden Rule. This outlook can easily be reconciled with Kant's claim that the only thing that is absolutely good is a good will. The apparent contradiction with the claim of the irrelevance of motivation can be resolved by admitting the possibility of different systems of ethical rules or institutions that might satisfy the Golden Rule (and the other rules of autonomy and pluralism). A system could conceivably be 'better' than another in the eyes of some observers in the sense, for example, that it encourages more benevolence, or more economic efficiency, or is likely to be more stable, or arises from good will, yet both systems could satisfy the Golden Rule.

This allows for variety in codes and institutions and allows for moral development. It does not allow for 'anything goes', but would have to agree to anything that satisfies the criteria. The values underlying different systems are related to basic beliefs about people and the world. This does not necessarily mean that existing codes of ethics always break Hume's law that values cannot be derived from fact, but it does mean that what are thought to be the 'facts' of the case profoundly influence people's view of what is possible. For instance, it is widely held that an unequal distribution of income is inevitable at the levels experienced. If nothing can be done, it makes no sense to say that something ought to be done. People's views do change as to what the facts are, man's place in nature and the nature of people and things. The views change (among other causes) with scientific development and with scientific fashions. In particular, the 'official' scientific views of the status of natural laws and of the constituents of matter have undergone very profound changes in the last few generations, and may continue to do so. When the basic beliefs change, development of codes and systems occurs. To this extent, the relativists are right to see ethical codes as situation dependent, but are wrong in believing that that is all they are, or that that implies that they are beyond rational criticism. The ground rules discussed in this chapter allow for variety, development and co-existence of more than one substantive code in the same nation at the same time. We need to see how far down the line this variety can go.

For example, can companies tolerate alternative values and codes within their jurisdiction? Can they tolerate or encourage dissent? Does this apply to trade unions or to institutions such as government departments? A great deal of work has been done by the analysts of group dynamics that has sought to test the limits to which deviant attitudes may be held. This work is illuminating. The issues of such toleration are far from luxuries. The relevant evidence discussed in the book so far includes: the leak of toxic gas at Bhopal; restrictive trade and labour practices; the causes and consequences of inflation; manipulation of official statistics; surveys on the extent to which managers are required to suppress their own ethical values; cases, such as that of Stanley Adams, in which a huge variety of value issues was uncovered; experiments such as those of Milgram showing how vestigial people's autonomy can become, even when they are under very light and ambiguous pressure to conform; the long lists of issues provided by, for example, the conference proceedings edited by De George and Pichler (1978) and by Van Dam and Stallaert (1978). The ground rules suggested in this chapter indicate that most of the material used provides many examples of actions, institutions, practices and ethical codes which would not completely satisfy the criteria. But this does not demonstrate that business and the institutions that surround it are typically unethical, or are incorrigible, or that standards are uniformly low and incorrigible. To do so is to make a substantive moral judgment. Indeed to attempt to discuss the matters is to adopt a moral standpoint. An attempt to apply the ground rules in detail to the examples already given would not be very fruitful, for several reasons. *First*, the examples have entered public discussion in the first place because someone regarded the acts, practices or institutions as 'wrong'. *Second*, very little constructive development is likely to follow from such an exercise. The examples do illustrate that the issues do exist in business ethics, and are real, rather than 'ivory tower' matters. They can be seen to be complex, and cannot be resolved by mere application of scientific technique (and often arise from it). Nor can the standard theories of ethics provide solutions that are likely to be compelling. *Third*, the examples show that in most cases (though not all) the issues arise not because the values of the various parties concerned have been shown to be fundamentally at odds with each other, but because they are not discussed at all until after the event. The belief that ethics is irrelevant to business appears to have become a self-justifying truth, partly because business became persuaded that positivism had the answers, and partly because the managers of business, being in the game of value enforcement without coherent values to enforce, have often fallen back on expedient, fashion, and fast-talking, ephemeral managerial cure-alls and instant solutions to the problems arising from the initial absence of coherent ethical values. This is not to say that all managers of companies are without such values. Clearly, there are many sources of commitment to values from outside the workplace. In some cases, attempting to work to standards is like the familiar problem of lifting oneself by the 'own bootstrap' method. In many cases, there is no scope for anything other than playing the organizational game according to the rules that have somehow emerged.

The key issues surrounding the sceptical question of whether there are any ethics in business ('ethics and business are contradictions in terms') have been given a positive answer: there are standards that are applicable to business, and some *are* applied. There is much scope for a (positive and negative) critique of the values that are implied in the running of business, the economy and the various support institutions. There is a growing literature, especially in America, which addresses the issues, and it is possible to suggest in the light of this literature and of the ethical traditions that precede it, some ground rules that take into account various insights provided by rival, incomplete, and often ancient ethical theories. Ethics in business is not just a matter of taste, or of group, cultural or historical norms. It can be a matter of the systematic handling of values, with a view to reconciling them, having first ensured that they are properly articulated. As De George puts it:

> Business ethics can help people to approach moral problems in business more systematically, with better tools than they might otherwise use. It can help them to see issues they might otherwise ignore. It can also impel them to make changes they might otherwise not be moved to make. But business eithics will not, in and of itself, make anyone moral. Business ethics just as ethics in general, presupposes that those who study it already are moral beings, that they know right from wrong, that they wish to be even better, more thoughtful, more informed moral beings. (De George, 1986, p. 19.)

In relation to the development of the role of business ethics, a further element is feasible: people are constrained by the institutional, legal and custom-and-practice framework within which business operates. The study of business ethics can indicate ways in which 'official' values can be more fully analysed and validated within business, and brought more into line with the unofficial ones, and vice versa in such a way that the defensible practices become more 'official' and more practised. This suggests that the emerging discipline might aspire to offering ideas for discussion in relation to the development of autonomy, accommodation of pluralism and widespread use of criteria for improvement, particularly those which satisfy the Golden Rule. Advisory roles have long been established in various ways, for better or worse, by a variety of disciplines in the physical and social sciences, all of whom have identifiable and dominant value sets. Business ethics might also aspire to helping these, highly practical, disciplines to come to terms with the consequences of their application, as outlined in the early chapters of this book.

Part Two, in an attempt to be even-handed, examines practices, statements and evidence taken from a variety of permanent institutions and organizations, including 'the City', company codes, government institutions and trade unions. Clearly, each of these would require more than one volume of business ethics for a full treatment. What is attempted here is necessarily selective and influenced by the author's own background and experience. It is, all the same, possible to examine some standard arguments in relation to these and to indicate areas in which they are likely to satisfy the ground rules, and using the ground rules, to indicate where the 'standard' critiques of the institutions, organizations or arrangements are valid, or are wide of the mark. One of the strengths of the ground rules proposed is that they are neither novel nor idiosyncratic. What would have some novelty would be a widespread acceptance that they are workable, combined with a concerted effort to put them to service, impartially.

PART TWO

The Ethics and Logic of Industrial Practice

Introduction to part two

Part One sought to identify and illustrate a number of key issues in business ethics, some of which were discussed in detail. It was concluded that the key issues are methodological (procedural) in nature, rather than substantive. Pseudo-sceptical attitudes as are exhibited in such questions as '*are there any ethics in business?*' were seen to be beside the point, being usually prompted by a variety of beliefs, for example that standards are everywhere deplorable because it is held to be the nature of competitive business to be unable to afford ethics, or because proposing higher standards is hopelessly idealistic or unworldly or unpragmatic, or because business is 'really about' something else, such as profit maximization or achieving pragmatic solutions to technical problems. These beliefs were seen to lack coherence, and to be weak of evidence, and rarely developed in detail. The 'key issue' of the possibility of an ethics of business was answered affirmatively. The systematic handling of values can replace the unsystematic attempts to ignore values or to impose unexamined sets of values on the community at large.

Whether people in general in industry behave well or badly is not offered here as a key issue; whether such judgments are sensible and of any use is worth considering, though. In part the matter is connected with the ancient debate on whether or not values and actions are simply matters of custom, or preference. It was seen that customs and practices are relevant to the discussion, but far from decisive.

Part One concluded that the continued coexistence of rival theories and classification schemes is no more a handicap in ethics than in other disciplines, and has positive advantages. Among these is a compelling ground for a pluralist approach to theories and practices. Business ethics could not be defended if it attempted to impose beliefs, practices or codes on industry, nor could an extreme pluralism that would accept *any* practice merely because it exists 'in nature'. Rejecting specific codes does not imply rejection of principles. In addition to the principle of pluralism, Part One proposed the use of the traditional 'Golden Rule' as criterion for judging business practices, and the principle that practices and institutions could and should be designed in order to increase the level of autonomy of individuals in their actions.

119

The evidence used to illustrate the key issues tended to refer to specific events, most of which have been discussed in public because they were thought by some to be examples of misconduct or of pathological processes.

Part Two is concerned with processes and institutions which, though not without critics, are widely held at least to be legitimate. These include the bureaucratic forms of management organization, trade unions, City institutions, and various kinds of groups. It is common in the literature to discuss the extent to which the capitalist or free market system or some other (e.g. 'socialist') is the embodiment of justice, or automatically promotes it. It will be seen in Part Two that the principles of pluralism, Golden Rule and autonomy can be fruitfully applied to different systems, or for that matter to different times and places. To this extent, the argument favours the 'objectivist' side of the debate with the 'subjectivists' and 'relativists'.

CHAPTER SIX

Codes of Practice

Ethics is a practical subject. One of its many aliases is 'practical reason', and as such figures in one of Kant's major works, *The Critique of Practical Reason*, in 1788. In recent years there has been an explosion of codes of practice in a variety of contexts, accompanied by an increasing number of commentaries. Some of these favour the use of codes, and others reject them on various grounds. Codes, codes of practice, sets of working rules, model procedures and procedure agreements are applied for example in industrial relations, in health and safety encouragement, and in general company policies. They are applied by governments, as in highway codes, or codes of behaviour during the currency of policies towards the control of aggregate incomes. They are applied by trade associations, and most notably by professional bodies. Codes can be formal, as when statutes are set out systematically in an attempt to avoid inconsistencies. Sometimes codes are expressed attitudinally rather than formally, as in 'codes of honour', and are in this form sometimes enforced as something extra or superior to the law, and, often, enforced more rigorously than the law itself, as was the case with duelling codes at one time. Company codes are sometimes called 'codes of ethics', but are often expressed as policy statements, for example, towards 'responsibility', or related to the 'social responsibility of business', or just as 'company philosophies.'

An examination of specific codes published by companies and of some recent surveys of corporate codes and of the uses of and attitudes towards codes is in order at this stage if only because of the wide range of attitudes towards them. A representative sample of attitudes towards codes would certainly include the idea that they are at best irrelevant to business, but more likely to be harmful, because they miss the main point of business. On this view the 'purpose' of business is to make, or often to *maximize* profit, on the grounds that all persons and institutions should do what they are best at, and business is held to be best at making profit, or offering goods and services with a view to making profit. This view has been presented and criticized often enough to make a detailed treatment un-

121

necessary here. Helpful treatments can be found in Beauchamp and Bowie (1988), in Velasquez (1988), and in De George (1986). The legitimacy of the idea that business may have 'social responsibilities' is one of those old debates in which the holders of pro- and anti- attitudes often appear to have little or no intention of listening to each other. It is sufficient to say that supporters of the view tend to base their claim (that businesses have no responsibilities other than to make profit and obey the law) on what they take to be Adam Smith's authority as expressed in his eighteenth century masterpiece, *The Wealth of Nations*. Some authors, such as Sen (1987), see such a claim as a considerable distortion of Smith's views. Even if Smith had an uncompromising doctrine of 'the hidden hand', and could prove conclusively that if all businesses that acted in the way indicated, economic welfare would be maximized, and even if all firms did act thus, the question still remained open as to whether the public good is merely an economic matter, whether economic outcomes are so easily specified (i.e. there is much scope for debate on the boundaries of economics), and finally, whether 'the public good' is meaningful at all, rather than merely empty rhetoric. Although much has been written on these matters, as witnessed by the huge list of references in Sen's book cited above, there are no grounds for thinking that the matter has been settled within the economic debate, or even that it could be. The concept of *profit maximization* itself is a highly metaphysical one, in which recognition of a profit-maximizing situation is purely formal, with radical ambiguities as to the status of the general and the particular assumptions needed to give a formal identification of a profit-maximizing situation. In particular, the matter of short-run versus long-run considerations is radically insoluble. Anything less than profit maximizing carries the implication that industry is wasteful of resources. The problem becomes vastly more complicated when the notion is challenged that firms 'have goals' or 'objectives'. Discussions of real organizations demonstrate a multiplicity of 'goals' or objectives that could be regarded as appropriately attributed to the organization. Each of these reveals a further multiplicity of goals, expectations, objectives, claims, and much else, held by individuals and groups within organizations or firms. The first problem is identifying the authentic and legitimate goals. The second is pinning down the responsibilities. The third, and most important problem is on whose authority legitimate goals and actions can be identified. Clearly, however technically skilled the pseudo-Smith doctrines of profit maximizing may be, the idea and its legitimacy are matters of value, and open to debate on their own grounds. To paraphrase Hume, it is not contrary to reason to claim either that firms do or do not have responsibilities, and if the claim is made that they do, then no particular set of responsibilities can be derived from any technical treatment of the behaviour, economic or other, of firms. The responsibilities of firms (or absence of them) are matters for grounded debate among those who are affected by the activities of companies to which technical and philosophical arguments can be relevant, but never sufficient. Our sample would need to include the view that there is an implicit contract (as in the notion of 'the social contract') between business and the wider community. The terms of the contract need to be constantly revised in the light of circumstances. This view, or something close to it, is discussed in Galbraith's *The New Industrial State* (1967), and in Beauchamp and Bowie (1988). There seem to be shared assumptions held by opposing doctrines: that the public good can be identified and exists in the first place, that company objectives are unambiguous, that the matter can be settled by means of technical or philosophical argument without finding out what the stakeholders actually want, and reconciling that with consistent, grounded, explicit moral/ethical principles. We saw in Chapter Two that the 'public good' is elusive, and apt to be used as a 'weasel word', that, for analytical purposes is better omitted altogether: who is to identify it and how is as problematical as the notion of profit maximization. If, therefore, it is not worthwhile to speak of codes in terms of whether they help firms to meet their (real or alleged) 'social responsibilities', and if it is merely dogmatic to assert that firms have no responsibility other than to maximize profit within the law, there is still the possibility of codes helping firms to ensure that they pursue legitimate activities in seeking profit, or whatever else their directors are trying to do. Here opinion is divided, for example between, on the one side, drafters of government legislation that includes non-enforceable, but legally relevant codes, the executive councils of professional and trade associations, and company boards who believe that codes can regulate extremely diverse behaviour, and on the other side, the critics, such as the British Member of Parliament and former Minister, the Rt. Hon. Enoch Powell who sees the proliferation of codes as a kind of twilight legislation made and supported without due legal process or checks and balances by increasingly powerful ministers. Studies of industrial relations codes have long shown a tendency for them to degenerate to become merely new battlegrounds on which old conflicts are fought.

Given the above debates on codes, it can safely be taken to be the case that the issue of whether to support or oppose the development and proliferation of codes is neither irrelevant to business nor trivial. Whether the contents of codes of practice are truly ethical, or merely rules of skill and prudence remains to be discussed. Their prevalence in the major professions and their continued attraction to governments, companies and trade associations can safely be taken to indicate that they are often thought to have practical value by people with practical responsibilities.

The Use of Codes of Practice

Because codes of practice are usually offered as highly practical sets of rules and guidelines, they are not usually accompanied by detailed arguments as to their purposes and uses. These are, typically, expressed in a form that is well protected from discussion, expressing aims in a matter-of-fact language. Varieties of codes are so diverse that attempts to define them are particularly fraught with difficulties. On most accounts, the Hippocratic Oath in medicine, the United Nations Declaration of Human Rights, the Geneva Convention, the American Penal Code and the proverb, 'don't count your chickens before they are hatched' would be codes of practice. So would the agreement said to exist in criminal fraternities not to inform on each other. It is feasible to offer an account of some of their main features.

(1) *Codes tend to be expressions of mixtures of technical, prudential and moral imperatives.* The inclusion of merely technical items alone would constitute part of the technique of a particular occupation, for instance, how to service a washing machine would be technique. How to behave towards customers would form part of an ethical code for a washing machine service employee, but may be ethical only in that the code may be mainly prudential, with ethical overtones. Such a code would be a technique from the point of view of a service training organization, which could have its own code in relation to what training contracts would be considered, and how the consultancy relationship with clients would be conducted. The principal use, ostensibly at least, of codes is to guide people, laying down rules to be followed. Their publication removes some doubt as to what is expected.

(2) *Codes vary in the extent and manner in which they can be supported or enforced.* They range from, at one end of the scale, enforcement which takes the form of obliging professionals to cease from practice as a result of decisions by disciplinary committees, to expressions of disapproval from within or without a profession. The enforcement is sometimes weak in trade associations, for example when their expulsion of members who break the codes does not prevent the ex-members from practising their trade.

(3) *Of company codes*, in particular, it can be seen that the single 'goal' of pursuit of maximum profit is neither admitted to nor aspired to. There is an ironical element in the contrast between this and so many academic and business disciplines which insist that companies do pursue maximum profit, ought to do so and would do well to use the academic techniques for that end, and that the advice is both value free and worth having. It seems to me that companies and their spokespersons are more realistic than their

academic advisors about what they are doing, its value content and its need for justification in terms of what are thought to be the legitimate interests of shareholders, customers, employees and public. Whether the attempts at justification typically succeed requires a great deal of research in depth comparable to the major studies of motivation, bureaucracy and restriction of output, such as that by Gouldner (1954), Roethlisberger and Dickson (1939a,b), Crozier (1964), Burns and Stalker (1961), Lupton (1964) and Woodward (1965).

Such studies are now unfashionable, and though it might be argued that they have had little direct effect on business behaviour, they have at least become part of the understanding of educated managers.

Company Codes: Some Examples

In one form or another, company codes have existed since the early days of the Industrial Revolution, no doubt replacing the traditional prescriptive rules of the feudal system. Tawney (1922/1961) shows the various ways in which the economic and business systems broke free from the old mediaeval values, in order to grow. From the present vantage point it may have been historically useful to develop the idea of value-free business, or, as De George terms it "the Myth of Amoral Business" (De George, 1986, p. 93). The office rules quoted in Chapter One date from 1852 and have very clear moral overtones. In the 1920s the Bell Telephone Company elaborated a very clear set of rules, and even called them the company's 'ten commandments'. They are listed by Roethlisberger and Dickson. An example from Britain in the 1970s is provided in a paper published by the (now defunct) Foundation for Business Responsibility, and written by the Public Affairs Director of IBM (United Kingdom) Limited:

> Social responsibility, social accounting, the responsibilities of business and other phrases have been widely used in speeches by businessmen, politicians, trade union leaders and others in our society who are looking for evidence of change. Alongside mounting attacks on many of the leading institutions in our society, there is a growing awareness within these institutions that a response is needed, not just to criticisms, but rather to the genuine demands of a rapidly changing social, political and economic environment. Because thinking on this subject still tends to polarise between those who, rightly believing that the business of business is business, think that this must lead them to eschew activities that are unrelated to the short term results of their organisations and those who indulge in a number of social activities for a variety of moral reasons but without much business rationale, two things are necessary. The first is that the subject of responsibility should be defined in a way that reflects more than an indulgence in good works. The second is that

it should be accompanied by a rationale that puts corporate responsibility within the mainstream, instead of on the periphery, of business activity. (Hargreaves, 1975, p. 1.)

Hargreaves goes on to identify three circles of responsibility, namely, basic responsibilities (paying taxes, obeying the law, satisfying the basic needs of employees, shareholders, and having honourable dealings with suppliers, creditors etc.). The second level, for Hargreaves, concerns responsibilities that go beyond the letter of the law, to its spirit. This includes, for example, avoidance of pollution arising from industrial activities, even where it is legal to pollute the environment. The third level, 'societal responsibilities', is summarized as

... the argument for third circle activities is that the healthier the environment the better the chances of success for the company (loc. cit., p. 2)

and

It is the suggestion of this paper that failure to invest in the solution of societal problems will, long-term, contribute to the effectiveness of business organizations. (loc. cit., p. 4.)

This, clearly prudential, theme is continued by Unilever's published statement in 1981:

The success or failure of a company—and Unilever is no exception—largely depends on its people, particularly its managers. Its reputation depends on the ways its managers behave (Unilever, 1981, p. 2)

but the statement adds some forthright moral commitments:

We never forget that our most important single responsibility is to keep Unilever profitable. Without profit we cannot discharge our obligations to shareholders, suppliers, customers and employees. Unilever's ability to create wealth in developed as well as developing countries increasingly depends on an understanding that our operations are beneficial to the countries concerned and that our behaviour is of the highest standard. (Unilever, op. cit., p. 10.)

In the pamphlet, the Company recognizes that the highest standards can be difficult to achieve, but expresses a commitment to the OECD and ILO guidelines for the behaviour of multinational enterprises, the United Nations Commission on Transnational Corporations, whose ground rules provide both for the conduct of international business, and for the conduct of governments towards business. The Company expresses commitment to the free enterprise system and the market economy. It is committed to recruiting, where possible, employees with appropriate qualifications "irrespective of differences in race, religion, or nationality" and on page 6:

Though we do not take for granted a social structure which contravenes this objective, we cannot break the law or deviate offensively from local custom in pursuing the goal.

The pamphlet expresses a belief that employees have a right to be consulted on issues which "directly affect their working environment" (page 7), and "a wish to be a good citizen" (page 8), "staying aloof from support for political parties" (page 9) and operates an anti-bribery stance. It expresses a willingness to operate with legitimate groups such as trade associations (page 9).

An American example of a company code is provided by the Cummins Engine Company, of Columbus, Indiana. Cummins, according to Williams (1982),

Consciously and deliberately strives to be a leader in the Corporate Social Responsibility movement

and, according to Williams, has a good reputation as a profit-making organization (as, indeed, does Unilever). The net sales of Cummins in 1980 amounted to 1.7 billion dollars, the Company had twenty-two thousand employees, and seven thousand common stock holders. The Cummins Practice on Ethical Standards sees ethics as resting on "a fundamental belief in people's dignity and decency" and states

Our most basic ethical standard is to show respect for those whose lives we affect and to treat them as we would expect them to treat us if our positions were reversed.

Specifically, Cummins is committed to obey the law; to be honest, presenting the facts fairly and accurately; to be fair, i.e. to give everyone appropriate consideration; to be concerned about how the Company's actions affect others, and to strive to make those effects as beneficial as possible; to be courageous enough to operate the code even when it means losing business. The Company claims that it rarely comes to loss of business. Accordingly, again, to Williams,

Over the long haul, people trust and respect this kind of behaviour, and wish more of our institutions embodied it. (Williams, 1982, p. 20.)

Having drawn attention to codes of ethics and practice from various international institutional and company sources, a number of questions arise. For example, how widespread are codes of practice or their equivalents? Is acceptance of their values typical of companies even if typical companies do not issue formal codes? How effective are the codes in promoting what they stand for? To what extent are they genuine and operational, rather than cynical or self-deluding claims to do what some people say business cannot do, even if they wish to? Should companies have codes at all? Do they make any difference? Would the issues raised in the study of business ethics largely evaporate if most companies were to adopt similar codes? How do the codes fare when tested against the three principles of pluralism, autonomy and the Golden Rule, identified in Chapter Five? How far do they reflect the standard ethical theories of deontology, utilitarianism, objectivism or subjectivism, for example? Many of these matters can be only conjectured in the absence of major research programmes, but some information, from surveys, is available, and much experience has been gained from the operation of codes of practice in wage regulation. Much of the latter shows that the effects may be the opposite of those intended, or which are officially said or implied to be intended. In particular, the counter-productive effects of policies designed to restrain the aggregate growth of incomes are now widely accepted as having produced rebound effects that put the rate of growth on to a higher path, in several widely different economies. Typically, these policies were reinforced with highly specific pay codes or their equivalent, often drawing on very sophisticated knowledge of the many ways in which pay can escape less specific controls. Specifically, when pay codes are published, the formulae themselves often contain the seeds of their own downfall, as for example when ministers assert that 'pay should rise in line with productivity growth'. At best, such formulae freeze the existing distribution of income, whose general fairness is thought by many influential bargainers to be unfair in a variety of ways. This is usually compounded by codes which attempt to freeze the situation as it is in any point in time, usually for reasons of short-term expedient. This inevitably creates anomalies, which cannot be dealt with because any attempt to correct them creates new ones. Thus for large-scale matters such as the control of incomes in the aggregate, codes tend to be counter-productive. Attempts at control tend to be, to use Wittgenstein's phrase, trying to repair a torn spider's web with one's fingers. Codes can produce downward revision of conduct, as in the case of 'time clocks' in factories. The procedure encourages both punctuality and clock-watching, and control becomes the enemy of improvement. Minimum standards become the norm, just as in incomes restraint policies, wage ceilings become wage floors, so far as rises are concerned. Codes and regulations can be used to avoid or evade responsibility or to shift it to others. On health and safety matters, protective clothing can be so uncomfortable to wear or can make work so difficult that pressure is on foremen, union representatives and employees to ignore regulations. In one plant known to the author, uncomfortable and therefore unused masks were required in conditions of glass dust, an extractor had a faulty bearing and was not used, and broken glass was stored in the middle of the floor. These conditions were eventually rectified, but they and the regulations provided ready reasons for disputes, since they could be deployed tactically. In the circumstances, responsibility was not accepted by anyone, and the matters of safety could not be formally discussed, although everyone was fully aware of them.

There are many reasons why codes may not be operated. In discussions and in work with and in industry, my own experiences include: employers who could not afford to comply with the requirements of the codes, or at least claimed so; sometimes there were powerful reasons known to some people in the system, but not admitted for one reason or another. Codes have been so complex or so vague that no one really knew how to enforce them. An example from the health and safety field includes a fire exit that for years was unusable, because the security officers insisted on the door being permanently locked, with a key held only by them, as the fire exit was seen as a security hazard. None of the above can prove that codes are worthless, or that they cannot raise ethical standards. What they do show, in my view, is that if codes are in conflict with other values, the code is likely to be the one to give way.

Norms, Codes and Ethical Standards

At this point it is appropriate to make explicit a distinction that is implied in the argument so far. The distinction is between (a) the particular set of values (often called 'norms') that a group of people, for example, managers, football players, students, politicians, or any identifiable group adopts as part of the process of group dynamics, (b) the set of values that is deliberately and openly adopted, for example by the directors of a company, designed to achieve their purposes efficiently, and (c) the set of values that emerges from self-conscious examination of alternative values and value systems. These categories can overlap to some extent, but in general, the first two sets are selected from within a situation which has a particular structure, usually by leaders. In group (a), any set of values that is consistent with the survival of the group may be adopted, and in doing so, the group will not encourage or permit revision, except from within the rules of constitution of the group (which may be formal), or in time of major crisis.

These values are moral in the sense that they represent the *mores* of the group, but may be at odds with the *mores* of the dominant culture in which they find themselves. Secret societies or criminal gangs could easily fall into this category. It is of course possible, though unlikely, that these groups may have more defensible or justifiable values than those of the wider community, or of its dominant groups. The values would, I suggest, be of an order that is liable to moral criticism on a number of grounds: the *mores* selected may be unjustifiable in the sense that they would not satisfy the three criteria of pluralism, Golden Rule and autonomy. It is always possible that groups in category (a) could produce a highly defensible account of their values, for instance, secret societies have sometimes existed as protection from intolerance of a kind that is indefensible, such as persecution. Most inhabitants of category (a) would include groups whose chosen value sets are merely instrumental in achieving questionable aims.

Category (b) could easily include a great many existing business value systems. For instance, company norms of profitability, efficiency, service to customers, technical excellence of product or service, care for employees in the sense of stability of employment, promotion possibilities, welfare funds, recognition of trade unions and much else. Such firms do exist. They too would hold to values which are moral in the sense that group (a) values are moral, representing the *mores* of their own group (e.g. directors) and their proximate groups, e.g. employees, customers. We might even admire or share the moral values embedded in the company's practices. It could nonetheless be open to criticism on grounds of paternalism, i.e. imposing its own values on others in what are thought to be the interests of the others. Such practices could also be open to criticism even if the code were indeed representative of the values of employees, customers and others. We might even be inclined to think that it would be a huge step forward if such companies were to become typical. Nevertheless it is still possible for the values of company, customers, employees and others to rate very badly on the three principles. For instance, employees and customers may have been indoctrinated into a set of values that are low on the autonomy scale, possessing, perhaps, what Marxists see as 'false consciousness'; or the values themselves can be inconsistent, or badly thought through or vague, as, for example, when people express enthusiasm for 'democracy', but on examination, mean very different things by it. The values can be of restricted application, for instance, when third world suppliers are excluded from the benefits of a self-consciously ethical company. Even if these are included, there is still an uneasiness in the minds of some ethical thinkers. Immanuel Kant, for example, held that the only thing that is absolutely good is a good will. Thus, it might be possible to have all the trappings of a fully ethical system, but to have them for reasons of expediency, because people think that it is possible, or even more likely to do well by doing good, as when people hold that 'honesty is the best policy'. For Immanuel Kant, such practices would not count as moral unless they are operated out of reverence for the moral law, rather than because they are held to be prudent or profitable. To put the matter simply, some moral theorists do not regard an action as fully moral or ethical if it is done only because it is held to be prudent or profitable. In this case, the ethical basis would be weak, and the ethical code would be liable to be withdrawn if some people came to think that it was no longer prudent or profitable. Some moral theorists, that is, claim that an act should be done because it is right, not because it is convenient.

In category (c) the set of values emerges from self-conscious examination of alternative values and value systems or sets. The actual values and codes that emerge in category (c) may be identical to those of category (b). The difference is that in category (c), the stance, for example, on honesty would not be merely that it is the 'best' policy, but it is the 'right' policy, even if it turned out to mean that contracts were lost, the business suffered loss of profit and the employees suffered lack of job security. It is possible to hold that the two principles can, in some circumstances at least, be true together, that business in general stands to gain more from application of justifiable ethical principles than by ignoring them, but may legitimately be called upon to sacrifice profit, stability, or growth in some circumstances. As Ryan puts it:

> ... many people believe *there is an absolute standard of right and wrong.* While some situations are clear-cut, many involve moral ambiguity. This requires a certain flexibility that challenges appeals to absolute standards. We all need basic principles that can be utilised in resolving moral dilemmas; yet, reasonable people may disagree about which course of action is correct in a given situation. Ambiguous situations often require trade offs that demand more sophisticated moral reasoning than blind adherence to unbending rules. Executives who believe business ethics is directed at absolute standards of conduct may have difficulty in discerning its relevance to the ambiguities found in business. (Ryan, 1989, p. 30.)

This is, I believe a development of the points that Ross made in *The Foundation of Ethics* that the alleged absolutes are *prima facie* principles which can and often do conflict. There is no stable hierarchy in the principles, and the facts of the matter, which, in formal terms provide the minor premises of moral argument, are often complex and ambiguous and difficult to disentangle from the value premises. Part One provided many examples. Perhaps it is possible to paraphrase Kant and say that the only thing that is likely to be absolutely good is a good procedure, so that judgments, codes, institutions, decisions, actions, attitudes and the like can be revised in the light of development of knowledge. Thus it follows that the contents of a code, no matter how much we admire them, are not sufficient: they must have been put there by due process, amendable by due process, and drawn up, operated and discussed by efficiently autonomous participants. The provision of such autonomy is the task of business ethics as a discipline, or in my view, it ought to be. What is to count as 'due process' is open to debate. My own proposal is that the principles of autonomy, pluralism and the Golden Rule are sufficient. Surveys of codes in operation in Britain provide some tentative answers to some of the questions raised earlier in relation to the prevalence, content and uses of company codes. Two British surveys, by the Institute of Business Ethics and by the University of Edinburgh Department of Business Studies, were both published in 1988. The first of the surveys involved a questionnaire sent to 'Chief Executives of the largest United Kingdom Companies' (300) and to 'members of the Christian Association of Business Executives' (100). The response rate was 36%, and, for various reasons, this was reduced to a usable figure of about 24%. Most of the replies came from 'the larger publicly quoted companies'. Somewhat over half of those who replied had a written code of practice or ethics (Webley, 1988, p. 4). The University of Edinburgh survey questionnaires were sent to 'the chairmen of the largest 200 companies listed in the Times Top 1000 Companies (1986/87) business directory' (Schlegelmilch and Houston, 1988, p. 9). The latter study records a response of 37% completed questionnaires. Of those who replied, somewhat less than half had introduced a code of ethics.

One of the surveys was prompted, in part at least, by market research findings that a small proportion of respondents (a published figure of 17% was cited) thought that top businessmen could be rated highly for honesty, as opposed to an estimated 29% who thought that their honesty was low. In terms of the principles of autonomy, Golden Rule and pluralism on the evidence presented in the surveys, the Golden Rule criterion appears to have been detectable in the background judging from the contents of the codes, but there is no evidence to suggest that the actual values of those subject to the codes' provisions were actively sought, as opposed to assumed by the drafters of the code. If this is the case, then the codes do not satisfy the autonomy criterion either. One reason for this conclusion is that, according to the Edinburgh study, only about 60% were circulated to employees, and some were circulated only to boards of directors.

As one journal put it:

> While originating codes would appear to be a "top down" exercise, the Institute of Business Ethics emphasises the need for wide consultation at the preparation stage. The IBE recommends that early consultation is needed with the heads of personnel and public relations, and with company secretary or legal officer. (Industrial Relations Review and Report 422, p. 14, August, 1988.)

The Insitute does indicate that in some cases, employees at all levels were consulted, and "their views taken into account" (Webley, 1988, p. 14) but the generally 'top down' nature indicates further that the practical expression of the Golden Rule as criterion, i.e. a value-reversal test, was rarely, if ever, applied.

The Institute of Business Ethics produced a model code that should be applied to

> ...all employees and that any non-compliance will be considered a serious disciplinary matter. (Webley, 1988, p. 12.)

Examination of the codes reproduced in the surveys discussed above and the codes referred to earlier leads to the conclusion that the codes often contain first-order values that would command widespread support as constructive and 'respectable' values to hold. These are more than simple statements of narrow self-interest that would be included in my category (a) above. They appear to include many 'civilized' values that we may reasonably expect to be included in any behavioural rules that conform to the three criteria that I have proposed, but in the absence of the procedures to elicit those values, we may only guess. One of the themes of this book is that the procedures by which rules and decisions are made are of equal importance to the values expressed in the decisions and rules themselves: the right thing for the right reasons with proper procedures is a state of affairs that is recognizable, even if not always obvious to casual observers. Thus, to repeat a conclusion reached in earlier chapters, the enforcement of morals or ethics is a denaturing process: forcing people to be good has no more merit than the Rousseauan prescription that in some circumstances, people need to be forced to be free.

There is very little scholarly research on the detailed generation, operation, monitoring and amendment of codes in business. Because codes tend to be expressions of mixtures of technical, prudential and moral imperatives, and because they tend to vary in the extent to which they are or can be (or can defensibly be) enforced, they cannot be regarded as the major vehicles for identifying and encouraging the practices that will raise the level of the systematic treatment of values in business and industry. We might go further and say that in addition to the criticisms that the proliferation of codes represents at the level of public administration a 'twilight legislation' that takes control out of the hands of elected representatives and gives it to irresponsible agencies, codes have many other well-canvassed flaws. As Bernard Shaw said, professions can be conspiracies against the laity, and their codes, it may be added, are widely held to be primarily aimed at the protection of the members of the profession, rather than the public. Further, as Donaldson and Waller pointed out:

> Clearly, the central attraction of an institutionally-backed professional code

is that it would enable individuals to follow the dictates of their consciences at greatly reduced personal risk. However, although such an outcome is highly desirable, if only for the practical consequence of reducing the incidence of death . . . it is difficult to see that it reflects much moral credit on those who are only prepared to act when supported by an established, power-backed code. The morally 'strongest person' is one who in Ibsen's terms 'stands alone' i.e. one who has the courage to act without institutional support and frequently in the face of it. (Donaldson and Waller, 1980, p. 45.)

There are, however, some dilemmas here. Is the justification of an ethical system that it produces people who are morally strong, or that it generates what people believe to be the right practices and decisions? Is unanimity essential, and if it does not occur, then whose morality should prevail? Should it be enforced, and if so, what enforcement procedures are morally acceptable, and on what grounds? These are related to the matter of whether the law enforces morality, or merely enforces norms. In turn this raises one of the central questions in traditional ethical theory: why should I (or anyone) be moral?

Is it because it pays to be honest, because there are penalties for being caught, or is it because we have a moral sense that ought to be obeyed, or because there are rewards in a later life? It seems to me that the general answer is a logical one: moral rights imply moral responsibilities, but there is no way of avoiding some ranking of actions and principles at the first-order level: some lapses are trivial enough to suggest that they do not imply the loss of all moral rights and claims, but to deny them to others does imply the loss of such rights to the individual. There is an unavoidable reciprocal nature in ethical claims, and the Golden Rule provides a compelling statement of it.

The conclusion seems to me to be unavoidable that ethical, as opposed to prudential, codes at their most defensible represent a stage in the development of identifying, reconciling and practising morally autonomous systems which can satisfy also the requirements of pluralism with procedural correctness in accordance with the Golden Rule. If they are not generated and amendable by reference to these principles, it is difficult to claim ethical merit in codes, however useful they are at the level of prudence or self-interest.

CHAPTER SEVEN

The Ethics of Trade Unions

The Regulation of Union Behaviour

From the point of view of the systematic handling of industrial values, the significance of trade unions is drawn from a variety of sources. Objectivity in analysing, dealing with or responding to the issues raised by the existence and operation of trade unions is difficult to achieve even by those who deliberately seek to do so, and in my experience, the attempt itself is a rarity. Their existence does not make much sense except in the context of some concept of pluralism, but at the same time, union activities raise issues that demonstrate how difficult it is to recognize and reconcile a plurality of values and of sources of authority and commitment. The difficulties relate to both the relations between trade unions and the state and other institutions, as well as between them and employers or employers' associations. The acceptance and role of unions in different countries shows extremely wide variations influenced, if not wholly determined by, the political and industrial history of the country, its geography, size, moral and religious attitudes and institutions and much else (Bean, 1985). Even unions themselves have at times stormy relations with other unions within their national boundaries, and tenuous ones with unions in other countries. The result is a network, or rather a tangle of inconsistent attitudes towards and within trade unions.

It would be overambitious to attempt to offer to disentangle the attitudes, but it is possible to attempt an explanation of some of the lines of thought, and to indicate the various points at which they become, apparently, hopelessly knotted, as a prelude to estimating how far they go to meet the three ground rules. Like companies, corporations, and trade and professional associations, unions operate within a framework of law, externally imposed codes, and codes of practice arrived at by consent or agreement.

It would be a mistake to infer that unions and employers are always at loggerheads. In some cases, amicable agreements are reached which

135

suggest mutual rather than adversarial modes (Sheldrake, 1988a, pp. 45–47). The British Department of Employment publishes strike figures that have led to the conclusions that about 95% of employees never experience a strike at their place of work during their whole working life. Typically, strikes exhibit a cyclical pattern associated with the economic cycle, and reactions to legislation, which, in Britain at least, exhibits cyclical patterns of its own, associated with the election cycles. Some unions and employers are accused of being too accommodating, as when the British Railways Board, not the Rail Unions, was successfully prosecuted in the European Court in relation to its attempts to enforce a closed shop ('union membership agreement') in 1981, or when the employers and union were accused by a breakaway group of employees of operating an agreement that was to the detriment of members (Lane and Roberts, 1971). Codes of practice imposed by government control pay movements during the currency of 'incomes policies' or other policies of pay restraint. That they work imperfectly and are often counter-productive was once held to be an invitation to redesign codes that work better. Thus, the idea of imposed codes has been, and still is, attractive to governments which seek to control union activities. They now extend to the conduct of strikes (codes on picketing) and on the operation of ballots for deciding on or against strike action, or election of union officers. These codes are often associated with legislation, and though compliance is not compulsory the consequences of breaking them amount to an element of compulsion.

The legal provisions vary from country to country. The patterns of conflicts are well known in the literature to be profoundly influenced by the patterns of legislation aimed at reducing them. For instance the American system, it has been shown, tends to lead to fewer, but longer strikes than in Britain. That public sector strikes are illegal in America raises a large number of ethical issues. For instance, an issue that turns out to be an example of a very general ethical dilemma is described by Gotbaum (1978): a union executive can be in a position to encourage or prevent an illegal strike. The power structure can be such that by not striking, the employees will always lose, even cases that objective observers would find in their favour. The executive, in a secure job, could obey the law (a moral imperative) and thereby condemn the people who have placed their trust in the executive to be permanent losers—a breach of trust. Whatever action is taken by the executive will break some moral imperative, but the cost, given that even a strike may be a failure, could easily fall on others. These are not hypothetical cases, but real issues faced regularly by union executives. If there is an ethically sound solution to this dilemma, there are several lines of approach that may be considered. For instance, a hierarchy of principles could be established, as for example when the concept of the 'rule of law' is cited to suggest that the law ought to be obeyed even by those who believe that a particular law is morally wrong. Another would be to attempt to assess the consequences of one action or another, and estimate which course would maximize the good. A third would be to insist that the law can be changed in favour of the disadvantaged employees, who should be encouraged to be patient until the law is changed. Other, more pragmatic courses of action might be considered, for example to find sympathetic arbitrators, to fudge the issue by generating allowances in the payment/compensation system that take the edge off the emergency. This latter has been a common way out of rule-imposed impasses, though not often in relation to lower-paid employees. There are practical solutions to such dilemmas posed by highly constrained circumstances as described above. Some indication will be offered in Part Three. For the present, it is suggested here that the method of describing moral dilemmas used in the example is a common one. It makes some assumptions that are not tenable. It need not be assumed in this kind of case that there must be one 'moral' course of action, and that a sufficiently well-trained and impartial observer should be able to see what it is. As Gotbaum points out in the paper from which the dilemma is taken, arbitration has been known to lose the trust of people subject to it, who become wary of trying it. Appeal to the law can be a soft option:

> Every evil can be justified by moral standards or by a law to the person who perpetrates it. (Gotbaum, 1978, p. 168.)

A problem with the method of setting up such dilemmas, whether to keep promises at the expense of having to tell a lie, or whether it is permissible to break the law in the act of doing good, is that they have no mechanism for operating any procedure that ascertains what the views are of the parties most affected. In other words, the moral agent is placed in a vacuum, with no ground on which to stand to make a decision. As Gotbaum puts it, "you have to make a decision" (*ibid.*, p. 168).

So far in this chapter the argument about unions has centred on their part in overt conflicts, such as strikes, but since most of their time, most employees and union executives are not striking or preparing for a strike, it is useful to point out that in addition to the legal requirements, unions have constitutions, rule books, and codes of their own. For instance, in Britain, union rule books are overseen by the Certification Officer. Rule books contain provision for revision, usually at special conferences of delegates from local branches. Elaborate codes govern the procedures at meetings (Citrine, 1984), and the Bridlington Agreement reached by British (TUC) unions in 1939 covers such matters as the conditions under which unions can recruit. For instance, non-members may not be recruited when the individuals concerned are on strike. Plants are operated by members of a union which will not be subject to competitive attempts by other unions to 'poach' members. The agreement has been broken in recent years, for controversial reasons and with (as yet) uncertain results. In general, the Bridlington Agreement has operated in ways reminiscent of employers' cartels, but for many years it effectively damped down inter-union conflicts. But why should there be inter-union conflicts at all? The general answer is given by many speakers at the Annual Trades Union Congress: the value is stated and reinforced that trade unions exist to further the interests of their members. This doctrine has been somewhat tempered by the notion that unions are 'cause groups', subscribing to the doctrine of 'the brotherhood of man'. In general, unions do not support each other much during the conduct of strikes, although there are many cases in which mutual support has been forthcoming. The high point in Britain for such concerted action was a period of nine days in 1926, during the 'General Strike'. Such 'sympathetic action' is currently unlawful in Britain. The general question of how far union activity can and should be regulated by law keeps recurring in different contexts.

An example from Britain in the early 1980s was the decision of the Trades Union Congress to agree to a 'day of action' in support of National Health Service employees. Such secondary action had been illegal in the 1920s, in the legislation that followed the collapse of the General Strike, and permissible from 1945, discouraged in the 1971 legislation, permitted in 1975, and legislated against in the 1982 Act. Without saying that the law formalizes moral codes (which is a partial truth), it is clear that opinion is divided and shifts from time to time, usually with changes of government, on 'secondary action'. A standard solution in moral and political theory is to propose that even if a person believes a law to be immoral, breaking it can only be morally permissible if the law is clearly contrary to justice, and oppressive, and when the democratic means of amending it are blocked, for instance if the government of the day declared itself to be a permanent dictatorship.

A standard reply in rebuttal is that the government in a democratic system cannot be afforded absolute powers by the electorate. There are limits, and legitimate pressure groups are entitled to use their powers of persuasion. Pragmatically, some laws are changed because of public revulsion and widespread disobeying of particular laws, and it is a matter for mature judgment on the part of all concerned where the limits lie in a particular case. Such issues are, sensibly, discussed only in terms of those matters, such as secondary action in furtherance of a trade dispute, which are so much at the boundary of decision that the law oscillates between permitting and banning the action. Such cases are best dealt with at the level of bargaining skills, and prudential calculations of the likely outcomes. It is stretching a point to see the enforcement of uncertain (and non-criminal) rules as having a greater moral force than the content of the rules themselves.

These issues in part explain why a great deal of opinion in Britain has favoured the exclusion of trade disputes from the law.

The existence itself of trade unions is rarely called into question in the serious literature and in public debate. Much of the criticism, most of which has substantial ethical overtones, has been of their methods of operation. Unions are often likened to monopoly companies, and indeed, are sometimes labelled 'labour monopolies'. This aspect will serve to introduce the more general criticisms of trade unions, that is, the criticisms that are not specifically focused on strike patterns and their regulation. This is appropriate because, as has already been pointed out, such overt and dramatic conflict is not the mainstay of union activity.

The underpinning of the rules governing the operation of competition among firms and corporations is the idea that monopoly is 'wrong' because it delivers economic power to a single company (or, on the more pragmatic interpretations, a small group of companies). This economic power is held to distort the pattern of production, and, on the analogy of political democracy, it is equivalent to buying votes, as a sum of money spent on a good or service is held to be equivalent to a vote for the product of service. Behind the economic theory is the moral concept of the sovereignty of individual consumers and producers and the notion of pure or perfect competition is usually defended as an ideal way of ensuring the democratic economic equality that ensures an undistorted pattern of production. The notions of 'competition', 'pure', 'democratic', 'sovereignty' and many others, such as 'optimal allocation of resources' are important clues to what must follow. As with the problems of regulation of restrictive practices described in Chapter Two, the moral and technical concepts in the economic study of the labour market have become seriously entangled, and often reversed. Nevertheless, the economic arguments about trade unions are derived from the idea that trade unions are labour monopolies, restricting the labour supply in order to maximise wages. Note that 'wages' also is a heavily loaded moral concept, which has often been surrounded with technical language (Donaldson and Philby, 1985, especially Chapter 1). As economic institutions, trade unions are held to raise pay—and unemployment—to levels which would not occur in the absence of unions. Curiously, estimates in America of the union wage effect tend to cluster around 10%, that is that unionized labour forces tend on the average to receive about 10% more pay than non-unionized labour forces (Hamermesh and Rees, 1984).

As one British Prime Minister once put it "One man's pay rise is another man's ticket to the dole queue". Since pay is usually associated with moral notions such as 'the rate for the job' and 'a fair day's pay/work for a fair day's work/pay' and has been in the technical economic literature linked with employment, and hence people's livelihood and well-being, people have expectations of just rewards that befit their effort or status.

The history of the notion of 'the just wage' is ancient and there have been many illuminating studies, such as that in Tawney's (1922) *Religion and the Rise of Capitalism*. What does emerge is that given mediaeval concepts of hierarchy, it was thought possible to deduce from first principles what the pay or reward ought to be for a person of a particular occupation and status. When labour market conditions changed, and pay was clearly influenced by what we now call supply and demand conditions, the notion began to emerge in the eighteenth century of a mechanism that would relieve decision makers and wage fixers of the duty of making such moral decisions. The market mechanism, or rather the concept of it, did not reach its full glory until the early decades of the twentieth century, since when it has remained highly controversial. For our present purposes, it need only be noted further that studies of trade unions and wage behaviour have tended (ignoring the ephemeral modes of treatment) to be divided between technical, but theoretical, treatments, involving much mathematics and little evidence; statistical studies, based on assumptions; and observational studies that seek to examine the behaviour of unions (and occasionally of employers). Virtually all of the work that has been done has been in the positivist tradition. The positivist nature of the statistical studies is well attested in the literature and will not be discussed further here. Within the 'social science' tradition, there have been many studies of the attitudes and orientations to work of trade union members and shop stewards. Much is known about the operation of rule books and the use of procedural rules to manage (or manipulate) meetings and negotiations. The process of revision of rule books is well known. Much, too, is known about the internal divisions of opinion, conflicts between groups with differing ideologies, power struggles, and attitudes to strikes. Attitudes towards employers, reasons for striking, motivations of members have all been intensively studied, along with the detailed operations of branches, shop stewards' committees, processes of formulation of pay claims and much else. Indeed, more is known about trade unions and their members than about the much smaller group of managers and public administrators, for example. The reasons are easy enough to recognize: it is much more difficult to get access to board rooms than to picket lines and trade union branches; there are more trade unionists than managers, and thus it is more likely that researchers will be able to find someone to survey or talk to. Few trade union members have much in the way of confidential or damaging information to defend. The literature on trade unions is far more descriptive than that on managers, and far more related to conflict behaviour. The literature on managers, perhaps in part because access to managerial decisions and meetings is more difficult, tends to be pre-scriptive, and geared to techniques of management for consideration by managers.

The knowledge of trade unions and their industrial relations content is so well distributed that for countries that have well-developed trade unions and industrial relations systems, the editors of some recent bibliographies of industrial relations have made the sensible decision to publish, for those countries, not lists of relevant books and articles, but lists of bibliographies (Bennet and Fawcett, 1985). The intense interest in trade unions can be seen from an inspection of the literature to be linked to a very large number of issues at the first-order level. These are all directly ethical or have major ethical implications or overtones.

It is germane at this point to ask why the kind and level of attention given to trade unions in the management literature is so different from that given to managers and management. The answers must include the considerations mentioned above, of access to the larger number of trade union members as opposed to managers. But there are some strong theoretical reasons. The standard techniques and theories of management are framed in such a way as to make it difficult even to claim that unions could be relevant. If decisions to expand are calculated from discounted cash flow or other 'optimization' techniques, the technicalities admit no role for the opinions of employees, who generally have neither the information nor the skills to perform the technical routines. Their contri-bution comes, if at all, in the stage of administering the plant closures or new methods of production, or perhaps in assisting with the communi-cation of management's intentions to other employees. The (possibly exaggerated) technical and confidential nature of management decisions then, makes it difficult to find a role for unions in management processes. Even the idea that they might do so seems just as alien to unions themselves. Managers dispose, and unions oppose, mitigate or bargain. They do not initiate much more than pay claims. The theories of manage-ment, from Taylor's *Scientific Management* in the early decades of the twentieth century, the economic theories of the firm, also perfected in the last eighty years or so, the criticisms of scientific management associated with the human relations school of management thought, the techniques of operations research and management science give no formal place to unions in their theories, because they are theories and techniques for managers about management. Some studies have built some bridges, but on the whole, management theories and methods are addressed to hierarchical and bureaucratic organizations.

The ideal of a union-free environment does exist, and is much stronger in some countries than others. Amongst the older democracies, the variations in managerial and public attitudes towards unions is reflected in the wide variations between countries of unionization of labour forces, with America (below 20% in the 1980s) and France (about 20% in the same period) at one end of the scale, and Britain (50%), Germany (40%), Canada and Australia all at the 'high' end.

It is against this background that the ethically based criticisms of unions should be considered. The sixth 'key issue' listed in Chapter One was: *can a clear boundary be drawn between business ethics and other matters, such as law, politics, economics or psychology?* The Bhopal case, the issues surrounding restrictive trade and labour practices, the ideas of 'economic growth', the continuing difficulties of control of inflation, the generation and enforcement of codes of practice demonstrate that any boundaries between these various disciplines are inevitably artificial.

There are some standard criticisms of trade unions that have recurred in ministerial statements, and have been implied in legislation and in the terms of reference of official enquiries, and which appear frequently in the mass media. Some suggest a questioning of the ethical right of unions to exist at all, but most criticize the operation of unions, usually seeing the operation as unduly restrictive of management or damaging to the national interest or to third parties, but occasionally alleging that unions do not go far enough in their opposition to the managerial and administrative framework. As one writer put it, reactions to the idea of unions range "from apoplectic to apocalyptic" (Armstrong, 1974).

Some Standard Criticisms of Unions

The moral criticisms of unions can be categorized:

1. The Argument From Labour Monopoly
On this argument, unions are thought of as acting just like monopoly firms, restricting labour supply by various means, in order to raise pay or maintain pay levels in the face of pressures from the market for reduction. On this view, union activity is held to be immoral in the same way as monopoly company activities are immoral. The action is regarded as reducing total economic output, and therefore total potential for economic well-being, as well as redistributing pay from those employees (labour units, workers) whose monopoly power is low or zero, as well as, in some cases, reducing the incomes of the unemployed to dependence on welfare

benefits. It should be no surprise that the argument from labour monopoly is identical in form to the restrictive practices argument discussed in Chapter Three, and suffers from the same problems, in that it raises more issues than it clarifies, mixes to the point of entanglement technical and moral matters, and has very little practical application in a world in which power over income determination is distributed between highly organized groups on the basis of political, moral, and traditional processes, as well as technical ones. It always has been so. Nevertheless, it does draw attention to the power-related processes of bargaining, and for that matter, to non-bargaining processes of pay determination. Whether unions aim to act like monopolies, and succeed in doing so, has become another of those 'tired old debates'.

2. *Trade Unions and Inflation*

Trade unions have long been held to cause inflation, which, broadly, is best described as the sustained rise in the general price level. The ethical problems of inflation are usually, and reasonably, taken to include particularly the redistribution of income on grounds of power and chance, rather than merit. In fact, students of income distribution have debated for a very long time the extent to which the distribution of income is based on merit even in the absence of inflation. This argument, too, is a mixture of moral and technical considerations, including, for example, the possibility that income is distributed on the basis of genetic endowments, power tactics, technical market processes, tradition, attitudes towards education, and much else. The debate shows no sign whatever of resolution, indicating that the matter is more ideological than rational. Unions do contribute, among other groups, to pressures on production: it is easier to manufacture demands on the output of an economy than to manufacture the goods (or supply the services) that can meet the demand, as has, to my mind, been convincingly shown by Machlup (1974) among others.

3. *Union Membership, Representation and Freedom*

In Britain, until the 1980s the 'closed shop' and its enforcement by unions and employers were permissible in law, without restriction other than that provided by the criminal law in the event of specific criminal offences. The 1980s legislation has reduced the scope of enforcement and in some cases has been instrumental in ending some long-established closed shops in particular companies, particularly in the newspaper industry. In mining, a 'breakaway' union has gained some recognition by the employers.

The American system, under the Wagner Act of 1935, permits 'union shops', and agency shops. In the latter, a union secures negotiation rights for persons who are not members of the union. (Such 'agency' representation is not unknown in Britain.) Union shops are permitted in some states but not others, suggesting that the matter is still unresolved (De George, 1986). In both countries, the number of employees covered by such arrangements runs to millions, but in ethical terms, the number bears on estimates of the nature and strength of attitudes, but is irrelevant to the determination of whether the practice of enforced membership is justifiable in ethical terms and to the grounds on which the principle can be established. Insofar as there is a standard set of arguments in the matter of enforced union membership, it surrounds several issues, ranging from heady notions of freedom and liberty, and collective rights, through to cynical estimates of the moves that can be made in 'the power game'. Pragmatic claims that, in fact, closed shops are convenient for employers and employees alike point to stability and relative freedom from conflict, possibilities of orderly resolution and the development of understandings between employer and employee representatives that outlast the presence of particular individual managers and union representatives. My own view is that the pragmatic arguments favour obligatory union membership in some contexts, but not others, but that such arrangements unambiguously restrict freedom. This should come as no surprise, as all law and all bureaucratic, hierarchical and legal processes restrict freedom. John Stuart Mill's criterion for establishing the legitimacy of such restrictions, though often criticized, has never been replaced with a sounder one. It is still apposite:

> The only part of the conduct of anyone, for which he is amenable to society, is that which concerns others. In the part which merely concerns himself, his independence is, of right, absolute. Over himself, over his own body and mind, the individual is sovereign. (Mill, 1859, Fontana edition, 1962, p. 135.)

Mill distinguished in the essay between 'self-regarding' and 'other-regarding' actions. Admittedly, Mill's distinction, like all dichotomies, cannot be decisive in all cases. He attempted to qualify the effects on others as pertinent only when people were affected 'directly and in the first instance'. In the case of enforced union membership the nub of the problem is how to decide whose freedom and rights should be encouraged or enforced: the union members' rights to bargain freely on terms of approximate parity with employers; non-members' rights to negotiate their own contract, if employers are willing to do so and in the cases of changes in contract of employment, requiring that existing, non-members who are employees be required to join the union as part of the new contract. The concept of consent to changes in contract seems to be established in the courts, including the European Court, which also ruled, in the case of a complaint against British Railways in August 1981, that the right to join a union implied the right not to join, but that there are circumstances in which a closed shop may be enforced without infringing the European Convention of Human Rights.

A running theme in this book has been that what *is* is not necessarily what *must be*, and not necessarily what *ought to be* a practice, ruling or law. The general problem, for supporters of the 'rule of law' is how to set about changing laws that are held to be mistaken or inappropriate. It is unlikely that a satisfactory resolution of the problem can be achieved at the first-order level. Ambiguities remain even when the Golden Rule, the principles of autonomy and the notion of pluralism are applied by writers, courts, arbitration panels and others. It is not suggested that such decisions are not proper or that they ought not to be binding. It is suggested that the ethical arguments are prior to the legal ones, and that it may be proper to abide by a rule that an ethical agent believes to be wrong, since that is an essential part of the concept of the rule of law, particularly when the institutions and procedures are trusted. As Gotbaum points out in his article, these conditions do not always apply. The problem then, is that satisfactory resolution of such problems will never be received if absolute certainty is sought. The prospects improve as the institutions develop towards ascertaining and evaluating the informed views of autonomous relevant parties or individuals. There is a long way to go before such institutions are developed in industry in general and in industrial relations in particular. Standard arguments for and against the closed shop are:

The Case For

1. People are entitled to benefit from the work of an association only when they contribute towards its advance.

2. It is therefore the duty of the employers to accede to the union demands for benefits for ALL workers.

3. National negotiations and government pay policies make it necessary for unions to seek assurances that their loyalty to agreements in unfavourable circumstances will not lose them members.

4. Many unions need a closed shop to maintain standards in their craft, trade or profession.

The Case Against

1. It is a violation of the freedom of the individual and his/her freedom of association. A person should be allowed to join a union, any union, and should also be allowed not to join a union at all.

2. The closed shop can harm the economy by limiting the employment of skilled employees and craft unions will not accept employees in government retraining centres.

3. Unions can refuse membership to anyone they please, do not need to give reasons, hence lack of public accountability.

4. Closed shops make unions non-voluntary organizations, which is

5. An employer deals with one organization representing the employees in that grade or establishment and can expect uniform action amongst members of that organization.

6. Union leadership has collective dissident minorities and deters unofficial/unconstitutional action by smaller groups.

7. A closed shop agreement limits the development of multi-unionism, and prevents unions competing for membership.

8. Members of closed shops show greater participation and interest in the activities of their union.

9. Employing non-unionists with union members causes a great deal of unnecessary friction.

10. A closed shop creates a better disciplined and more tractable labour force.

11. A closed shop strengthens the union bargaining skill.

12. A worker who does not join a union is evading responsibilities to other workers.

13. Closed shop removes the need for union officials to justify activities of the union to potential members.

against the principle of modern trades unionism.

5. Closed shops can be nepotistic, i.e. the dock workers 'sons and brothers' list.

6. Employees who are forced into a union are not only passive, they are also focal points for disaffection and disruption.

7. Closed shop causes capital to leave the trade and markets to be lost abroad.

8. Closed shop forces up costs.

9. Powers which closed shop confers are abused.

10. Because the notion of the closed shop is thought to be unpopular with the public, employers are often reluctant to accept that it can be done in a mutually advantageous way.

The above points for and against the closed shop indicate that in this matter, as in others, the mixture of pragmatic, prudential, ethical and legal issues should at least advise caution to any moral agent who is prepared to take an absolutist stand.

It may be safely asserted that a closed shop situation is more pluralist than a union-less situation would be where there are disparities in power between employer and employee, but limits pluralism to the extent that individuals are required to conform to company and union rules. On grounds of autonomy, the more individuals know about company and union policies, the more they can make up their own minds about them. There are, however, processes in companies and unions which militate against this condition, ranging from secrecy, bureaucratic decision making 'behind locked doors', back-room deals, and apathy of members. All of these are interconnected. In terms of the Golden Rule, the value-reversal test will not be decisive if guessed at by a single observer or committee. It cannot be expected to give absolute certainty, but can increase trust, and provides for revision on an agreed basis.

In short, the moral, prudential and technical issues in this matter, as in others, have become entangled, and the entanglement is not relieved by the current industrial relations institutions. Until then, the judgment of a Conservative Secretary of State for Employment seems to have summed the matter up in 1980: "it is horses for courses".

4. *The Challenge to Legitimate Managerial Authority*
The argument here is that since managers have the right and duty (or responsibility, obligation or similar) in law and in principle for producing efficient, maximized production, unions can only be disruptive. The more efficient an industry is, the more there is to share out in potential welfare. There is ample evidence that unions resist change, possibly out of a mixture of conservatism and other motives. The image of the nineteenth century machine-wreckers, held to have been unable to see the writing on the wall of progress, is still potent. It is not difficult to see that, as usual, there are many moral issues involved. In terms of the three criteria, there is no pretence in the argument of applying the Golden Rule, autonomy or pluralism. If managers have the duty and skills to maximize and optimize, there is no theoretical room for unions, ethical doubt, autonomy of employees or pluralism. There is, of course, no evidence that managers do typically maximize production or efficiency or anything else. There is much evidence that they balance a whole range of demands from various sources, using whatever skills they possess. The circumstantial evidence from early 1974 in Britain is that during a period in which power was available to factories only for three days due to an industrial dispute, after a shock effect, many factories were producing in three days what normally took five days plus overtime. When due account is taken of the likelihood that in the short term employees would exceed normal long-term effort levels, there is an implausibility in any assumption that in general, output is maximized or optimized, even if, in the aggregate, such concepts have a useful application. The argument applies also to highly disaggregated units of production. There is no evidence, to my knowledge, that during the period there was a detectable difference in output of unionized as opposed to union-free factories, or that union-free factories consistently out-

perform unionized ones. Even if it could be shown that unions in general restrict aggregate output to a level below that of a union-free economy, for instance on the grounds that employers sometimes successfully prefer to take their factories to union-free economies, the argument from potential welfare, which was the original ground for criticism of the unions, is much weakened, if not destroyed by the long-term stability of income distribution in advanced economies, and by the extremes of wealth and poverty in most underdeveloped ones. The argument from potential welfare thus rests on the belief that union-free environments are more efficient, and on the implication that potential welfare will be equitably distributed, once achieved. Both are doubtful propositions. Even if the doubtful were to become true, the potential welfare benefits of maximized efficiency represent one set of values as opposed to others, such as autonomy and pluralism. In other words, the 'economic' criteria of efficiency, even if satisfied, are representative of some values among many, and are themselves subject to much uncertainty, as shown in Chapter Two.

5. Internal Control
There are many examples of 'undemocratic' procedures and decisions in unions. Their internal operations are said, with much evidence, to follow the 'iron law of oligarchy' in which small, self-perpetuating groups of active and informed members make decisions and attempt to decide policies, suppress internal dissent and opposition. There are many examples of such actions. The (then) General and Municipal Workers' Union, involved in a strike at Pilkington Brothers Ltd, glass manufacturers, excluded all but shop stewards from branch meetings (Lane and Roberts, 1971). Earlier, accusations of ballot rigging were proved in the courts against the Electrical Trades Union, and the election set aside. In America, the Landrum–Griffin Act, 1959, provides for internal opposition, in an attempt to reduce the power of union bosses. The more general case in Britain is one in which opposing groups within unions, usually accepting such labels as 'left' or 'right' or 'moderate', compete for control. Whoever wins, there is evidence of unions imposing fines on members, through such exotica as 'kangaroo courts'. Evidence of most of these processes can be found in companies and other institutions also. Of course, that others do it does not legitimate any action, but it at least shows the scale of the problem.

6. The Challenge to the State, and the Argument from Strike Violence
These two arguments are often linked and can usefully be taken together. Unions are seen as both encouraging strikes that cause employees to be in breach of contract, but also of condoning, conniving at, or failing to

control violence during strikes, usually involving offences against the criminal law. Since both undermine the authority of the state, as for example when strikes are in opposition to new laws, or are in pursuit of claims that infringe legislation aimed at control of incomes and their increases, the moral objections and the legal ones are legion. As it happens, leaders of unions can occasionally be found who appear to endorse strike violence, on the grounds that strike breakers started it, and the strikers were only acting in legitimate self-defence, and appear to approve of the defeat of the government of the day, if not its replacement. As with many other examples, the facts of the matter are often in dispute. In the case of strike violence, claims and counter-claims are made that the violence was originated by professional agitators, and encountered by claims that professional *agents provocateurs* were involved. In the nature of things, the facts of such matters are hard to come by. My own view is that such problems are capable of mutually satisfactory solution at the second-order level, using procedures that encourage autonomy rather than groupthink, using jointly agreed codes, with stated principles. If this seems like naive optimism, it should be set beside the notion of self-fulfilling prophecies: if some groups believe that violence and win–lose are the 'name of the game', then they can make it so, and group fantasies become realities. Whether any agreements in situations where the potential for such self-fulfilling fantasies could ever be honoured is a problem in what can be called 'the moral psychology of industry'.

7. *Effects on Third Parties*

During industrial disputes, and as a result of restrictive practices, persons who have no part in the dispute or practice are often inconvenienced or worse. Injury or death, loss of income or job, or loss of job opportunity can be seen as causally linked with disputes as consequences. On what ethical grounds could it be thought justifiable to permit these? The instinctive, and, I believe, correct, answer is that in the case of physical injury or death, no justification is possible. On whom does the duty fall to avoid such injuries by calling off the dispute?

We are here concerned with the moral duty, and not with what happens to be the current law and its *rationale*. Bearing in mind the old saw that 'it takes (at least) two to make a quarrel', it seems obvious that the duty is upon all the direct participants, at least. Whether the rule is workable depends upon the institutional arrangements for ascertaining the facts of the matter, and the principles involved in the dispute. As Gotbaum points out in the passage quoted at the beginning of this chapter it is possible for some parties to lose faith in the procedures. In practice, public opinion or the intervention of conciliators, mediators, government officials, and, as a last resort, use of force by police or armed forces is available, and sometimes, in some countries not always as a last resort. This reinforces one of the propositions of Part One, that morals are not enforceable, even though rules, group norms, or even the moral convictions of some may be forced on others in terms of compliance without acceptance. The more sinister activities, such as brainwashing, do not cast doubt on this proposition, since they clearly break the principle of autonomy. If there is an acceptable solution, it will not be found by drafting legislation, though that may help. The decision to refrain from physical injury to third parties follows from acceptance of the Golden Rule, autonomy and pluralism, but the industrial relations institutions that can encourage that are as yet undeveloped, even though they are on the whole more efficient in prudential terms, in the second half of the twentieth century in the older developed economics than they were before.

Damage to the economic interest of third parties presents more ambiguous problems. The causal sequences are more difficult to trace, and claims more difficult to sustain. As with most of the cases and practices discussed in this book, first-order solutions which take the form of statements of what is good, bad, right, wrong, justifiable or unjustifiable practice are highly problematic. Some of these problems are: on whose ordering of values is the judgment to be made? The lawyers' pragmatic test of what a reasonable person would decide, or what was decided earlier are not decisive in this context, because the question at hand is what is the ethically correct thing to do? The subjectivist or relativist view that the customs of the current culture should decide is not helpful, because the customs have told us nothing, which is why we have the problem. The standard solutions are to identify the values *assumed* to be held by reasonable people, and who is to be counted as a reasonable person is profoundly influenced by whoever makes the decision, which is whoever has the power. Thus justice becomes, in the words of Thrasymachus in Plato's *Republic*, truly "the interest of the stronger". The matter of damage to the economic interests of third parties becomes, as usual, a tangle of prudential, technical, factual and moral arguments. The untangling must rely on authentic information, but if the parties concerned have no voice (as in the cases of businesses damaged at the end of a long sequence of events) and there is no procedure for hearing it, the result inevitably becomes the 'shabby compromises' that are observable. The situation can be equally problematic even when third parties happen to be on the spot and are able to articulate their views.

A clue to some possible resolutions can be provided by making a distinction between causal and logical consequences. The first is, broadly, a utilitarian view, which seeks to judge what action would produce the best result. The second is a sequence of arguments, taking account of evidence and principles, and is much more rare.

Before that can be explored, it is worth noting that even when third parties are present on the spot, and are able to articulate their views, if proper procedures are not available, the problem can become more, not less entangled.

A recent example is provided by the British dispute over pay in late 1988 and early 1989 between the Association of University Teachers and The Committee of Vice-Chancellors and Principals, representing the employers. A favourable ballot held by the Association empowered its executive to call for, in effect, a complete boycott of all processes connected with the setting, marking and administration of examinations. The boycott was to begin on January 9th. By mid-January, reports appeared in the press to the effect that the Committee's ranks had been broken by a pay offer by one University to its staff. The Association's ranks had been broken by staff at some universities continuing to hold examinations as normal. The Association had been prepared to make exceptions to its general instructions, and did so, on the grounds, for example, that some students re-entering examinations would not be permitted, under the regulations of one University, to take the examinations at all if they were not taken in 1989. This is a clear enough case of recognition of damage to the interests of third parties, and willingness to avoid such damage. But the Association went further, in making exceptions in the case of possible escalation if the threatened action were to be pursued too vigorously. This holding back from the consequences of decisions made could be seen as tactical, prudential, or merely inconsistent, depending on the point of view of the observer. The difficulties of both sides in holding their constituents together are by no means unusual in disputes, and seem to be particularly noticeable in white-collar disputes, as noted by Sheldrake (1985) in relation to the Local Government Comparability Dispute of 1980 and visible in the ethical dilemmas posed by industrial action in nursing.

It suggests not only that threats, once made, cannot always be carried out, but that it can be difficult to admit either that they are or are not being carried out, or that the 'action' is not unanimous. At the same time it is difficult to insist that they be carried out to the letter, in case of escalation, or to admit they are not, because of the need to appear decisive and resolute. If the ethical emotions become diluted, the action can collapse, if they are not it can get out of hand. The third party considerations could be seen as either moral or tactical. This pattern appears to have been repeated locally, as some members of the Association carried out normal examination duties, while others made no recognition of noticing it. The threat from the employers' side is worth considering, since it was based on individual teachers' contracts.

The idea was that refusal to participate in examinations constituted a serious breach of contract, and was thus grounds for 'sending employees home', docking of pay, or even dismissal. As it happens, for at least some teachers the contract was very unspecific. Employees were required to perform 'duties as required by the head of department', and subject to local agreements. In some cases, the Head of Department had issued no instructions whatever, and no local agreements existed. It was assumed that the Head of Department's powers had been delegated to other members of the union, who were placed, or thought themselves to be placed, in the difficult position of ensuring that the examinations went ahead, while at the same time called upon to support the 'action' and withhold cooperation. Some incumbents solved the problem by retaining ambiguity. Local colleagues were reluctant to do anything to bring the situation into the open, and therefore remained silent. In the meantime, local meetings were being held at which no decisions of any kind were taken, and no intentions expressed. Nor did employees know what the contract of employment meant so they were not in a position to know whether any action would be in breach of contract or not. The apparently unlimited powers in the printed contract according to the Head of Department, presumably, would be limited by customs and practice, but even there doubts existed, for instance in the case of appointments to boards which did not previously fall within the employee's normal duties. It was not known whether appointment to new duties required consent on the part of the employee.

Three points emerge at this stage: (1) the lack of knowledge of what it meant to be in breach of contract, and the reluctance to confront the matter of action or inaction, are fairly common in white-collar disputes; (2) in addition the relationships between staff in universities generally require that conflict should not be expressed or become overt; (3) in many disputes involving several departments, units or sites, the quality of the relationships is variable, and in some cases, local cooperation with employers can occur to the extent of limiting the effect of the dispute, while at the same time conforming to the requirements of their representative institutions, or at least appearing to do so. This was illustrated in detail in Barlow's study, 'Some Latent Influences in a White-Collar Pay Claim' (Barlow, 1969). In terms of the Golden Rule: the matters were hardly discussed in an open way, for the reasons explained. The values of participants were assumed, rather than identified, and as large-scale ballots are very rudimentary forms of consultation, this could not convey the variations in attitude among members. There is, of course, no suggestion that the ballot was anything other than properly conducted.

One further point should be included: one 'third party' group whose interests were directly affected, the group of current students, was, in most cases on the premises. The students' own union, nationally, advised support for the university staffs 'action'. In some local units, student unions assured the lecturers that they supported the *principle* behind the action, but believed strongly that the *form* of action was inappropriate. They thanked those academics who had not supported the action. In this case the representatives of the third parties, in not recognizing that the action had been decided upon by due process, and was thus mandatory, seemed to be exhibiting the ambiguity also seen in the attitudes of the lecturers and their employers. This interpretation is reinforced by the wording, which appears to offer support at the rhetorical level, but implies a weakening in the tone of the message. It seems that even if third parties are in a position to participate, this does not ensure that agreed and justifiable procedures will be applied, or even sought by any or all parties. In the circumstances it is difficult to avoid the conclusion that when the contracts, procedures, issues and values are not clearly specified, the tendency for principle to give way to expediency or to calculations of win–lose is irresistible. Even worse, the possibility of admitting or correcting 'wrong' principles does not occur.

The Ethics of Unions: A Summary

The eight kinds of criticism of trade unions lead to the unsurprising conclusion that unions, like managers and business corporations, are often no better than they ought to be. The discussion of the various criticisms suggests that the criticisms themselves are caricatures, based on some evidence, but not giving a balanced view. For instance, unions are not alone in making demands on the economy that cannot be easily met, or in restricting supply to keep prices up (wages can be regarded as the price for labour). They are sometimes associated with destructive conflict, but this forms a small part of their activity, and it takes at least two to make a quarrel. A more tenable proposition is that union structures and attitudes follow, often with a lag, those of managers. As one Government Minister put it in the British General Strike of 1926,

> It would be possible to say without exaggeration that the miners' leaders were the stupidest men in England if we had not frequent occasion to meet the owners. (Quoted in C. L. Mowat, 1962, p. 300.)

If unions and employers between them do not give due weight to the interests of third parties, the third parties themselves may be no better than they ought to be, joining in the game of seeking what is expedient, rather than what is justifiable. The third parties with no voice to be heard inevitably lose most.

Against the frequently made suggestion that unions are agents for the destruction of the political order should be set the observation that they are, if anything, too conservative to permit much movement at all, and that, by institutionalizing 'left/right' conflict they are absorbers rather than instruments of radicalism. This absorption is an instance of pluralism that is rarely seen in other institutions, whose franchise is typically much more limited. The greed, as expressed in pay claims, can be set against the corporate swindles reported daily in the mass media.

Union members overwhelmingly occupy the lower half of the income distribution. Their power, in the heydey of the boom of the 1950s, 1960s and 1970s, can be set against the fact that the powerful and largest unions organize a high proportion of low-paid employees, as opposed, for example, to professional associations.

A more cogent criticism of the ethics of unions has been made by Sheldrake in a paper to the Seminar on the Teaching of Business Ethics at King's College (1988b). The argument may be summarized as, *first*, since unions form part of an industrial relations system, they are best considered, not in isolation, but as shaped by as well as helping to shape the system. *Second*, there are two contrasting myths, which, like most others, are founded on some evidence, but go much beyond it, becoming the presuppositions of some elaborate ideas which, in turn, inform the theorizing, research, legislation and conduct of industrial relations. They need to be confronted, since they form the core of what might usefully be called 'the Whig interpretation of industrial relations'. This interpretation is no 'straw man', but can be seen in legislation, and in official reports.

> ...the question of ethics in the teaching of industrial relations has been pushed to the margins and that the literature on industrial relations and management has attempted to force a unitary view which does not exist, namely that working life is characterised by conflict and an adversarial relationship between management and workers. Such a conclusion appears mistaken, because the literature draws on landmarks dating from periods of conflict whereas little is written about periods of non-conflict. Two myths are being perpetuated: a) work is based on exploitation, and the relationship of workers and management is based on conflict; b) the purpose of collective bargaining is to redress an inequitable balance of power, and collective action constitutes a step towards a collectivist or socialist society. Such ideas, however, do not correspond to most people's experience of working life. Before the emergence of the Labour Party, there was a body of literature

stressing the ethical view of the relationship between workers and management. (Sheldrake, loc. cit., 1988b.)

The myths do not correspond to most people's experience of work, since most people never become involved in a strike in the whole of their working career, and 'most' is estimated by the British Department of Employment as about 95%. Much less than 5% of trade unionists are active in the sense of attending branch meetings and participating in union affairs. Since at their peak, British unions organized slightly over half of the working population, the active participation in industrial conflict is minuscule. This is supported by the estimates of 'man days lost' due to industrial disputes in a year which are typically much less than 0.25%. As Fox (1974) has pointed out, the experience of most manual employees, other than skilled craft workers, is less well articulated than is required for a 'conflict model'.

On the other hand, what Fox called the 'unitary model' of industrial relations, in which employers' representatives such as company chairmen express the 'team' nature of work, is wide of the mark in its own way. Some employees do seem to experience such an identification, but the failure of the 'participative' schemes to take root and develop in the 1970s illustrates how little manager/worker relationships are 'team' based. Further, the hierarchical structure of industry is designed, above all else, to provide a stable system and structure in which competition for advancement through the levels is limited, providing what in the economic literature are sometimes called 'positional goods', which are only available to some people on condition that other people are excluded. Recognition that the system is neither to be characterized wholly by conflict nor cooperation has appeared from time to time (Charles, 1973; Currie, 1979).

These reports have had too little discussion in the industrial relations literature. What has been called the Whig interpretation of industrial relations is related to these observations in that its assumptions are implicit in the British report in 1969 of the Royal Commission on Trade Unions and Employers' Associations—the Donovan Report. The drift is the idea that there are two systems of industrial relations, a formal one which includes national bargaining between employer and employee representatives, national arbitration systems, laws, and training institutions; and an informal system in which practices are developed, largely unchecked, as employers at local level play games of tactical advantage with union representatives. In the American system, local negotiations are more systematized, and involve a commitment to carrying out the contract during its currency. Part of the argument in the Whig interpretation is that the system as described is close enough to a maturity that suggests something akin to permanency. Thus, if the two systems could be better matched, for example through professional personnel departments, or training for large numbers of persons in collective bargaining, the legitimate needs that the national system cannot satisfy could be satisfied by more orderly local processes.

The problem is a general one of attributing to what is happening now permanent features. According to Galbraith, President Coolidge saw a plateau of prosperity stretching from 1929, just before the Great Crash. The esoteric economic articles as well as the popular media and politicians saw no possibility of anything other than a permanent dollar shortage from the 1950s onwards. Informed opinion was that the trade cycle had disappeared as a result of Keynesian demand–management techniques of the 1940s through the 1950s and 1960s.

The apparent maturity of the industrial relations system in Britain can be seen to have been a feature of post-World War II prosperity. As a result of it, some market power switched to unions, who gained, on the whole, the prosperity of a rise in incomes about equal to the growth of overall income. Thus, pay rises coped with inflation, for those unions who were well organized enough to maintain pressure, but the distribution of income has shown no major, permanent changes, and few major changes at all (Donaldson and Philby, 1985). The system was known at least to some oberservers as 'the pay race that no-one wins'—because the leaders keep on overtaking each other, to be overtaken themselves later. As a result, most groups through shifting coalitions or exploitation of tactical advantage managed roughly to keep up. As the growth phase of the trade cycle slackened, the existence of occupations and industries in which employees had barely been able to keep in the race became more apparent. This was exacerbated by the world-wide rise in unemployment (generally larger in Britain than elsewhere in developed countries) leading to solutions such as abolition of the (vestigial) minimum wage protection in Britain in the expectation of market clearing in the labour market, if pay could be allowed to be flexible enough downwards. The annual speeches of delegates at the Trades Union Congress, to the effect that it is their duty 'to defend the interests of their members', necessarily defines the agenda to preclude cooperation.

In short, the 'normal' system of industrial relations, in Britain at least, was a system that was supported by the transient boom phase of the trade cycle, and which served large numbers, but by no means everyone, well. The transient nature of what was thought to be a permanent system is underlined by the ease with which the Conservative Government in Britain since 1979 has been able to set the scene for major changes that up to the 1970s were thought to be impossible. It is true that many of the old features remain, including closed shops and accelerating pay rises in some industries. How far the transformation will go before it is itself transformed by macroeconomic pressures is still a matter for speculation. That it will is one of the few certainties in industrial relations. The conclusion, from the point of view of the ethics of industrial relations, is that the faults attributed, with limited justification, to unions are the faults of the system itself, guided by its myths. The justifiably discernible issues are, in my view, those that pertain to the opportunities missed for more integrative work in the area. These, in turn, are related to what might be called 'the moral psychology of industry', to which we now turn.

CHAPTER EIGHT

The Moral Psychology of Industry

Moral Psychology

Why do some people perform those acts of omission or commission which are held in the literature of business ethics to be improper, unethical or worthy of critical attention? Why do others support them, acquiesce in them, connive at them or simply ignore them? Why are others disturbed by the acts or omissions, sometimes to the point of action; for example in proposing legislation, or 'whistleblowing'? When people give reasons, are the reasons usually the 'real reasons'? How can we tell what are the 'real reasons', and how can the individual actors be aware of their own reasons or motivations, especially in view of the tradition which accepts the potency of unconscious motivations or 'sleepwalking' (to use Koestler's evocative phrase)?

How can we tell what the real reasons are when people offer motives, or grounds for action or inaction, decision, acquiesence, opposition or protest—as opposed to supposed justifications in terms of what the audience wants to hear, or will find acceptable? Are business and industry mere political systems, and if so, is there only one kind of political behaviour, such as is prescribed by the 'laws' of competitive manoeuvring for advantage among individuals and groups? When people are 'taken in' by malpractice or by performatory utterances that are at odds with action (i.e. by what in plainer language amounts to hypocrisy and lies), is it because they wish to be 'taken in', or because they believe that they have no choice?

This small sample belongs to the explanatory category of the moral psychology of industry. On the principle that 'ought' implies 'can', if people's behaviour, and therefore business behaviour, can be explained in terms of the inevitable processes of group dynamics, or of maximizing behaviour, we will be obliged to conclude that what happens is inevitable. It is, of course, not a consequence of being able to predict behaviour that therefore the behaviour is inevitable (because causally determined by the laws of group dynamics, for example).

The above questions also form part of the stock-in-trade of a variety of disciplines in the social sciences, in psychology, and in hybrid disciplines such as social psychology. Summaries of the managerial literature in these areas are readily available in many text books (Luthans, 1985). Rather than attempt a comprehensive review, at this stage of the argument, of the managerial, psychological and social science literature, it is possible to extract characteristic examples of various viewpoints for the purpose of identifying some of the assumptions and perspectives that they share, or in which they differ. As will be seen, some contrasting viewpoints, such as the 'classical' or 'command and control' model of management have important assumptions in common with those of their most serious critics, the human relationists. Whether the descendants of the human relations school of thought (which originated in the 1920s), the exponents of behavioural science, have succeeded in breaking away to form a truly 'scientific' approach to behaviour is still controversial, but in my view is something of a 'red herring', in that whether an explanation is scientific or not is subordinate to the much more important questions as to whether it is true, relevant and cogent.

There are, thus, several separate traditions in the attempts to explain behaviour. They can usefully be compressed to three; the philosophical, the social science and the behavioural (or behavioural science) traditions.

The Philosophical Tradition
Doctrines such as utilitarianism, deontology, objectivism and subjectivism, which were taken in Part One as examples of the most widely used explanatory frameworks, are designed mainly to identify those rules, customs or practices, decisions, expectations and institutions which are 'good' or 'right' from those which are 'wrong' or 'bad', and to show how such judgments can be explained and justified. Thus, utilitarianism seeks to show that justifiable actions, etc. are those which are likely to produce the most good and the least harm or damage in terms of pleasure, pain, utility, liberty or some other 'end', the answers in this mode of thought being sought by some kind of cause–effect calculus. Deontologists seek the answers in terms of duty, which could follow a rule, or a logical process, and could be recognized by intuition or by strict logical deduction from axioms, such as the Golden Rule. In Part One, it was concluded that the various rival philosophical approaches are incompatible in places, incomplete, and at the same time, necessary, and that the prospects of any one producing conclusive proof of its superiority over the others or of refuting the others are negligible. All of the doctrines have something to contribute, but there is little to be said for attempting to produce some eclectic

amalgam. The three principles of pluralism, autonomy and value reversal (Golden Rule) were identified as between them capable of producing criteria for judging processes, customs, institutions and the like, and for improvement in these.

All of the doctrines have a moral psychology content; for instance, Bentham's view that mankind is governed by the pleasure/pain principle, and Kant's view that the only thing that is absolutely good is a good will, or the principle of intuitive recognition evident in the work of Moore (1903) or Ross (1939).

The older tradition, dating to the classical Greek philosophers, recognized many schools of thought, including some whose influence is still present in the main philosophical doctrines. From the point of view of the sample questions posed at the beginning of the chapter, and the three criteria, most of the questions centre upon what drives individuals to believe in certain things, or to act. The relation between thought and action, though important, is answerable only in terms of ideas developed from basic principles, since thoughts can be hidden or confused, and action cannot be wholly explained by reference only to observation by others. Actions are usually, and rightly, described as having a component of intention, as well as physical indications. On this matter, the crucial issue is that of whether people are so constructed as to be able to act in ways other than those which, truly or mistakenly, are intended to produce or maximize gain of some kind for the individual, and to minimize or avoid some kind of loss or displeasure.

As Mahoney succinctly put it:

> The eighteenth-century theologian, Joseph Butler, is perhaps best remembered today for the realistic recognition which he accorded to the twin drives within each of us to self-love and benevolence, and for seeing that ethics is not necessarily a matter of antagonism or inner struggle between these drives, but more a matter of achieving and maintaining the right mix between self-regard and other regard. And perhaps this gives us a clue to identifying the fact that it is not self-interest in itself which may be morally reprehensible, but that it is self-interest when it oversteps the mark, to get out of proportion in one area of our lives, or to be pursued at the expense of others. (Mahoney, 1988, p. 33.)

A general problem for philosophers is how to recognize particular 'volitions', intentions, motives, drives, needs, feelings or beliefs. People can dissemble or deceive, say one thing and do another. It is not normally difficult to recognize discrepancies, but identifying motives or 'the springs' of action is problematic. It forms the subject matter of 'attribution theory' in psychology, in which it is recognized that motives, drives, intentions and the like are not empirically observable, but are *constructs*, that is, explanatory concepts.

The philosophical tradition has a number of ways of dealing with the unobservability of moral thoughts, motives and feelings. Intuitionism provides one move towards a solution. Bentham's pleasure/pain principle appears to have been derived from introspection. Plato in *The Republic* sets up models which invite us to make a recognition from introspection or self-knowledge, or perhaps simply from seeing what the correct answer must be—another form of intuition. Speaking of the possibility of reconciling morality with prudence, Hare observes:

> Plato seems to have thought it relevant to the argument that if, by putting on our finger a 'ring of Gyges', we could render ourselves invisible, this would enable us to escape detection for crimes which we could not, as things are, get away with; he thought that the moral act had to be shown to be prudent even in those circumstances . . . But one supremely important empirical fact is that there are no rings of Gyges. And there are many other empirical facts which are relevant, not all of them so indisputable. On such matters I can only give my opinion; they are not the province of the philosopher. (Hare, 1981, p. 194.)

Philosophers, then, can point to inconsistencies in argument, or in behaviour, including the gap between claimed intention and action. They can provide explanatory frameworks and insights gained from them and from contemplation of them and from discussions. The evidence is the province of the empirical researchers. This division of labour to which Hare refers is defensible enough at the theoretical level, but there is a strong case in applied disciplines such as business ethics for some cross-fertilization between philosophical ideas and empirical research. As it is, the philosophical basis of much management thought has not been systematically explored, though there are forays from social scientists into 'epistemology' (the theory of knowledge) which is traditional philosophical territory; and philosophers sometimes make forays into historical research or into organizational behaviour, as for example in MacIntyre's work discussed in Chapters Three and Four.

The Social and Behavioural Science Traditions
From the point of view of the established management and business studies, the behavioural work falls into several categories. The older studies and practices such as the *Scientific Management* of F. W. Taylor in the early decades of the twentieth century were aimed at demonstrating that management could be a 'true science', which could raise output

generally and dramatically, to the advantage of everyone. The first proposition, the dramatic raising of output, has rarely been doubted, but its significance has remained controversial at least since the House of Representatives Committee reported on scientific management in 1912 (Sofer, 1972). The work was permeated by a high moral tone, and the psychological assumptions were only those that were relevant to ensure that industry operated on the basis of command and control exerted by the owners of industry or their agents, the skilled, hierarchical, scientific managers, through their technical expertise.

This hierarchical and technical approach has been a notable source of bias: a manufacturing bias which still encourages the (now dominant) service sector to behave like mass-production factories, bequeathing a set of managerial practices that is appropriate to the special case of the age of mass production of physical goods, and even then always controversial (Donaldson and Sheldrake, 1987).

For present purposes it will be assumed that the issues of moral psychology in industry are independent of stage of development and of sectoral type. I know of no principle or research that suggests the contradictory, other than the standard subjectivist argument that the behaviour of 1910 may only be analysed in terms of the values on 1910, which in our case is irrelevant because the values still dominate in the form of large, bureaucratic, hierarchical organizations.

One major, and apparently unanswered, set of criticisms of these is provided by Chris Argyris (1964) who sees the practices associated with the outlook as at odds with the needs of mature individuals. As he sees it the result is one of permanent and major frustration for most people at work, with consequent losses in performance and a potential for chronic conflict at all levels in industry. According to Woodward (1965), the model used prescriptively is a special case theory, appropriate only to production line technologies. Some studies, for example that of Mintzberg (1975), have suggested that managers tend to spend little time in planning (planning as a practice has undergone a vogue, followed by much disillusionment among managers). Bennis (1972) provides many reasons for believing the model to be out of date, and unable to cope with economic and technical turbulence or with the changing aspirations of labour forces.

The more technically minded theorists, such as operational researchers and management scientists, have long been concerned with the problem of the 'low rate of take-up' of their proposals by line managers. Human relations theory is in the process of transformation to 'behavioural science' but has not yet, in my view, demonstrated that it is much used by managers or has shaken itself free from the accusations of management bias levelled by authors such as Silverman (1970) or Dahrendorf (1959).

Despite much talk of the importance of the organizational environment, the subject has not yet been analysed in much detail in relation to the external/internal interactions in organizations. The internal orientation of organization theorists and the external orientation of economists provide a division of labour that has maintained outmoded and, arguably, contradictory dichotomies. The 'open system' theorists such as Lawrence and Lorsch (1969) in the U.S.A. and Lupton (1971) in the U.K. do not seem to have been heeded often enough by managers. These models, too, concentrate on manufacturing industry. In short, the older and less sophisticated theories (the two categories do not exactly coincide) seem to provide 'foundation myths', and supply the need for a managerial rhetoric; while the newer and more technical models seem to be mainly of interest to academics. The moral, psychological and other criticisms that have been applied to the managerial practices worked out in the early decades of the present century do not seem to have wrought much change in the face of a changing world. Their longevity could be due to their serviceability, or to their convenience to those who gain most from them. Their survival in the face of such sustained criticism suggests that the latter explanation is likely to be the case.

In the light of the authors' criticisms outlined above, the sources of biases are many and varied. It is appropriate to group them into two categories.

(i) *Scientism* In this set of beliefs it is held that the only worthwhile kind of knowledge is 'scientific' knowledge. This requires precise definitions, measurable quantities of things, and stable relationships. All these can be guaranteed to be found in nature, because if they are not to be found in relation to specific topics, then the topics do not refer to 'real' matters at all, and are therefore not 'scientific'. This process of reasoning characterizes a great deal of scientistic thinking in management and economics. It begins with the logically contingent proposition that 'real' things, states and processes can be measured and moves imperceptibly to the analytic (and arbitrary) proposition that only those things that can be measured are real (or important). Such scientism excludes a great deal, if not most, experience. The logical errors in such reasoning are obvious. They have in any case been exposed by many writers—Isaiah Berlin (1964), Arthur Koestler (1959) and H. A. Burtt (1924) provide some of the best known critiques.

Such scientism tends to lead, as Tawney pointed out, to sciolism, but the most important point is that it has underlined a great deal of modern thinking and practice in management.

(ii) *Specialism/Functionalism* The tradition of dividing firms into functions, such as marketing, production, personnel, finance, etc. has led to some well-known problems. The conflicts between *production and marketing* have been discussed, for example, by Lawrence and Lorsch; those between departments by these authors and by Burns and Stalker, Cyert and March (1963) and many others.

The consequences include oscillation between *centralization and decentralization* and, for example, the conflicts that lead to Burns and Stalker's (1961) *'pathological processes'*, of the *'mechanistic jungle'*, the *'ambiguous figure system'* and the *'superperson'* or *committee*. Very little of this material has been taken up in the discussions and in practice, presumably because it is not very flattering to managers, whose task is often complex enough, and whose culture so often requires that mistakes and unfortunate events are not admitted, hidden, ignored or when unavoidably visible, attributed to someone else.

In terms of the list of questions with which this chapter began, the general philosophical answers vary according to the school of thought. In the philosophical tradition it is possible by introspection and argument to attribute motives and to judge the adequacy of justifications offered or grounds stated by confronting what people say with what they do. The explanatory categories include motivation, intention and much else. The tendency among some linguistic philosophers to reduce the issues to linguistic analysis, though illuminating, has left most of the key substantive issues and methodological issues unresolved.

The social science and management traditions tend, for understandable reasons, to have a relatively narrow focus upon models of motivation and attitudes, the factors affecting leadership and its effectiveness, selection, training and the enhancement of performance. By-products, such as frustation or alienation, are seen in terms of the above categories, and of the impact, for example of technology upon individuals. These have been very productive concerns, and have, to say the least, been associated with the substantial rises in output and improvements in working conditions that have been widespread, though by no means universal in industry and business in recent decades. However, their focus has not been on moral psychology. As Argyris has argued (1979) there is a mismatch between the demands of formal systems and the requirements of mature individuals, in that for most poeple, work experience is designed to minimize autonomy. That is the point of the command and control model, and of bureaucratic forms of management. Weber, one of the early theorists of bureaucracy, thought that as a procedure it had the potential for reconciling efficient administration with 'rational' and accepted authority. If it does, it would appear not to have been realized yet on either count. Much of the literature of organization theory has been concerned with what came to be called 'the dysfunctions' of bureaucracy, in which rules were promulgated but not obeyed, even by the promulgators; where official systems often degenerated to gamesmanship, and 'micropolitical systems'.

The topic of the moral psychology of industry has not been ignored, but it has often been set in terms of the investigation of group processes or individual motivations. Kohlberg's (1972) work on moral development and its stages has been widely discussed, as for instance by Baxter and Rarick (1987) and Cooke and Ryan (1989). Exceptions such as these apart, the tendency when moral issues have been touched upon, has been to discuss them in cause–effect terms, or in prudential terms. There is an important tradition of business ethics education in America, and there are innovative moves to integrate it into the business curriculum (Dunfee and Robertson, 1988) but the dominant managerial tradition as represented in the literatures described above is one of cause–effect relationships around maximizing, or at least prudential behaviour of individuals in relation to employers or to groups. Experiments such as Milgram's indicate circumstances in which people subordinate what are usually thought of as strong moral values to authority, and are much influenced by context, finding it apparently difficult to stand alone. I find the experiments convincing, but the psychological and social science explanations both rely on theoretical constructions, such as motives, needs, conditioning, systems and structures, which do not set out to provide grounds for moral or ethical judgments, and there is no difference in logical status between a scientific, but unobservable concept, and a moral, or for that matter, a metaphysical one.

To return to one of the first of the 'key issues', the systematic handling of values in business and industry is no more impossible in principle than is the systematic treatment of problems of motivation, order and control in the empirical management literature.

I conclude that the explanation of industrial behaviour is not only a matter of individual motivation, group dynamics or ways of overcoming resistance to the implementation of managerial rules, although it may sometimes include these.

Explanation involves the rendering clear of ideas or processes, and the justification or otherwise of them, in rational terms. Out of this process, prediction and at least some degree of control is possible. There is no reason in logic why business ethics should not contribute to making these more firmly grounded in the systematic analysis of values. Part Three will explore some possibilities of designing practical ways forward, but there are some concepts from the traditional disciplines that seem to me to go a long way towards explaining the way in which the moral beliefs and commitments of individuals are subordinated to group and institutional pressures. These are various forms of self-sustaining processes.

Persuasive Labels and Self-Sustaining Processes

The idea that persuading people to accept being placed in a particular category provides much potential for control has long been known. Old proverbs such as 'give a dog a bad name . . ', the classical tale of Pygmalion who brought to life his own sculpture, the experiments that achieve remarkable performances from individuals or groups which had been written off as incapable of achieving 'normal' standards of educational or work-related performance, and the industrial relations wrangles over whether an event is a strike or a lock-out illustrate a few of the many processes. The label matters a great deal when justification is at stake. Many of the key terms in use in management and administration are ambiguous, and often radically so. In an extreme form this may be seen by contrasting the expressions 'professional killer' and 'unprofessional conduct'. In one case we are drawing attention to the claim that the individual is capable of performing efficiently illegal and unethical 'duties' without asking whether or not they are justifiable. In the other case we are describing conduct that falls short of a legitimate ethical code. The ambiguity extends to the possibility of the mercenary having a strong personal or group code. The unwillingness of professionals to criticize a fellow professional, or a professional code has often led to the conclusion that professions are as G. B. Shaw put it, "conspiracies against the laity". In recent years, there have been not a few examples of individuals who have taken on the task of supporting professional codes against powerful pressures not to do so. Examples of professional dilemmas will be given in detail in the next section. The idea of self-sustaining processes takes in what the sociologist Merton called "self-fulfilling prophecies", as well as self-justifying truths, and self-creating situations. The area is one in which the moral concepts of the Golden Rule, autonomy and pluralism, and the standard vocabulary of ethics can usefully supplement and be supplemented by the considerable amount of empirical research. 'Persuasive labelling' is a development of a term coined by C. L. Stevenson in an article in *Mind* in 1938. It became part of the theory of emotivism which sought to explain moral concepts in terms of expressions of emotions. The theory had a vogue in the period up to the 1960s. The ambiguity extends to the idea of managers as professionals. Are professional managers those who show a single-minded determination to pursue the interests of their employers, or those whose conduct is governed by managerial or personal codes? When managers speak of responsibility, is it 'responsibility to' owners, or 'responsibility for' what happens, good or bad? Is it unprofessional to admit errors or to push the blame on to subordinates?

Self-generating and self-sustaining processes occur in a wide variety of contexts in business and industry. In industrial relations, it is possible to distinguish between a variety of outcomes of collective bargaining. Walton and McKersie (1965) distinguish between distributive and integrative bargaining, the former describing typically the cases in which there are gains and losses, with usually one party making most of the gains. The idea of integrative bargaining allows for the possibility of all parties gaining, for example through producing better methods that increase available resources, removing restrictions which no one wants but had been placed as part of some historical tactical sanction. In many cases of collective bargaining, the conduct of the various parties leads to the conclusion that integrative possibilities are ignored because one or more parties is unable to recognize them, mostly because the parties simply do not have the concept. Bargaining situations, once defined as win–lose become win–lose, and stay that way.

Self-generating processes occur in a variety of ways, and result from beliefs that people hold. Thus, if firms are defined as 'micropolitical' systems by some members (whether or not they use the term), the members will act as though their view is the correct one. There are 'organizational cultures' in which such a view, whether articulated or not, would be regarded as obviously true, but insignificant because the internal power structure is open, visible and accepted. In others, the 'secret' would never be admitted openly, leading to what in the behavioural literature is termed, somewhat euphemistically perhaps, a distinction between formal and informal systems. This gap between the 'official and unofficial doctrines' is important and provides some clues towards methods of improvement, which, broadly, require more business and industrial firms and administrative bodies to recognize and deal with the disparity, as indeed, some do. J. A. C. Brown (1954), in a classic study, summarized the work done in the area of 'formal' and 'informal' systems. Subsequent work, for example by Burns (1963) and Pettigrew (1973), has described some 'micropolitical processes', and Morgan (1986) discusses the idea of 'organizations as political systems' in his book, *Images of Organization* (1986). Morgan writes in the social and behavioural science traditions, adding perspectives from general philosophy and political theory. His general or 'basic premise' is that

> ... explanations of organizational life are based on metaphors that lead us to see and understand organizations in distinctive, yet partial ways... For the use of metaphor implies a *way of thinking* and a *way of seeing* that pervade how we understand our world generally. (Morgan, 1986, p. 12.)

Clearly, the idea that people do use metaphors is a useful one.

Weber's analysis of bureaucracy, or Taylor's *Scientific Management* can be understood in part, in terms of attributing the assumption to them that businesses can be run like machines in essential respects. Silverman (1970) criticized the notion that organizations are like organisms, and warned against what he called 'reification' of organizations (but which perhaps would be better described as 'personification').

There are some logical problems in pressing metaphors too far, as Morgan recognizes, but there are also problems in pressing the idea that people's thinking about organizations is only a collection of partial insights through metaphorical language. It is the problem of phenomenalism in a new way: if we can comprehend only through metaphor, we have no reason for thinking that the reality is other than metaphor, as Kant pointed out in the *Prolegomena*, and as Hume pointed out in relation to his own theory that the mind is only a collection of perceptions. Hume's self-imposed difficulty was of specifying how a collection of perceptions could be aware of itself as a collection. Kant's was that if we can never know things 'as they are', but only as they seem, then we have no grounds for asserting even that they exist at all, since they cannot be perceived, let alone know what they are 'really like'. If we can know organizations only as collections of metaphors, and each metaphor has enough limitations to require that we use several, possibly contradictory metaphors, how can we know what the limits to each one are, except by confronting the metaphorical claim with evidence that is independently validated? Part of the problem is that most language has strata of meaning, and uses metaphors and figurative meanings which present problems for empirical description and for hypothesis testing, but there are ways of dealing with this (Ryle, 1949; Waismann, 1953; Austin, 1962).

Organizations, then, are in part at least, 'micropolitical systems', and part of the process by which political decisions are made to work is through people accepting that some decisions are legitimate and properly made and that compliance is therefore obligatory. That people are sometimes deceived by the withholding of essential information or by manoeuvring is a ground for criticism in ethical terms. That people do comply is testimony to the force of moral commitment.

I conclude that the self-generating systems and the self-sustaining systems are part of the processes by which moral commitments are drawn upon or manipulated in business, industry, administration and the unions. This has aspects which encourage the ethical malpractices discussed in the literature, but also suggests possible ways forward.

Cases

The first group of cases (all British) concern a newspaper, a productivity bargain at a continuous process chemical plant, the horse-racing industry and social security administration. I believe that they show that ethical issues can arise even though, initially at least, there is no evidence of generalized malice, ill-will, wilful negligence, personal greed, lies, hypocrisy or other of the standard symptoms of turpitude, though there is ample evidence of some of them developing by stages.

Case 1: 'Newspaper'
This first, and briefest case in 1986 describes a situation in which a journalist noted for taking what can be described as a 'hard-nosed', 'no-nonsense' approach to his work, including the belief that there is no such thing as a nervous breakdown, had one. Whatever the medical diagnosis of the problem, certain observable behaviour characteristics were present; a tearful state, and word blindness. Patched up and returned to work, the journalist pointed out that the conditions that caused the original difficulties should be avoided. The response was to provide protection in the form of a phlegmatic colleague, who could deflect the problem. The procedure worked well for a day, after which the phlegmatic colleague dropped dead from overwork. From the very limited data available, a provisional conclusion is that the task was the winner, and the human beings the main losers. Presumably, not all newspapers are like that, but certain features of the account fit well with those of Argyris' study of 1974, of the 'Daily Planet' in his book, *Behind the Front Page*. We do not know what the effect was upon the readers of the paper, or on other groups. In Argyris' case, the nature of the output was considerably influenced by the internal processes.

The case suggests that the differential distribution of gains extends to impersonal interests, such as that of 'the task'. (Reported in *The Guardian*, 1986.)

Case 2: A Productivity Bargain
In the early 1970s a relatively small, continuous process, chemical plant negotiated a productivity bargain. This was a job-evaluated, work-studied bargain that involved: a number of redundancies; a substantial pay increase for most of those who remained; an intention under the 'income policy' of the day to share out the proceeds of the productivity gains equally between the company, the employees and the consumers (the latter to be in the form of price reductions).

The job evaluation scheme used the standard procedures, under the advice of experienced and respected consultants.

The outcomes were: a substantial recorded rise in productivity; a substantial pay rise; a reduction in pay for stacker-truck drivers; some redundancies (about 15% of the manual employees).

Gains estimated at about: 90% for the company, 10% for the workforce, who thought that the gains were about evenly shared with the company; the consumers, not being present at the bargaining, received nothing.

The case is a counter-example to the widely held belief that the productivity bargains of the late 1960s and early 1970s in the U.K. were merely ways of evading pay controls without delivering any real productivity advances.

We conclude that the case supports our hypothesis, and shows that a number of winners and losers can be identified. Some were not party to the proceedings (e.g. consumers).

It might be thought that in an interconnected, complex economy, virtually everyone would, in principle, be affected: if the prices of the chemical had been lower, then final prices would be lower. This problem is merely a technical one. There are ways of consulting consumers—by market surveys, or consultative committees, for example. Insofar as some of the redundant employees could easily find jobs elsewhere, they would gain. A further proposition is that the consequences could not be regarded as unambiguously an improvement or a disimprovement. It depends upon whose point of view is adopted, whether it is an informed and legitimate point of view, and much else.

Case 3: The 'Stable Lads' Strike of 1975
The article in the *British Journal of Industrial Relations*, by Jack Eaton, is the principal source of information on this case. The essentials were: a ten-week strike in 1975, from April to June, by stable lads, who had not taken such action before. The claim from a low-paid group was for a pay rise of £4.70. In the event, the settlement was reached at £4.40 after an increasing number of parties was brought into the dispute. In this case, the number of parties directly involved was substantial. The analysis can begin with the TGWU claim to the Newmarket Trainers' Federation (two parties). As Eaton shows, some of the stable lads were not union members (a third party), some of the union members did not strike (a fourth party). The TGWU organizer can be seen to have a different need from that of the union as a whole: in his case to maintain standing with the union. In the event, a breakaway union was formed (an incalculable loss in prestige to a trade union) and the (then new) Advisory, Conciliation and Arbitration Service was brought in. So was the Horse Race Betting Levy Board, and the Association of Cinematographic and Television Technicians (ACTT)

(industrial action in support of the TGWU). The stable lads' breakaway union was in turn broken away from, as the stable girls came to the conclusion that the breakaway did not represent their interests. There were many other parties: the public (denied TV coverage of horse racing); TV watchers who dislike horse racing received a windfall gain. The bookmakers presumably lost money; some gamblers would have lost losses.

The case supports the initial hypothesis that there are winners and losers, and adds that the long-term consequences can be to add more gainers and losers, and to increase the number of parties. It begins to look as though the notion that there might be sound criteria for improvement, or for comparing one state with another, is more problematic than it appeared at first sight. Not only is the number of parties capable of substantial change, it is not apparently determinate, except by making arbitrary assumptions about who has legitimate interests, and what the interests are allowed to be (Eaton, 1977).

This provides a clear reason for the oversimplifications in the management literature, in the stances of political parties, and in the mass media.

Case 4: The DHSS (Department of Health and Social Security)
The fourth case describes a government department and a minor administrative matter that was rendered incapable of any resolution other than continuous loss by the client. This was achieved by (a) routine letters issued by the DHSS with 'strike out' clauses; the letters were used whether or not any of the paragraphs fitted the circumstances; (b) a set of rules that made it impossible for the Department to admit errors of any kind, or to re-assess decisions in the light of new evidence; an (apparently genuinely held) belief by members of the Department that errors could not be corrected: "not even the Prime Minister can overturn a decision once made" (this comment was made by an apparently sympathetic official to the client, by telephone); (c) increasingly bizarre evasions by the officials; (d) an easily rebuffed Member of Parliament; (e) a determination to accept all concessions and conciliatory attempts by the client anxious to make progress, and to give none in return.

It should be noted that one of the original causes of the problem was a strike at the DHSS. The client's attempts at resolution were, apparently, further rendered difficult by the DHSS headquarters' telephone being permanently engaged during which time a further strike was in progress at the London office. These seem to be symptoms not only of low morale, but of seriously pathological conditions in the London office.

The parties involved included at least: the DHSS at the Newcastle headquarters (several officials, and the DHSS adjudicator); the client; the London office; the client's Member of Parliament; the law (cast in a 'Spenlow and Jorkins' role, since the issues never reached the courts); the Government (apparently helpless to change the systems or procedures).

The outcome: capitulation by the client, whose sole 'error' was to accept the DHSS's wrong estimate, which it had calculated while in possession of the 'right' information; absence of reform of procedures; withdrawal by the Member of Parliament; no investigation of the sources and consequences of the errors, or of the conduct that the client objected to: the Department was unable to recognize any points made by the client, and persistently ignored them.

It should be noted that the original error was in September 1984, and the correspondence ended when the client finally realized that continued attempts at an orderly solution would be both unsuccessful and very costly, in time as well as money.

In brief, the main points of the case are:

(1) DHSS makes error, even though in possession of the proper information.

(2) DHSS blames the client.

(3) DHSS demands money back—unless the Department can show that the client operated with 'lack of due care and diligence', the Department is not entitled to reclaim the money. This is the nub of the case: the client expresses a wish to pay the money, even if the Department is not entitled to it, but objects to the accusation. The DHSS continues to claim that the problem was merely a matter of applying the language required by the law. The client is concerned with what appears to be a matter of substance.

(4) The Department appears to have hustled the problem to its adjudicator (who is not independent) with inadequate information. The next move is to claim that the adjudicator's decision cannot be altered (then proceeds to alter it).

(5) The adjudicator apparently rubber-stamps the original decision, and subsequently the revised decision.

(6) The Department realizes that the first decision is an error, then amends the figure and returns it to the adjudicator, blaming the client.

(7) The Department responds to the client's correspondence by sending a representative 'to explain our side'. Representative privately agrees with client, who does not see the representative's report.

(8) The Department sends misleading statement to the Member of Parliament.

(9) The Department telephones the client, in effect saying 'we sympathize, but there is nothing we can do'.

(10) Client accepts the verbal sympathy and capitulates.

The case illustrates, among other things, the already well-attested inflexibility of bureaucracies, classic symptoms of low and declining morale, unambiguous examples of turpitude on the part of officials, a classic example of an institution that is judge and jury in its own cause, use of obscurantism and evasion, a supine 'watchdog', the Member of Parliament, and fatalistic myths put to service of the bureaucracy.

The cases illustrate some major points:

(1) Very few of the interested parties were consulted. The higher the level of consultation and the more frequent, the more pacific and more stable the cases.

(2) There were in all cases gainers and losers.

(3) The gains and losses were differentially distributed.

(4) The more interests were taken into account, the more potential for mutual gain, even if it was not realized, and even in confused situations such as that of the 'stable lads' strike'.

(5) Organizational processes can be characterized.

(6) Outcomes of organizational processes can be characterized (but not in straight 'profit', 'production values' or 'people values' terms, with much conviction).

(7) It is possible to identify states, and move from one to another.

(8) Undesirable and unintended consequences are more likely to occur than not to occur.

(9) Identifying the interested parties and recognizing their rights and duties, views and expectations is possible and need be neither a luxury for 'socially responsible managers', nor a vital necessity to avoid economic collapse, but both are useful and proper.

The range of outcomes can be depicted in terms of a diagram:

States such as the (a) and (b) subcategories are not necessarily mutually exclusive. The descriptions are drawn from the cases used above, and from other management research reported in the literature.

1a is 'good' for the gainers;
1b is harmful to everyone;
1c is good while it lasts, but often traumatic when change has to occur;
2c is good for some while it lasts;
2d can be traumatic, and is rarely resolved completely;
3a usually satisfies most participants;
3b produces many traumas (bankruptcies, layoffs, strikes, etc.);
4 abounds with missed opportunities, and is very similar to 1a;
5a seems to be the best possible, but rare;
5b is useful for some.

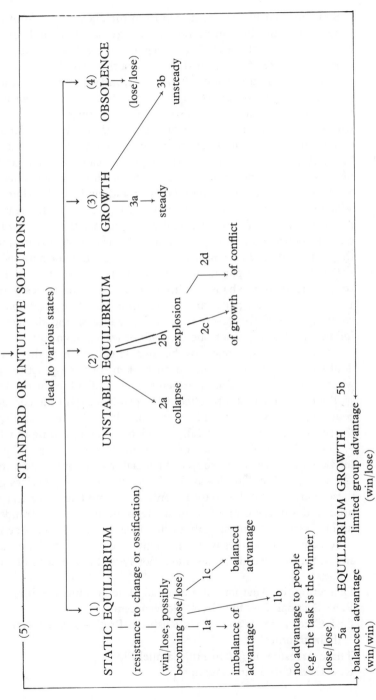

DIVERSITY OF INTERESTS/ASPIRATIONS

(ALSO OF GROUPS/CONTACTS/LINKS)

COMMUNICATIONS AND COORDINATION ISSUES

STANDARD OR INTUITIVE SOLUTIONS

(lead to various states)

(1) STATIC EQUILIBRIUM

(resistance to change or ossification)

1a → imbalance of advantage

1b

1c → balanced advantage

(win/lose, possibly becoming lose/lose)

(2) UNSTABLE EQUILIBRIUM

2a collapse

2b explosion

2c of growth

2d of conflict

(3) GROWTH

3a → steady

(4) OBSOLENCE

3b unsteady

(lose/lose)

5a balanced advantage (win/win)

EQUILIBRIUM GROWTH

5b limited group advantage (win/lose)

no advantage to people (e.g. the task is the winner)

(lose/lose)

Source: Donaldson and Sheldrake (1987, p. 40).

Some inferences may be drawn from the above cases from the point of view of the questions in moral psychology listed at the beginning of the chapter. One of these is that in general, the selfish, moral or malicious motives that are often implied in the idea that morals and business do not mix, are far from dominant, often absent, and sometimes arise as a result of feelings of hopelessness, or of being caught up in a system in which the most that can be hoped for is some form of coping. Taken in conjunction with the 'standard' models of motivation, it is possible to infer also that the idea of motives and motivation in the managerial literature has tended to be limited to the extent to which people can be persuaded to accept managers' decisions with as much enthusiasm as can be generated by the techniques derived from the models of and evidence bearing on motives. When people give reasons, it is sometimes the case that the reasons are not, from their point of view, the 'real ones', but are the ones required by the official doctrines or rules or power structure in the institution in which they are located. The reasons why the rules and expectations are as they are may not be apparent to any of the actors, or indeed may remain controversial after exhaustive discussion. The moral issues remain, and, if I am right, do not necessarily arise from proactive intentions, but from cobbling together excuses, relationships, face-saving devices, or simply following what appears to be the path of least discomfort.

Some further cases may now be considered, in which there is little or no doubt that formal rules have been broken, but the practical problem of what action to take, if any, presents many difficulties at the level of skill (will a proposed action be effective?); prudence (will the consequences be counter-productive, or lead to undesirable back-fires?) and morals (will the proposed action be ethically justifiable, and according to what rules?).

The area which is the last of the major business areas to be covered in the book, involves that group of financial institutions known in Britain as 'the City', and in America as 'Wall Street'. Financial services generally in these countries, but by no means only these countries have, in recent years, produced a heavy crop of scandals, legislation, reforms, frauds and institutions, reported almost daily in the press and mass media generally.

Some press headlines will help to give the flavour; and the year could be any in the last decade. They were mostly within a month of each other:

Dissecting the Anatomy of a Scandal (The Guinness Affair)
Bank Scandal Test for Greek Government
CBI Chief Attacks the City's Rush for Profit—Fund Chiefs 'would sell their grannies'
Three Arrested in £60 m Hill Samuel Plot
Row Over City Flares Again

New Merger Body 'Essential'
For Whom the Bell Tolls at Lloyd's
   (Allegations of widespread fraud, underwriters with luxury yachts, villas
   in the South of France, and strings of racehorses)
War Declared on £3bn a Year Pinstripe Fraud
Auditors may get Crime-Busting Role
How Will the City's Mini Policemen Stop Tripping Over Each Other's
   Big Flat Feet?
Former JMB Staff Linked to Nigeria Fund
Fraud Measures 'Let Off' City
Minister Was Member of a Syndicate Which Made Profits for a Select
   Few (and, by contrast, £1 (approx. 2 dollars) an hour Workers 'Exploited
   and Abused')
£400,000 Whistleblower on Dole
Bail in £853,000 False Accounting Case
Brittan Plans Action Against City Fraud
Whitehall Helped Company Evade EEC Law
   (from *Guardian*, November, 1985)

Headlines are not always so dramatic, and may even play down, rather than play up the problems to which they refer, as for example: "Depositors Given Reassurance over US Thrift Crisis" reported criticisms of some of America's largest accounting firms, ". . . three of whom were being sued by federal regulators for allegedly failing to detect fraud and mismanagement of various thrifts" (*Financial Times*, 28 January 1989). The article added "The plaintiffs are seeking hundreds of millions of dollars of damages from the firms to cover financial losses they suffered in subsequent rescues of the failed institutions" (loc. cit.).

In some of the issues to which the collection of headlines refers, some examples of illegal behaviour were proved. This raises again the matter of where the line should be drawn between unethical and illegal behaviour. Should, for example, the law simply enforce those ethical values which, it is believed, people will not have the moral strength to live by if not backed by sanctions? Should it be assumed that because an act or omission is unlawful, it is therefore unethical? Or should ethics be confined to those matters on which the law is silent? For instance, if a substance or practice is known to be dangerous, but has not been legislated against, would it be unethical to continue to use it? Should a practice that is thought to be unethical be discouraged, even if there are strong reasons to believe that legislation would be counter-productive? If so, how should it be discouraged? Should, for example, professional institutions take on a regulatory duty in cases where the law cannot be used?

Given that evasion is possible, given the complexity and privacy of company activities, especially in financial institutions, enforcement is not always possible. A solution is to create general regulations, and to set up enforcement institutions, equipped, for example, with codes. According to Kintner and Green (1978):

> This approach to law enforcement sets up a vicious circle: the broader laws and regulatory agencies will inevitably uncover an increasing number of law violations, and this discovery will, in turn, engender still broader laws and regulations and even wider enforcement activities. IF this trend is carried to its logical conclusion, it will produce the sort of iron statutes which will eliminate the flexibility that is necessary if the law is to be effective, and its enforcement just and nondiscriminatory (Kintner and Green, 1978.)

Kintner and Green advocate the development and self-enforcement of effective codes of conduct.

This contrasts with the first group of cases in which the acts and events which can be criticized on ethical grounds were not obviously illegal, and some were obviously not so. The criticisms on moral grounds are those of responses to a situation in which the harmful or culpable practices seemed necessary to the parties concerned. The moral psychology of the cases does not amount to deliberate wrong-doing, and in some cases the actors personally regretted actions which they could see no way of avoiding, in the circumstances in which they found themselves. Selfishness, egoism, greed and the other traditionally less admirable motivations were mostly absent. The law could have little place in two of the cases, and, if the officials were right, it actually caused the problem in the Social Security case.

The next example is some light thrown on the moral psychology of fraud. Reflecting on a number of investigations, Bosworth-Davies makes the observation:

> Greed was a fairly regular feature in most investment-related scams... greed on the part of the investor did play a significant part in bringing the investor and the fraudsman together. I was to discover that one of the most appealing influences in the decision to invest money in a speculative scheme was where the investor believed that the particular investment was dishonest or illegal. (Bosworth-Davies, 1988, p. 5.)

Bosworth-Davies attributes the experience that individual victims, including directors of large companies, often turn their anger on to the investigator out of the fear of ridicule, which is also powerful enough to persuade people to stand the loss, rather than admit that they have been taken in (loc. cit.).

The size of the problem can only be guessed at. What is clear enough is that unlike the earlier cases, people are usually aware of the ethical implications in this area. According to Goldsmith and Clutterbuck (1984), a high value is placed on integrity by top executives, who frequently appear to believe that ". . . without absolute integrity their businesses simply could not operate" (op. cit., p. 123).

The passions roused by any doubts as to the company's absolute integrity, it seems are often extreme, and perhaps echo the apoplectic passions roused by the thought of strikes and trade unions, discussed in Chapter Seven.

It would seem, therefore, that there are several categories into which the ethical issues of business and industry can usefully be separated. Some are controversial, some unforeseen in particular cases, some arise from the logic of some institutions and their rules of operation, and some involve the deliberate flouting of the known ethical rules, in the expectation of gain. There are hopeful signs in this, and I believe that the cases support the proposition that there is a balance to be struck between self-regarding and other-regarding actions. The standard sceptical claim discussed in Chapter One, that there are and can be no ethics in business, looks more and more tenuous. The evidence is that people do know the ethical rules and sometimes try to operate, or change, or circumvent them. Sometimes people are willing to dissemble, and cover up lapses, but this does not argue for the absence of ethical rules, but for their tenuous hold in some places, and ambiguous role in others. We may not all approve of the particular rules and standards, but it is implausible to deny their existence.

PART THREE

Prospects

Introduction to part three

Part Three suggests ways, compatible with the three principles of pluralism, Golden Rule and autonomy, of bringing the 'official' versions of what the various institutions do, as expressed by their images and espoused values, closer to the reality and vice versa. If, for example, the belief, often expressed by 'top managers', that integrity and other ethical qualities are indispensable in business is at odds with the daily reports in the media of malpractice, then the rhetoric could be abandoned and the reality recognized, or the reality could by diligent action by industry become nearer to what it is supposed to be. If what it is supposed to be expresses values that are acceptable to the community at large, the problems of reconciliation will be so much easier. If there is a discrepancy in the values themselves, the prospects are less sure, but there is nothing intrinsic to business that precludes the powerful values that drive it from being rationally justifiable, and reconcilable with general ethical or moral values in the community, including the international one, or at least amended to fit them.

Chapter Nine identifies a number of procedures for improvement of practice, and attempts to indicate ways in which they could be operated, having regard to principles of ethical behaviour. Chapter Ten, the concluding chapter, summarizes the argument of the book, and identifies and tries to respond to arguments which discount the possibility of establishing procedures for improvement. Two kinds of scepticism are identified, the kind which, as a result of familiarity with the standard arguments, is sceptical of dogmatic assertions of ethical viewpoints. The second kind is one which affects a quizzical scepticism as an alternative to systematic thought or to action. The first is, in my view, an imperative in its own right. The second, being indefensible, tends to evaporate when challenged.

CHAPTER NINE

Procedures for Improvement

Standards of conduct in business and industry are neither generally beyond reproach nor universally deplorable, and it is possible to suggest and defend criteria for judging them in terms of better or worse, defensible or indefensible, justifiable, proper and the like. It is possible also to make grounded judgments about the verbal and emotional superstructures by which values are pursued, enforced, insinuated or inveigled into practice and into the technical literature, or protected from rational discussion. It is possible to suggest explicit criteria which can guide the progression from less defensible to more defensible practices. It is commonplace among the theorists of organizations that there is always a formal and an informal system, and there is always a discrepancy between the two. Insofar as this represents a set of high standards and imperfect means to achieve them, the gap presents no serious problems, but the evidence in the literature, some of which has been discussed in the earlier chapters, gives many reasons for doubting both the end values and the means in an indefinitely large number of contexts and cases. Procedures suggested for improvement will include as elements processes by which the formal (or official) rules and procedures that govern (or are supposed to govern) practice are brought into line with the realities. This could involve more realistic and less grandiose claims as to the purposes and skills of managers, and a raising of sights, aspirations and skill levels so that they can meet the criteria. The criteria used in the following argument will be the ones adopted in Part One. It is not claimed that no others are possible. It is claimed that they are constructive and consistent with the principal ethical theories, at least up to the point at which the theories claim, or have claimed for them, exclusive recognition of moral truths.

This is not to say that existing practices and ideals present the only possibilities. Progress in business and management thought and practice is far from continuous, and newer ideas are not necessarily better than old ones, or more informed, despite the 'knowledge explosion', but new ideas and new variations on old ideas do appear from time to time in the literature and in practice, sometimes as would-be panaceas, and sometimes as potentially valuable innovations which are abandoned, often because hopes are too high for them. It seems likely that the notions of participative management developed by the human relations theorists such as Elton Mayo (1949), and by the enthusiasts for institutionalized methods of participation in the 1970s fall into both categories.

It is often claimed that there is an inevitable trade-off between profit and ethics or morals. Examples are easy to find, and some have been discussed in earlier chapters, as has the notion that business has as its role, the only task of making profits, and that if it does so, all will benefit. This is a version of 'doing good by doing well'. The counter-claim is sometimes made, that behaving ethically is good business: 'honesty is the best policy' or 'doing well by doing good'. 'Virtue is its own punishment' is often nearer the mark, but in the case of whistleblowers, the punishments are sometimes reinforced by the victims of the practices on which the whistle has been blown.

Before the suggestions for procedures for improvement can be developed, there are some prior questions which need to be addressed: *first*, if defensible principles can be enunciated and put into operation, does this mean that we can characterize 'the ethical firm', or provide lists of good and bad practices, or good and bad values? It is no easier and no more difficult to describe and identify 'the ethical firm' than it is to describe and identify 'the profit-maximizing firm'. 'Profit maximizing' can be, and has been, given elegant formal treatments in the economic textbooks, but like Weber's bureaucracy in its pure form it is an abstraction containing many non-empirical characteristics, such as the notion of 'equilibrium', for example. There is little to be gained from attempting to profile 'the ethical firm'. It is analogous to the attempts to describe the good life, or a happy person ('call no persons happy until they are dead'). From the point of view of business ethics there are more fruitful options. One proposition, consistent with pluralism, the Golden Rule and individual autonomy, is that an ethically defensible firm or institution is one which has developed procedures for identifying and reconciling the values (interests and aspirations) of those who have to do with the firm or institution, and has similar procedures for amending the procedures. This means that no individual or group is able to impose values on others. If it so happens that the procedures are manipulated following the 'iron law of oligarchy', as is often suggested to be the case in companies and unions, then it is certain that the procedures fall short of encouraging autonomy, and shortfalls in relation to Golden Rule (principle of reciprocity) are almost certain to be consequent on it, if only because the oligarchs will assume that they know best what values should be pursued.

The proposition does not commit anyone to holding the view that there are no principles other than the methodological ones required for reconciliation, or that respect for other people's values amounts to the proposition that values are subjective, or that anything goes. It means that each value should be taken seriously and that people are entitled to be in a minority of one, with an opporunity to persuade or be persuaded on what can be counted as defensible values, and on what attitudes towards them are defensible. It means, for example, that the group dynamics process by which 'deviants' are brought into line can degenerate into the irrational processes of 'groupthink', but should be prevented from doing so.

Just as a firm does not need to be a perfectly competitive one in an ideal environment to be competitive, a firm does not have to be fault-free in order to be counted as one with some defensible values. In this sense, Gouldners's 'representative bureaucracy' would be an advance on the 'mock bureaucracies' in which rules are announced, and largely ignored, and on the 'punishment-centred' ones in which rival groups take whatever tactical advantage they can without concern for the costs imposed on others.

Second, since it requires no proof that people's values can be seriously at odds, whose values should prevail? The temptation is to say that in a democratic system, the minority should be prepared to be outvoted. Few firms are democracies in any meaningful sense, but even if they were, their procedural correctness, if used to suppress alternative views, would not be sufficient to satisfy the autonomy criterion, since majorities and minorities alike can be mistaken about the relevant facts, or inconsistent, or even hypocritical, which is an inconsistency pursued in full knowledge that it is inconsistent. The suppression of views would also be at odds with the Golden Rule, and with the principle of pluralism. To the question, whose values should prevail or be encouraged, the answer must be, those which procedural correctness permits, provided that decisions are open to reversal in the light of argument and evidence. Thus, some philosophical scepticism is required by procedural considerations as well as by the lack of grounds for dominance of any particular philosophical theory. This is standard stuff in the theory of democracy, to which appeal is made often enough, for example in the Editorial in the London Times (*The Times*, 7.9.82).

Third, not all values are of the same kind, or of equal importance. How, then, is it possible to assign priorities to values, and which ones can be recognized as important or overriding, which should be regarded as trivial, which should be regarded as 'good' values, and on what grounds? Similarly with 'bad' values, which are they, and how should they be recognized and dealt with? Are moral values superior to technical or prudential ones, or vice versa, and why?

This ground is covered in much detail in the various philosophical theories discussed in Part One. Ross (1939), Nowell-Smith (1954) and Frankena (1963) provide stimulating treatments of the topic. The short answer is that the ones that satisfy the three criteria are 'better' values than those that do not. The traditional imperatives of keeping promises, telling the truth, respect for others are the most likely to do so. The elegant but artificial dilemmas that demonstrate that there can be no stable hierarchy between them can in any case be bypassed by the same philosophical scepticism that underlies the principles of pluralism. The idea that there can and should be such a stable hierarchy seems to me to reflect an urge to find some mechanical rule that will relieve individuals of the responsibility for decision. The same argument applies to any demand for grades of values. Hume may have been wrong in claiming that "it is not contrary to reason to prefer the destruction of the world to the scratching of my finger", but proving it at least to some people's satisfaction involves the whole debate between the subjectivists and the objectivists.

These philosophical matters aside it is possible to suggest specific procedures for improvement. These are any procedures which satisfy the three criteria and replace others which do not. Again, the precedence in case of conflict between the criteria can be problematic, but not insoluble. If people choose not to make the effort required to become autonomous, preferring to be dependent upon others, should they be forced to become autonomous against their will? It is unlikely that any grounds could be found for doing so, but the issue does arise in matters relating to forced union membership. Does person A (a trade unionist) have the right to force person B to join, though B is faced by an alternative threat from the employer if he or she does join the trade union, when A believes, perhaps rightly, that if B does not join, the consequences will be loss of autonomy and rights for A, and others? If B refuses to be autonomous and to operate the Golden Rule, then B is in a position similar to Thrasymachus in Plato's *Republic*, and the solution is the same: non-joiners lose the claim to the protection of the rules. B's most defensible course would be to join the debate and become autonomous, if escape is not possible. This leaves open the possibility of proposing that the rules be abandoned and a new set substituted for them.

In practice, the problem is much easier to solve given the great scope for improvement, as I hope the following examples will show, some of which are explained below. Others are self-explanatory.

Some Procedures

The proposed procedures are first listed, then detailed in turn. Some are based on research programmes and on consultancy experience, and reflect a particular concern which had clear value implications. Others are backed by much precedent, and some have hardly been tried at all, to my knowledge.

(1) Matching values to strategies.

(2) Adoption of and publishing of codes of practice which seek to identify and reconcile the values of 'stakeholders', and which are not imposed 'top down' and have published procedures for amendment.

(3) Legislation to encourage experimentation in ways of bringing formal and informal systems and procedures closer, and acceptably.

(4) A substantial expansion of business ethics into professional examination courses, business school programmes and in-company training. The progress in this area is much advanced in America, compared with other countries, and in comparison with past decades. Some of the work is encouraged and supported by industry (Dunfee and Robertson, 1988).

(5) More open procedures and less secrecy in decision making could be developed within firms and in relation to public policy. There is much evidence of processes which restrict agendas and options in ways that prevent constructive solutions to persistent problems, such as inflation and incomes control. Safety, low morale and stress, and equitable pay and opportunities are specific issues at the level of the firm and industry.

(6) Encouragement to relinquish or at least modify the bureaucratic and hierarchical forms of business and business-related institutions. These have been heavily and persistently criticized, but there have been few well-developed alternatives.

(7) Raising of public awareness and more responsiveness from the teaching and research institutions to public concerns, whether manifested, for example in low public opinion ratings in relation to business (and unions), or in environmental or consumer pressure groups.

(8) More encouragement of detailed research into values and value-related matters in business and in public institutions, preferably of a case study nature.

(9) Developments in these areas should reduce the need for 'whistle-blowers', but insofar as they do not do so, the risks and difficulties should be more widely discussed. More support for whistleblowers would raise problems of trust and motivations. The individual at odds with colleagues or employers is not always right, but there are genuine enough cases (not all from profit institutions) to support the view that the problems have not yet been thoroughly aired, despite some attention from the mass communications media and from academic research, as well as the courts, both national and international.

(10) What Mahoney (1988) calls the 'de-absolutizing' of ethical concepts.

In other words, the procedures are developed from experience and reflections of many writers on business ethics and of practitioners in business and in research and consultancy, and business-related institutions, including unions.

Matching Values to Strategies
One of the standard criticisms of bureaucratic forms of industry and the principles that seek to provide its rationale and justification is that it makes no provision for 'juridical' processes, that is, there are no formal mechanisms which can modify as of right the decisions made by members of the hierarchy. Informally, higher authorities within the firm may be persuaded to intervene, but many, if not quite all decisions made by managers and owners of businesses are their 'responsibility' and theirs alone. Some managers, with great powers in particular plants, may themselves be subject to transfer for misdemeanours or unacceptable performance, by decisions from 'higher up' the 'chain of command'. This is modified to some extent by the existence of external directors, or in the case of universities and schools, boards of governors or outside representatives, with varying powers and titles. Further modifications are made in the form of outside 'watchdogs' (but not usually for employment relations), 'ombudsmen' and other regulatory agencies. In the case of plants that are union organized, there are agreements covering matters of discipline, though these vary from country to country and from industry to industry. Employment tribunals, private and public arbitration, conciliation or mediation, labour courts, media publicity, and disputes are all used with varying degrees of success in mediating between conflicts between various parties. In some cases, the criminal law can be involved. Consumer watchdogs such as the Press Council, and the various consultative councils for some public service industries (whether privately owned or not) provide another source of modifications. Thus the powers of managers and business are far from unlimited, being checked by many regulatory processes. These institutions vary in their effectiveness and in the persistence of their critics. At this stage in the argument, it is not proposed to attempt a review of their effectiveness. Many such reviews are available. What is more relevant is the explosive growth of business ethics issues and of the awareness of them. It would suggest that, at the very least, some of the institutions need to be examined with a view to designing major improvements. The area for manoeuvre in business, industry and related institutions by the various regulatory agencies remains vast: the value-matching processes described below operate in this area.

In the cases, as so often happens, industrial relations difficulties were consequent upon changes in company policy, and in the external economic environment. Case One concerns a large company which operated in England, and made and imported products for sale in its own chain of retail outlets. Population movement and fashion in planning had indicated that the company should expand its capacity in its distribution warehouses, and expand to take advantage of the new shopping facilities and the enlaraged client base. The problem was that expansion was constrained by physical capacity at the warehouse, and by the need for a very substantial increase in labour productivity. The view was that the labour quality as determined by past hiring standards was not sufficient to cope with the changes, as incentive schemes seemed not to work. A policy-imposed constraint was that the pay bill should not be allowed to go up. The union policy for the industry was for a very substantial rise in pay levels. There were some serious anomalies in the pay system, in particular one group, whose job demands were widely thought not to be very high had, for some years been allowed a more generous bonus than had been intended, due to an uncorrected clerical error. One option before the company was to 'buy out' the 'mistaken' bonus payment by means of a lump sum. The problem was what was a fair offer of a lump sum? A second possibility was to hire a consultant to deal with the matter on a 'turnkey' basis, and to hand the agreement over to the company to run. The company decided to solve the problem itself, with the support of technical work study specialists and pay system design specialists. As it happened, the outcome was a major rise in output, profit and pay, and a fall in unit labour cost. The process differed from a standard productivity bargain in that the parties concerned began to see that the physical constraints were not as serious as at first thought, and that led to a reassessment of a whole range of assumptions about labour quality, employment practices, equitable pay and an agreed basis for change. The solution involved abandonment of the idea of buying out the mistaken bonus payment, and basing the pay system and structure on an agreed, equitable set of principles. A problem for the union was that the persons who emerged at the top of the pay hierarchy after agreement had been reached on the equitable procedures were not members of the union, and had no intention of becoming so. There was no acceptable choice, having made the agreement on a stated set of values for either the firm or the union, but to accept the logic of the situation, which they did. The unit in the case was relatively small. It is not suggested that productivity bargains do not have an ethical element, but it is suggested that the success of the case was largely due to the ability to separate matters of interest between the various parties from matters of principle, and to recognize that some of the factual assumptions were not only false, but were consequences of moral evaluations to do with labour quality. In sum, the success stemmed in large part from the skill in separating factual, prudential and ethical matters. The case is described in detail in Donaldson and Philby (1985, Ch. 13).

Procedures for ascertaining the values of relevant parties within companies are readily available in, or adaptable from standard practices, such as attitude surveys, negotiating or management/union meetings, staff meetings and staff councils, practices such as quality circles can be developed in this area, although in Britain and America at least, all of these present problems.

In particular, one British engineering company some years ago sought to discover why the work pace was declining slowly, but measurably against a background of unfulfilled orders, a recession and of high-grade products. One conclusion from a survey was that employees were apathetic and that they were ashamed to work for the company. It was said that people removed the company's car park stickers from their car when parking outside the company's premises. The company was unionized, and all bargaining was on an adversarial basis, leading to an apparently inexorable rise in pay, relative to output. The company decided to embark upon an interview programme. Its results were directly contradictory to the results of the survey. Instead of being apathetic, it appeared that employees were deeply concerned with the future of the company, recognized the high quality of the product design (for some products at least), and felt themselves to be enmeshed in a system in which workflow and information flow complications were insoluble, and worsened by attempts to install improved computerized information systems, of which there was a succession. The interview programme sought to identify every interest and occupational group within the company, and to discover what the values and expectations of the groups were, and how they thought they might be met. It should be said that the company, as a result, was able to raise productivity through a participative scheme, and this ensured survival in the short term. The plant is still operational with a much expanded revenue and profit, after at least a decade, but has eroded its participative system to the extent that management and production are conducted on traditional lines, having identified and corrected the major problems.

From the above it should be clear that it is possible to set up methods of identifying and adjusting the acceptable values of groups, subgroups and individuals. It is not claimed that there are no hard choices, or that 'right' decisions are always reached, or that companies embark on the process with no thought to whether it is profitable or not, or that there is no element of short-term expediency in the decision to seek and reconcile values. It is claimed that attempts to identify and reconcile values are not incompatible with enhanced performance on the traditional performance criteria.

There are well-established techniques for conducting interview programmes, many of which have an ethical content. It needs to be made more explicit, and care must be taken not to raise expectations that cannot be met. Technically it involves what might be called a matrix of values and strategies. The values of any work group can be listed. It is almost certain to be the case in any such listing that some of the values will be obscure and some will be contradictory. Some will be incompatible with those of other groups, which in turn will count some obscure and contradictory values among the list. Inevitably some possible company strategies will make it easier to satisfy and reconcile the values than can be achieved with others. Some will lead to the various dynamics described in Chapter Eight. At the very least, company policies will be capable of justification in terms of open values, free from the temptations of assuming that managers always know best by definition, followed by the cover-ups and transfers of blame and risk that are so common in industrial relations when decisions go wrong. Such transfers are very potent sources of the self-generating and self-sustaining pathological processes described in Chapter Eight.

Development of Codes of Practice
Procedures such as those described above would render codes of practice in the area redundant. There are many areas in which, despite criticisms in Chapter Six, codes can be an advance in that they set down rules where otherwise none may be possible. Traffic regulation codes are examples of these. The Social Security example in Chapter Eight would be an appropriate example of a situation in which codes of a sort have been generated, but have degenerated as a result of pressures from the system. An adjudicator who is integral to one of the parties, and whose decisions can be claimed to be final, yet amended *de facto* is an inappropriate device that could not satisfy the three criteria, and is at a much more basic level inconsistent with common justice. There are many similar cases. In some universities, though not all, students who fail examinations, and who appeal (perhaps on medical grounds) have their appeal heard by the Board of Examiners which made the original decision. My point is not that such boards abuse their privilege (although some undoubtedly do), it is that since no reasons need be given, there are no elements in the process which satisfy any of the criteria, or even require a demonstration of rationality or fairness even at the most elementary level. Other codes, for example covering treatment of individuals who are in the nature of things unable to articulate their view and values in such a way as to influence practice, may be the best available means. Examples are to be seen in the codes of travel associations, which recommend to many agents, behaviour towards a very large number of non-interacting clients. The publishing of such codes, and of procedures for amending them would go some way towards meeting the, perhaps cynical, suspicion that codes exist to protect the suppliers, not the

clients, or merely supply a smoke screen behind which it is 'business as usual'.

The matter of the development of codes is bound up with the matter of enforcement. As a matter of logic, ethics, once enforced, ceases to be ethics, and becomes no more than imposed values. On the other hand, codes which are not enforced might be thought to be no more than cynical expressions of pious hopes. Worse still, the obeying of the ethical codes of a professional association even when backed by law can be costly to individuals to levels which it is unreasonable to ask them to accept. For example: in 1985, an accountant refused to ratify the accounts of a British defence contractor, warning his colleagues of the consequences of over-charging the Ministry. The contractor, after an investigation, was made to repay £400 000. The accountant was made redundant, given moral sup-port by the professional accounting body and the Institute of Directors, but the client offered thanks, but no help to defray expenses caused as a result (Norton-Taylor, 1985).

In 1988 another British example involved an accountant who communi-cated to the Inland Revenue knowledge of some dubious reinsurance transactions, and thereby lost his job. The following dilemma is expressed by David Lindsay of the English Institute of Chartered Accountants:

> The accountant in industry is in a *Catch 22* situation. Either he says nothing and compromises himself, or he puts his livelihood at stake . . . even if he is proved to be right, he is branded as a trouble-maker. (Quoted in Irvine, 1988.)

An alternative view was put by a spokesman for another institute:

> Our advice to members—and I am afraid it may sound a bit cold is that they have to act ethically. This is the price you have to pay for being a professional and a member of a professional body. (loc. cit.)

Two practical suggestions and schemes from within the accountancy profession have been a legal advice and consultation scheme, and an insurance scheme to support whistleblowers.

Another perspective on the problem is one that has cropped up several times in this book: the individual in this position is morally stronger if able to act without the shelter of a professional institute, but the point of ethical values and ethical theory cannot sensibly be to provide tests for people in extreme circumstances or to develop powerful ethical muscles. Individuals in the circumstances can and do make hard choices, sometimes at very great personal costs. It is unlikely that solutions short of major reforms in attitudes will raise personal ethical standards much. Part of the problem is the secrecy with which managers are required to make decisions. In the

case of military contractors, this is presumably inevitable. Part of the
problem is the lack of juridical process in bureaucratic organizations,
which permits behaviour to go unchecked, concentrating great influence.
The existence of the whistleblower is a consequence of the bureaucratic
form of management. In much lesser ways as well as in the ways described
above, bureaucracies produce the self-generating and self-sustaining
systems which magnify issues of dissent at any level. This presumably
explains the apoplexy of company executives (at the suggestion that there
might be problems of an ethical nature) reported by Goldsmith and
Clutterbuck (1984, p. 123). Presumably also, the length of time which a
practice which may be objected to has to develop unchecked is a factor in
making it appear legitimate to those who support it. The case of Stanley
Adams in relation to Roche Products (Newbiggin, 1984; Adams, 1985;
Hughes, 1985a, 1985b) suggests that the events might be explained at least
in part, on these lines. In the event, the case demonstrated the lack of
development of procedures in the European Community up to that date,
and the underdevelopment of regulations in relation to multinational
companies, in relation to international law.

Bureaucratic Reform
The discussions of bureaucracy in the academic literature have generally
been divided into two camps: the critics of bureaucracy, such as Bennis
(1972), Burns and Stalker (Burns, 1963), and Argyris (1964) have drawn
attention to the gap between 'official' and informal practices and their
consequences. Argyris sees normal firms as typically placing individuals in
positions of passivity and dependency that are at odds with the needs of
mature individuals. For Bennis, and Burns and Stalker, bureaucracies are
too inflexible to be able to adapt to changes in increasingly volatile markets
and to better educated employees. The supporters of the idea of bureaucracy, such as Jaques (1977), see it as the institutional means by which
people can reach their potential. The career opportunities offered by
bureaucracies are seen as democratic in that people can achieve through
education the skills and qualifications necessary to compete.

Now, in terms of the notion of pluralism, it appears that it has no place
at all in the bureaucratic theory as originally offered by Weber. There is
one source of loyalty, which is the rational–legal constitution of bureaucratic organizations. Decisions and orders are handed down from the more
qualified, more experienced, more suitable people at the high levels in the
bureaucracy. Where alternative sources of loyalty appear, as in trade
unions, bureaucratic theory has no provision for them. In practice, of
course, when bureaucratic organizations are faced with unions, one way
of dealing with them and preserving the bureaucratic appearances is

to compartmentalize them, as manifestations of industrial relations. We cannot say in bureaucratic theory whether unions are or are not part of the organization. Yet, insofar as juridical procedures exist in them, they are as a result of procedure agreements between managers and unions. My own view is that shop stewards are part of the control system of bureaucracies (where shop stewards exist), but are clearly part of independent institutions, i.e. unions. The terms of reference of the bureaucracy debate have been set in the social science tradition: in terms of business ethics it can be seen that the autonomy is necessarily restricted. Bureaucracies reserve decision making to the top of the organization, and decisions are handed down. The evidence from the surveys discussed in Chapter Six identify the discrepancies between company values and those of individuals, as do the cases of the whistleblowers. Much research shows that bureaucracies in fact tend to appoint officials from limited constituencies, limited by the 'halo effect', in which people appoint others who are like themselves in many cases and use 'old boy' (and other) networks to replace the pre-bureaucratic practices of nepotism. Participative schemes are sometimes introduced, but can be withdrawn by company officials without hindrance. The autonomy accorded to members of production lines has traditionally been low, and the problem in the social science literature has usually been referred to as one of 'alienation', whose cure is usually, and reasonably, thought to be some form of 'participation'. Despite this, participative schemes have had an uncertain history, with a vogue in the 1970s in Britain which culminated in a Committee of Enquiry's proposals for company boards to be made up equally of representatives from shareholders, employees and outsiders. The recommendations were not implemented, and the concept lost support. This loss of support coincided with, but was by no means a sole consequence of a change of Government. Bureaucracies, then, of necessity restrict autonomy to a few. The extent to which their internal decisions and processes can be partially justified by use of the Golden Rule is unknown, and dependent upon the specific moral or ethical character of the directorates. The felt need for codes, and the daily reports of practices and decisions which are questioned on ethical grounds, suggests that the ethical standards that exist are contingent on not only the ethical standards of directorates, but on the ability of professional associations that have to do with industry to set standards. It is, of course, a cause for a certain amount of optimism that firms have their defensible practices supported and sometimes generated from outside, because firms exist in the community and not apart from it. But there is surely a case for business to generate its own methods of ethically grounded improvement, rather than waiting for criticism and legislation. Codes, for all their weaknesses, and something like the 'values–strategies matrix', even though its use is rare and its hold tenuous, are potential ways forward. Whether this amounts to 'industrial democracy' is another matter, which requires specialized discussion.

As De George puts it, speaking of American industry:

The movement toward some form of corporate democracy may be taking place. But if it is, it is taking place slowly and in a piecemeal fashion. No head-on movement for corporate democracy has as yet caught the conscience or consciousness of the public at large. In a typically American way, the corporation is changing slowly as it meets new situations and encounters new problems. (De George, 1986, p. 415.)

In a British survey in the late 1970s by Heller and colleagues, the (plausible) conclusion was reached that most employees do not wish to take on the responsibilities of management, but do like to know from time to time what is going on.

For the present, it seems that bureaucracy is not able in theory or practice to satisfy the three criteria unaided. To the extent that it does, the impetus comes from professional institutions, the law, and the personal ethical standards of managers, of which it is safe to say that they are unlikely to differ much from those of the community at large.

In terms of industrial democracy, it is worth noting that there is a very considerable literature on the concept and practice of democracy. One conclusion that emerges is that the concept is empty unless associated with practical arrangements as indeed the philosopher Kant thought to be the case for all concepts.

In the case of democracy, the notion is best described in terms of institutional arrangements, such as ballots, meetings, meeting procedures, representative institutions and their rules (and much else), and a spectrum of choices, between, at the 'anarchist' end, complete autonomy of all individuals and absence of authority, through to a Rousseauan democracy, in which roughly equal participants in small units apply something akin to the Golden Rule, within an established constitution, and on to a Schumpeterian model in which two competing oligarchies compete periodically for support, and finally to a pressure group model in which the inter-group rivalries are recognized and adjusted, more or less continuously. These notions are taken from political theory, and insofar as corporations are 'micro-political institutions' (albeit, sometimes very large ones), have much potential for adaptation.

In the mean time, it would seem to be a practical proposition to suggest legislation that permits different styles of participative and democratic processes to be attempted in industry. As it is, the structure of authority and responsibility required by law may well be inhibitive of moves in this direction.

CHAPTER TEN

Prospects for Improvement

Scepticism

The confident statement, 'there are no ethics in business', has as its sceptical or (often) pseudo-sceptical counterpart, the question, '*are* there any ethics in business?' In question form it has a more sophisticated ring to it, but at the same time can express mild surprise that anyone could think that there are, taking shelter from the linguistic protection afforded by the quizzical format. In this form, as Hume puts it, the sceptic has "no citadel to defend" (or at least not one that can be found). A slightly more positive, but essentially sceptical variant is, ' . . . but that is (only) your opinion, is it not?', or ' . . . but these are (merely) subjective matters, are they not?'. These attitudes belong to what can be called 'casual scepticism', and as such are notoriously ambiguous. The standard counterpoint to the more confident assertion is ' . . . and there are no businessmen in heaven', or one of its variants. De George accurately labels the assertive form "the Myth of Amoral Business" (De George, 1986, p. 3). To the more sceptical version, there are no standard counterpoints, presumably because it offers no targets to aim at. The huge variety of issues and cases discussed in the expanding literature and in the mass media—a small fraction of which has been discussed or referred to in this book—suggest at least that there are many ethical matters raised by business and industrial activity. The language of strike propaganda from both sides in disputes is full of ethical references and accusations. We can go further: the executive apoplexy to which attention was drawn in Chapters Seven and Eight in response to the occurrence of 'industrial action' or to any casting of doubt upon the integrity of enterprises, suggests at least that the executives are wont to *claim* that there are 'ethics in business', and that they are vital. In short the evidence is very strong that business and industry and their support institutions are redolent of, pregnant with and dependent upon values, both moral and non-moral.

The problem is not that ethics is irrelevant to business, but that the ethical issues have usually been left to fend for themselves, with little in the way of systematic treatment. The growing concern manifested in the literature, and in the setting up of new institutions, centres and networks, could be a positive sign that times are changing, but even this notion is open to sceptical treatment. For instance, a casual sceptic could ask whether, granting that values are relevant, industry simply uses them as stalking horses, so that they can be used to require behaviour in accordance with 'official' principles from others, such as competitors, subordinates and suppliers, so that they can be cynically manipulated? This form of scepticism is not so easily countered. It is possible that any particular act, statement, omission and the like could be hypocritical, but it is not possible that all could be. This is another version of the famous logical paradoxes (e.g. the Cretan who said that all Cretans were liars). If all moral claims were hypocritical, they could have no function whatever, as the deception can only work if there is a true concept for the phoney one to be confused with. It is much more likely that the gap between ethical pretensions and actions arises from a variety of causes. That a claim or statement might be false, or a lie, or hypocritical does not mean that it is, or must be. Even if it is not possible to tell from casual inspection which is the case, it does not follow that it is impossible to tell, given a variety of evidence, over time. The very senior educational executives who, faced with 'industrial action' by staff insisted that it was a breach of ethical standards and asserted that they would be taken into account in due course when it came to increments, where there was discretion, or promotions, or leave, or who claimed that such industrial action was in breach of contract which could lead to dismissal are more likely, in my view, to have been unable to see the irony of their position. As it is, senior administrators do not typically receive any education in ethics or industrial relations practice. Judging from surveys of industrial executive training, very few top industrialists, in Britain at least, have any knowledge, other than of the casual kind, of industrial relations. As it happens, the training in industrial relations for union members has a long tradition, and has some very skilled exponents, but the likelihood of persons involved in industrial disputes having the requisite skill training is low enough to be negligible. The ability to call upon persons with the skills in emergencies often exists, but the role of the experts is very often one of fire fighting. Prevention can sometimes be better than either the disease or the cure, but in areas in which strong values are at stake, it is important to be able to distinguish situations in which it is so from those in which it is not.

Another variant of casual scepticism is the idea that although values can be taken seriously, industry cannot, in the nature of things, afford to pursue them, on the grounds that 'the good guys always come last'. The view is also a variant of the self-justifying truth. Again, though there are examples of cases in which no other conclusion can reasonably be drawn, there have been no serious research studies that have indicated the prevalence of the situations. Once again, 'could be' is not 'is'.

Many firms do, as the surveys quoted in Chapter Six showed, have explicit codes of practice which, though not immune from criticism, do represent a recognition of the potency of values. The values which the codes usually promote tend to be those which are generally thought in the community to be desirable, amounting often to prescriptions to be honest, avoid bribes, tell the truth, keep promises. These are the traditional prescriptions that crop up in many contexts and eras. Companies, and unions, often do stick to contracts and agreements, and to agreed ways of amending them. Health and safety procedures are not universally adhered to, but there are many examples in which they are. Consumers are often 'loyal' to suppliers because they like the product and are satisfied that dealings with the suppliers have been fair.

In terms of comparisons with the practices of the nineteenth century, as was seen in Chapter One, the ethical basis of industry has shown considerable progress. In particular, the doctrines of property rights from the early industrial revolution left factory owners with scope to exploit and abuse. Some owners took advantage, and some did not. Reformers, such as Lord Shaftesbury and Francis Place, Sir Robert Peel, and many others objected to the dominant standards of the day, and changed them. A sceptic could still argue that despite the evidence, Shaftesbury, Peel, Beatrice Webb, Seebohm Rowntree, Charles Booth, Robert Owen, Abe Lincoln, Elton Mayo, the Quaker cocoa magnates and many other reformers, were all pursuing some personal drives that needed to be satisfied, rather than making ethical judgments and setting ethical examples. The triumph of the casual sceptic is complete at this point, because we cannot know the individual moral psychology and drives of the persons concerned. We cannot know in principle because they are no longer with us. But we cannot know in principle also because the drives and motive are constructs and not observables. The triumph of the sceptic is complete, but empty, because by the same token, the reasons which prevent the ethical theorists from ascertaining what the motives of business people and reformers are also prevent the sceptic from knowing.

From historical sources, it is possible to build a picture of the lives and statements of the people concerned. There can be little doubt, from Bready's (1926) account that Shaftesbury's justifications of his behaviour and proposals for reform were closely tied to his Christian beliefs, Robert Owen made his own secular beliefs widely known, yet in their different ways were working towards setting up practices that could satisfy the imperatives for autonomy and for the Golden Rule. In terms of evaluation of business behaviour, and of proposals for reform, criteria based on comparing expressed belief with action are far sounder than a methodological commitment to searching for non-ethical or non-moral motives for every action.

The above reasons are, I believe, sufficient to justify rejection of casual scepticism as an approach to the matter of standards and values in business and industry and their systematic treatment.

There is another form of scepticism with regard to values which can be claimed to be worth recommending. This can be called *informed scepticism*. 'Informed' in this context implies familiarity with some of the issues of business ethics and of at least some systematic attempts to explain them. There is no suggestion that, in this sense, 'informed' commentators are more entitled to hold an opinion, or are thought to be more worthy in any sense than anyone else. What is suggested is not even that it makes sense to propose that being 'informed' is likely to make an individual's intuitions and judgments more 'correct' than anyone else's. There is plenty of evidence of the syndrome of 'trained incapacity', and no real evidence that I know of that knowing ethical theories and cases makes people better, or that grading people in ethical terms has anything to commend it. It is possible, as has often been thought to be the case, that a commitment to behaving ethically is not derivable from a study of ethics, but arrives from a moral sense, religious experience, of a theological or secular kind, or from early training, or some mixture of some of these. There is, and has historically been, a strong connection between morals and religion, or even reaction to it. The service that informed sceptics can provide is that of providing reminders that the great philosophical traditions of utilitarianism, deontology, and the others, are limited in their explanatory powers, and potentially highly dangerous when allowed to become dominant. The career of philosophical radicalism in the nineteenth century, and not a few doctrines of the twentieth century, are testimony to that. This suggests that it is imprudent to discourage scepticism and ethical philosophizing alike.

It is possible that informed sceptics are more likely to admit it when proved wrong on particular points than some people are, but even the notion of proof may be out of place: evidence can be overwhelming, and ethical proposals can be shown to be inconsistent, but the nature of arguments in ethics is that the more general and abstract the proposition, the more difficult it is to prove or refute or to demand major modifications of it, at least so far as the traditional doctrines go.

Could a sceptic, casual or informed, consistently hold to scepticism and to the three criteria of autonomy, Golden Rule and pluralism? In the case of pluralism there is clearly no conflict, since scepticism is its ground. In terms of autonomy, the sceptic is not required to doubt everything all the time. For the casual sceptic, the doubt is either a result, it may be guessed, of having no views at all, or it could be a mask hiding strong views and an inability to articulate them. For philosophical sceptics, as Hume suggested, scepticism is a method, not a way of life. It is best left 'in the study', as its uses in daily life are quite limited.

Progress

In claiming that in some forms scepticism provides a useful service, the notion of 'useful' and 'service' are clearly values. Part One, especially Chapter Two, attempted to show that ethics has to do with adjusting between the legitimate values, interests and ideals of individuals. There is little merit in *defining* an 'ethical firm'. It can be said that one which develops procedures for identifying and meeting legitimate values and aspirations of those who have to do with it can be regarded as ethically defensible. Such a firm would not need to be conflict free, or devoid of questionable practices or decisions, or employ only individuals of exemplary purity, if they exist. All that is needed is a readiness to operate the procedures in such a way that it is open to rational discussion and amendment of decisions and practices when convincing arguments are put. It is always possible, of course, that managers can refuse to recognize a convincing argument when they are confronted with one. It is common enough for people to use reasoned argument up to the point at which they are likely to have a decision go against them, and then abandon pretence at rationality and assert hierarchical authority or resort to manipulative games. The ways in which even 'high-reputation' and 'high-performing' institutions have protected themselves from such re-examination in the light of experience and argument are well described in the literature of group dynamics. A detailed example is provided by Argyris (1974) in the American newspaper industry. It is natural enough to speak of movement in firms towards the development of such procedures as 'progress'. The term itself is clearly value laden, and the values it carries are many and complex. The word 'progress' is currently unfashionable, but was well used in the nineteenth century, as exemplified in Porter's book, *The Progress of the Nation* (Hirst, 1912). As late as 1940, economics texts used the notion as in Colin Clark's seminal work, *The Conditions of Economic Progress* (Clark, 1940). Modern expressions such as 'economic growth', 'economic development', 'growth of science', 'management development', 'growth of scientific knowledge', 'scientific and technical advance', demonstrate the continued use of the idea. It is not suggested that because people still use the idea that it must follow that it is true. It does raise the problem of explaining why scientists, economists, managers and others indulge in the activities at all, other than in pursuit of either the values they so often assert or some others that they cannot admit to or are unaware of (Koestler, 1959). 'Development' and the like suggest a progression to a norm or desired state. 'Progress' suggests a movement along a path towards some ideal or ideals.

Values are not all of one kind. The distinctions between moral and non-moral values (Frankena, 1963), and between *rules of skill, counsels of prudence* and *categorical imperatives* (Kant, 1785; Paton, 1965) are still highly serviceable. The deletion of moral values from science, physical and social on the grounds that they are 'subjective' or unmeasurable entails the deletion of all other values, rendering science literally worthless. Yet the scientific culture requires that values be treated externally, as after-thoughts, as when ethical committees are set up to ameliorate the moral consequences of technique.

A further distinction should be made, between interests and ideals or principles. In his essay under the title, 'Ethical Managers make their own rules', Sir Adrian Cadbury observes:

> The rise of organized interest groups makes it doubly important that managers consider the arguments of everyone with a legitimate interest in a decision's outcome. Interest groups seek publicity to promote their causes and they have the advantage of being single-minded: they are against building an airport on a certain site, for example, but take no responsibility for finding a better alternative. This narrow focus gives pressure groups a debating advantage against managements, which cannot evade the responsibility for taking decisions in the same way. (Cadbury, 1987.)

In the previous passage, Cadbury had referred to the interests of potential employees, which should be taken into account at the wage bargaining table. Many, though not all, union bargainers have supported this stance, which I believe to be highly defensible. At stake here, however, are much more than interests. The principles, such as those used by Cadbury in the essay, are integral. The principle that people's interests should be considered is an ideal. That they should be given due and equal weight with those of other individuals is also an ideal. But people's aspirations extend much further than interests. On the whole, conflicts of interest can easily be bargained, given the current state of knowledge of bargaining procedures and skills. Conflicts of ideals are much more problematic, and are responsible for the bitterness that accompanies so many industrial conflicts. Symptoms of the seriousness of principles or ideals that have been ignored or opposed to each other are the procedural wrangles on the meaning of every phrase, word and comma in agreements, the increased incidence of latin phrases, such as 'the *status quo*' clause, '*ad hoc* committees', '*ex gratia* payments' and the like. The ideals represent a summary of the relationships and the basis on which they operate. 'Justified claims', 'management's right to manage', 'management's responsibilities', appeals to precedents, comparisons that support the justice of the case, 'hard realities' are bursting with ethical norms, intended to be persuasive. That they are sometimes settled to the satisfaction of the parties testifies to the genuineness of the ideas, and to the ethical commitments present at least on some occasions and held by both (or all) parties. That they are sometimes used in ways that are cynically manipulative, confused or lacking in foresight does not imply that they always are. The ethical and technical skills are available, but underdeveloped in quantity and extent. Progress in this area is dependent upon the willingness of the people concerned to use the methods available. The massive shortfall of training of business executive and union representative alike is an indication of the extent to which progress is possible. But bargaining and determination of pay, or compensation, is done only in a minority of instances. This is especially true of America, as opposed to Britain, because of the much smaller proportion of employees unionized. (The proportion appears to be falling in both countries.) In the absence of representative institutions, the techniques for proper adjustment are necessarily different, but the principles of equity remain the same. The likelihood of the outcomes being much different on the average in the total absence of representative institutions is difficult to assess. Most studies put the 'union wage effect' at about 10% above the levels in non-union establishments (Freeman, 1979; Hamermesh and Rees, 1984). At the lower levels of the income distribution the effects can be much higher, and qualitatively very different (Donaldson and Philby, 1985). But the bargaining process is not merely a matter of management–union relations. Studies of organizations have often pointed to the many contexts in which bargaining is conducted, between departments, for instance, over budgets (Burns, 1963; Lawrence and Lorsch, 1969; Cohen and Cyert, 1975). The case of the Chrysler Loan (Velasquez, 1988) provides a good example of bargaining between many parties.

Barriers to Improvement

The most serious barriers to improvement are not in the nature of people or business and industry, but are attitudinal. The grounds for casual scepticism and for cynicism based on some interpretations of moral psychology have been shown to be less than firm. The self-generating and self-sustaining systems that lead to destructive politicking in business and business-related institutions are 'dysfunctional' (to use the standard technical term for the zany and irrational processes endemic in bureaucracies). They would be wholly destructive in the absence of self-sustaining processes that encourage people to make the system work, despite the difficulties they find themselves in. Many studies have demonstrated the ease with which commitment of employees can be gained. These form the core of the behavioural science methods (Luthans, 1985). The techniques are often, and legitimately, criticized as being potentially manipulative. The absorption of business ethics into the discussions of the techniques and their uses has much potential. The constructive self-sustaining systems are capable of being reinforced in this way. The absence of ethical reasoning in the development of management from the early twentieth century has, as argued in detail in Chapter Two, been a major factor in allowing technique to displace, rather than supplement, ethical reasoning in management. There are encouraging signs that the uses of positivism in these contexts are giving way to more thoughtful methods, as witnessed in the growth of the business ethics literature.

A further barrier is to be seen in the sheer size and variety of the first order issues as depicted in the literature. On this, Tawney's general answer in context of the notion of equality, is worth remembering:

> It is true, indeed, that even such equality, though the conditions on which it depends are largely within human control, will continue to elude us. The important thing, however, is not that it should be completely attained, but that it should be sincerely sought. What matters to the health of society is the objective towards which its face is set, and to suggest that it is immaterial in which direction it moves, because whatever the direction the goal must always elude us, is not scientific, but irrational. It is like using the impossibility of absolute cleanliness as a pretext for rolling in a manure heap, or denying the importance of honesty because no one can be wholly honest. (Tawney, 1931/1964, p. 56.)

This applies also to the proposition that the making of value or policy decisions, and the investigation of causal relations and development of techniques can be sharply distinguished, and that specialized roles develop on that basis. The inevitable result is the bolt-on morality to which reference was made above. The sheer size of the problem suggests caution in claiming what might be obtained from the integration of formal and systematic ethical thinking into business, but the existence and development of codes, the willingness of most firms to operate broadly within safety rules, and the generally pacific nature of industrial relations and customer relations show that progress and improvement have occurred, and can reasonably be claimed to be superior to standard business practices in the nineteenth century. Of course, even then there were companies that deliberately chose to operate to higher standards than the average in these respects. To claim that their motives were always and only prudential or self-centred would, then as now, be unprovable in principle, but unlikely in practice. Then, as now, managers or owners of business imported their own values into a system rich in values, but poor in opportunities for criticism, however constructive. The standards that were criticized by Shaftesbury, Owen, Marx, Kingsley and others were not 'the standards of the nineteenth century', but those of a particular group of people, who chose to ignore relevant arguments and evidence. In plain fact, opinion even among manufacturers was divided, and well known to be so (Bready, 1926, p. 204).

The lack of juridical process in bureaucratic organizations which still dominate business has long been noted. The slow development, and uncertain operation of the alternative forms to bureaucracy provide a major challenge in the development of business ethics. These forms, such as 'matrix' management, 'free-form' management, and cooperatives, either operate within a bureaucratic framework, or, in the British context at least, tend to be last resort operations, attempting to keep alive bureaucratic businesses which are due to close for commercial reasons.

The direction from which the developments are likely to come is best described as some form of 'industrial democracy', which takes into account the principles from one or more of the theories of democracy, self-consciously, and combines them with a variety of institutional arrangements. The bureaucratic habits of hierarchy, ranks, and narrow distribution of power have little support in ethical theory, and, judging by the mass of evidence on 'bureaupathology', incline organizations to be vulnerable to the kinds of practices identified in the business ethics literature. That is, they incline without necessitating, to use Leibniz' phrase (Leibniz, 1686).

Source of Improvement

The likelihood of new ethical theories being developed that are capable of guiding business and industry without serious difficulty to the position in which major ethical issues are definitively solved is extremely low. It can be said with some confidence that major new ethical theories rarely appear, and when they do, they have easily recognizable forerunners, usually dating to classical antiquity. One of the major challenges for ethics is to adapt the theories that represent concerns that have been evident for millennia to modern conditions. Novelty by itself has little merit, nor does tradition for tradition's sake. It is a considerable advance that the matters are now being discussed, but this has itself brought some criticisms. The suspicion that business ethics is 'just another fad', and that its use is to find ways of attacking business, was voiced by the eminent writer on management, Peter Drucker (1981). In the article, Drucker voices a suspicion that it could be used, alternatively, to support highly dubious managerial decisions. His criticisms are, however, not centred upon the idea of ethics, but upon what he believes the subject is being used for, namely to defend a kind of casuistry that could easily degenerate to a kind of moral laxity. Drucker's own view, as Williams (1982) suggests, appears to fall on the deontological side of the debate with utilitarians or other teleological theorists. Williams himself defends the element in casuistry which recognizes that general principles need to take into account the uniqueness of particular situations, preferring a combined or, in Frankena's (1963) terms, a mixed deontological and utilitarian doctrine.

My own view is that business ethics as it has developed in the last decade has neither been generally hostile to nor unduly subservient to business. The possibility remains that it could be hijacked by business and put to service in providing a respectable face to malpractice, or at least to complacency, or which would probably be no more appealing, it could be hijacked by academics and used to solve esoteric and trivial puzzles, i.e. imprisoned in the notorious ivory tower. Indeed, some combination of the two is not impossible. Other disciplines have often enough been accused of something of the kind, as when, to take an example remote from our own time, Nassau Senior in the nineteenth century argued that a working day of shorter duration than twelve hours would be ruinous, because all the profit is made in the twelfth hour. It is true that the evidence of the modern industrial psychologists was not available then, but evidence that shorter working periods would raise output and lower costs was readily available at the time, and was in fact used by Shaftesbury in his speeches to parliament. The point is not that Senior was wrong (which he was), but that the argument was used despite the evidence.

As it is, the volume of work now available in the area, the rise in numbers of specialized institutes, centres, and networks, and the variety of disciplines from which practitioners come are, in my view, hopeful signs.

According to Leo Ryan, speaking of the United States:

> My larger confidence rests on the belief that the waves of concern are now more frequent and less theoretical, with lessening of mere exhortation and greater attention to specific suggestions and their implementation. I note also the simultaneous convergence of different interests. This is a quantum leap from the earlier cycles of concern, building up a sustained momentum which is bound to develop ethical acuity in business leaders. We have here a

maturing of business ethics, which, like the good seed, has the ingredients to improve business behaviour a hundredfold. (Ryan, 1988.)

If I am right in thinking that the major issues are procedural in nature, rather than substantive, the solution to the problem of how to recognize and operate 'good' values, and to avoid and discourage 'bad' ones is likely to be more constructive in prospect than the ancient rivalries between advocates of particular values.

Values drive business and business-related institutions. They underlie rituals, attitudes and beliefs. There is nothing in the nature of people or of business which makes the mutually acceptable adjustment of interests, values and principles impossible, and there is a vast literature, stretching back for millennia, which can help. The fact that it has not been much used is testimony to the confidence placed in scientific, particularly positivist modes of thought, in the past. The consequent growth of ethical issues is testimony to the need for ethical reasoning.

References

Ackoff, R. (1962) *Scientific Methods: Optimising Applied Research Design*. John Wiley and Sons, New York.

Adams, S. (1985) *Roche Versus Adams*. Glasgow. Fontana/Collins.

Argyris, C. (1964) *Integrating the Individual and the Organization*. John Wiley and Sons, New York.

Argyris, C. (1974) *Behind the Front Page*. Jossey-Bass, New York.

Argyris, C. (1979) The impact of the formal organization on the individual. In Pugh, D. (Ed.) *Organization Theory*. Penguin Books, Harmondsworth.

Aristotle (1961) (Ed. Thompson, J.) *The Ethics of Aristotle*. Penguin Classics, London.

Armstrong, E. (1974) An anatomy of strikes: some basic incisions. In Preston, R. (Ed.) *Perspectives on Strikes*. SCM Press, London.

Ayer, Sir A. (1936 and various editions) *Language, Truth and Logic*. Gollancz, London.

Ball, R. and Doyle, P. (Eds) (1974) *Inflation*. Penguin Books, Harmondsworth.

Barlow, G. (1969) Some latent influences in a white-collar pay claim. *Journal of Management Studies*, Vol. 7, No. 2.

Baumhart, R. (1961) How ethical are businessmen? *Harvard Business Review* (July–August).

Baxter, G. and Rarick, C. (1987) Education for the moral development of managers: Kohlberg's stages of moral development and integrative education. *Journal of Business Ethics*, Vol. 6, No. 3.

Bean, R. (1985) *Comparative Industrial Relations*. Croom Helm, London.

Beauchamp, T. and Bowie, N. (Eds) (1979; 3rd edn, 1983) *Ethical Theory and Business*. Prentice-Hall, Englewood Cliffs, New Jersey.

Bell, D. and Kristol, I. (Eds) (1981) *The Crisis in Economic Theory*. Basic Books, Inc., New York.

Bennet, J. and Fawcett, J. (Eds) (1985) *Industrial Relations: An International and Comparative Bibliography*. Mansell Publishing, London and New York.

Bennis, W. (1972). A funny thing happened on the way to the future. In Thomas, J. and Bennis, W. (Eds) *The Management of Change and Conflict*. Penguin Books, Harmondsworth.

Bentham, J. (1789) *Introduction to the Principles of Morals and Legislation*. (Quoted from the Fontana edition, *Utilitarianism* (Ed. Mary Warnock), 1962.)

Berlin, Sir I. (1964) Does political theory still exist? In Laslett, P. and Runciman, W. (Eds) *Philosophy, Politics and Society* (Second series). Blackwell, Oxford.

Bernstein, R. (1983) *Beyond Objectivism and Relativism*. B. H. Blackwell, Oxford.

Blackaby, F. (Ed.) (1981) *Deindustrialization*. Heinemann/NIESR, London.

Bose, A. (1989) Union Carbide Agrees to $470m Payout. *The Guardian*, 15.2.89 p. 10.

Bosworth-Davies, R. (1988) *Fraud in the City: Too Good to be True*. Penguin Books, Harmondsworth.

Boulding, K. (1969) Economics as a moral science. *American Economic Review* (March).

Braben, D. (1988) Science and Economic Growth (Letter). *The Independent*, London, 9.5.88.

Braybrooke, D. (1965) *Philosophical Problems of the Social Sciences*. Macmillan, London.

Bready, J. (1926) *Lord Shaftesbury and Social–Industrial Progress*. George Allen and Unwin, London.

Brown, J. (various editions since 1954) *The Social Psychology of Industry*. Penguin Books, Harmondsworth.

Burns, T. (1963) Industry in a new age. *New Society* (31 January).

Burns, T. and Stalker, G. (1961) *The Management of Innovation*, Tavistock, London.

Burtt, E. (1924) *The Metaphysical Foundations of Modern Physical Science*. Routledge and Kegan Paul, London.

Business Ethics Research Centre, Kings College 'Report on the One Day Seminar on the Teaching of Business Ethics' (1988) Kings College, University of London, London.

Cadbury, Sir A. (1987) Ethical managers make their own rules. *Harvard Business Review* (Sept.–Oct.).

Cartwright, D. and Zander, A. (1962) *Group Dynamics*. Row, Peterson and Co., Evanston, Ill.

Chapman, R. (1988) *Ethics in the British Civil Service*. Routledge, London.

Charles, R. (1973) *The Development of Industrial Relations in Britain, 1911–1939*. Hutchinson, London.

Churchman, C. (1961) *Prediction and Optimal Decisions: Philosophical Issues of a Science of Values*. Prentice-Hall, Englewood Cliffs, New Jersey.

Citrine, Lord (1952) *The ABC of Chairmanship* (Eds Cannell, M. and Citrine, N., 1984). NCLC Publications, London.

Clark, C. (1940) *The Conditions of Economic Progress* (2nd edn, 1951). Macmillan, London.

Cohen, K. and Cyert, R. (2nd edn, 1975) *The Theory of the Firm*. Prentice-Hall, Englewood Cliffs, New Jersey.

Cooke, R. and Ryan, L. (1989) The relevance of ethics to management education. *Journal of Management Development*, Vol. 7, No. 2.

Crozier, M. (1964) *The Bureaucratic Phenomenon*. Tavistock, London.

Currie, R. (1979) *Industrial Politics*. Oxford University Press, Oxford.

Cyert, R. and March, J. (1963) *A Behavioral Theory of the Firm*. Prentice-Hall, Englewood Cliffs, New Jersey.

Dahrendorf, R. (1959) *Class and Class Conflict in Industrial Society*. Routledge and Kegan Paul, London.

De George, R. (2nd edn, 1986) *Business Ethics*. Macmillan, New York.

De George, R. and Pichler, J. (Eds) (1978) *Ethics, Free Enterprise and Public Policy*. Oxford University Press, New York.

De George, R. (1987) The status of business ethics: past, present and future. *Journal of Business Ethics*, Vol. 6, No. 3.

Devlin, P. (1965) *The Enforcement of Morals*. Oxford University Press, London.

Dolecheck, M. and Dolecheck, C. (1987) Business ethics: a comparison of attitudes of managers in Hong Kong and the United States. *The Hong Kong Manager* (April–May), p. 33.

Donaldson, J. (1974) *The Paradox of Incomes Policy*. Manchester Business School Occasional Paper, Manchester.

Donaldson, J. (1978) *Incomes Policy: The Continuing Paradox*. Imperial College Occasional Paper, London.

Donaldson, J. and Philby, P. (1985) *Pay Differentials*. Gower Publishing Co. Ltd., Aldershot.

Donaldson, J. and Sheldrake, J. (1987) *The Management of Services: A Coherence Approach*. School of Management Research Paper No. 1, Imperial College, London.

Donaldson, J. and Waller, M. (1980) Ethics and organization. *Journal of Management Studies*, Vol. 17, No. 1.

Dray, W. (1957, 1979) *Laws and Explanation in History*. Oxford University Press (1957) and Greenwood Press (1979), New York.

Dray, W. (1964) *Philosophy of History*. Prentice-Hall, Englewood Cliffs, New Jersey.

Dray, W. (1980) *Perspectives on History*. Routledge and Kegan Paul, London.

Drucker, P. (1981) What is "Business Ethics"? *The Public Interest* (Spring), Vol. 63.

Dunfee, T. and Robertson, D. (1988) Integrating ethics into the business school curriculum. *Journal of Business Ethics*, Vol. 7, pp. 61–73.

Eaton, J. (1977) The stable lads' strike of 1975. *British Journal of Industrial Relations*, Vol. 14, No. 2.

Elbaum, B. and Lazonick, W. (Eds) (1986) *The Decline of the British Economy*. Clarendon Press, London.

Elliott and Lawrence (1985) *Introducing Management*. Penguin Books, Harmondsworth.

Farnham, D. and Pimlott, J. (3rd edn, 1986) *Understanding Industrial Relations*. Holt, Rinehart and Winston, London.

The Financial Times (1989a) Depositors Given Reassurance Over US Thrift Crisis. *The Financial Times*, 18.1.89, London.

The Financial Times (1989b) Three Guilty in US Defence Deals Scandal. *The Financial Times*, 28.1.89, London.

Finnis, J. (1980) *Natural Law and Natural Rights*. Clarendon Press, London.

Finnis, J. (1983) *Fundamentals of Ethics*. Clarendon Press, London.

Flew, A. (Ed.) (second series, 1973) *Logic and Language*. Basil Blackwell, Oxford.

Flew, A. (Ed.) (1984) *A Dictionary of Philosophy*. Pan Books in Association with the Macmillan Press, London.

Foot, Paul (1987) Agony of Horror Factory Workers. *The Daily Mirror*, 9.7.87, London.

Foot, P. (Ed.) (1967) *Theories of Ethics*. Oxford University Press, London.

Fox, A. (1974) *Man Mismanagement*. Hutchinson, London.

Frankena, W. (1963; 2nd edn 1973) *Ethics*. Prentice-Hall, Englewood Cliffs, New Jersey.

Freeman, R. (1972/1979) *Labor Economics*. Prentice-Hall, Englewood Cliffs, New Jersey.

Friedman, M. (1953) *Essays in Positive Economics*. University of Chicago Press, Chicago and London.

Galbraith, J. (1958) *The Affluent Society* (2nd edn, 1961). Mentor Books, New York.

Galbraith, J. (1967) *The New Industrial State*. Hamish Hamilton, London.

Gauthier, D. (1987) *Morals by Agreement*. Oxford University Press, Oxford.

Gellerman, S. W. (1986) Why good managers make bad ethical choices. *Harvard Business Review*.

Goldsmith, W. and Clutterbuck, D. (1984) *The Winning Streak. Britain's Top Companies Reveal Their Formulas for Success*. Penguin Books, Harmondsworth.

Goodman, N. (2nd edn, 1965) *Fact, Fiction and Forecast*. Bobbs-Merrill, Indianapolis.

Gotbaum, E. (1978) Public service strikes: where prevention is worse than the cure. In De George, R and Pichler, J. (Eds) *Ethics, Free Enterprise and Public Policy*. Macmillan, New York.

Gouldner, A. (1954) *Patterns of Industrial Bureaucracy*. Free Press, New York.

Grayeff, F. (1980) *A Short Treatise on Ethics*. Duckworth, London.

Grice, H. and Strawson, P. (1956) In defence of a dogma. *Philosophical Review* (April), Vol. 65.

Griffin, R. (1987) *Management* (2nd edn). Houghton Mifflin, Boston.

Hahn, F. (1982) Reflections on the invisible hand. *Lloyds Bank Review* (April), No. 144.

Hamermesh, D. and Rees, A. (3rd edn, 1984) *The Economics of Work and Pay*. Harper and Row, New York.

Hare, R. (1963) *Freedom and Reason*. Oxford University Press, London.

Hare, R. (1981/1987) *Moral Thinking: Its Levels, Method and Point*. Clarendon Press, Oxford.

Hargreaves, B. J. A. (1975) *Policy for Responsibility*. Foundation for Business Responsibilities, London.

Harré, R. (1972/1976) *The Philosophies of Science, An Introductory Survey*. Oxford University Press, London.

Hart, H. (1963) *Law, Liberty and Morality*. Stanford University Press/Oxford University Press, London.

Health and Safety at Work Act (1974) HMSO, London.

Heller, F., Wilders, M., Abell, P. and Warner, M. (1979) *What do the British Want From Participation and Industrial Democracy?* Anglo-German Foundation, London.

Herzberg, F. (1966) *Work and the Nature of Man*. World Publishing Co., New York.

Hirst, F. (Ed.) (1912) *(Porter's) Progress of the Nation*. Kelley, London.

Hobbes, T. (1651) *Leviathan*. Collins (Fontana Library) Edition, 1962, London.

Horrigan, J. (1987) The ethics of new finance. *Journal of Business Ethics.*

Hospers, J. (1978) Free enterprise as the embodiment of justice. In De George, R. and Pichler, J. (Eds) *Ethics, Free Enterprise and Public Policy*, Oxford University Press, New York.

Hughes, R. (1985a) European Court Awards Damages to Adams. *Financial Times,* 8.11.85, London.

Hughes, R. (1985b) Victory for Adams in 12-Year Battle. *Financial Times,* 8.11.85, London.

Hume, D. (1739/1965) *A Treatise of Human Nature.* Clarendon Press, Oxford.

Hume, D. (1777/1962) *Enquiries Concerning the Human Understanding and Concerning the Principles of Morals.* Clarendon Press, Oxford.

Hume, D. (1779/1947) In Kemp Smith, N. (Ed.) *Dialogues Concerning Natural Religion.* Bobbs-Merrill, Indianapolis.

Industrial Relations Review and Report 'Business Ethics Codes: A Moral Majority?' (16 August 1988) No. 422, London.

Irvine, Julia (1988) Professionals in a Catch 22 Situation. *The Independent,* 12.1.88, London.

Jackson, D., Turner, H. A. and Wilkinson, F. (1975) *Do Trade Unions Cause Inflation?* Cambridge University Press, Cambridge.

Jaki, S. (1978) Ethics and decision-making in business. In Van Dam, C. and Stallaert, L. (Eds).

Jaques, E. (1977) *A General Theory of Bureaucracy.* Halstead/Heinemann, London/New York.

Johnson, C. (1988) Desperately Seeking Sounder Statistics. *The Independent,* 27.6.88, London.

Johnson, H. (1967) *The Economic Approach to Social Questions.* London School of Economics Inaugural Lecture, London.

Kant, I. (translated by P. Lucas) (1783/1962) *Prolegomena to any Future Metaphysics.* Manchester University Press, Manchester.

Kant, I. (1785/1965) *Groundwork to the Metaphysic of Morals* (see also Paton, H. (1948) *The Moral Law.* Hutchinson).

Kellner, P. (1988) I See No Armies of Unemployed. *The Independent,* 27.6.88, London.

Kenny, T. (1976) '*The Asbestos Situation or Whose Safety First?*', *Personnel Management.*

Keynes, J. M. (1936) *General Theory of Employment, Interest and Money.* Macmillan, London.

Kinter, E. and Green, R. (1978) Opportunities for self-enforcement of codes of conduct: a consideration of legal limitations. In De George, R. and Pichler, J. (Eds) *Ethics, Free Enterprise and Public Policy.* Macmillan, New York.

Koestler, A. (1959) *The Sleepwalkers.* Penguin Books, Harmondsworth.

Kohlberg, L. (1972) A cognitive–developmental approach to moral education. *The Humanist,* 4.

Koontz, H. (1961) The organization theory jungle. *Academy of Management Journal* (December).

Korner, S. (1960) *The Philosophy of Mathematics.* Hutchinson, London.

Kuhn, T. (1962) *The Structure of Scientific Revolutions.* University of Chicago Press, Chicago and London.

Lane, T. and Roberts, K. (1971) *Strike at Pilkingtons.* Fontana, London.

Laslett, P. and Runciman, W. (Eds) (1967/1978) *Philosophy, Politics and Society* (third series). Basil Blackwell, Oxford.

Lawrence, P. and Lorsch, J. (1969) *Organization and Environment.* Richard D. Irwin, Inc., Illinois.

Leibniz, G. (1686) *Discourse on Metaphysics.* In Lucas, P. and Grint, L. (Eds) (1961). Manchester University Press, Manchester.

Leibniz, G. (1765) *New Essays* (Everyman Edition, London, 1963).

Levi-Strauss, C. (1958/1972) *Structural Anthropology.* Penguin Books, Harmondsworth.

Lipsey, R. (1963; 6th edn, 1983) *An Introduction to Positive Economics.* Weidenfeld and Nicolson, London.

Little, I. (1950) *A Critique of Welfare Economics.* Oxford University Press, London.

Lupton, T. (1964) *On the Shop Floor.* Pergamon Press, Oxford.

Lupton, T. (various editions since 1971) *Management and the Social Sciences.* Penguin Books, Harmondsworth.

Lupton, T. (Ed.) (1972) *Payment Systems.* Penguin Books, Harmondsworth.

Lupton, T. and Donaldson, J. (1985) Wage bargaining and wage costs: alternative models and methods. In Donaldson, J. and Philby, P. (Eds) *Pay Differentials.* Gower Publishing Co Ltd, Aldershot.

Luthans, F. (1973; 4th edn, 1985) *Organizational Behaviour.* McGraw-Hill, New York.

Mackenzie, P. (1967) On fact and value. *Mind,* Vol. 76, No. 302.

MaCarthy, W. (Lord McCarthy) (1985) *Freedom at Work.* Fabian Society, London, No. 508.

McGregor, D. (1960) *The Human Side of Enterprise.* McGraw-Hill, New York.

McHugh, F. (1988) *Keyguide to Information Sources in Business Ethics.* Nichols Publishing, New York.

Machlup, F. (1978) *The Methodology of Economics and Other Social Sciences.* Academic Press, New York.

Machlup, F. (1974) Cost push versus demand pull. In Ball, R. J. and Doyle, P. (Eds) *Inflation.* Penguin Books, Harmondsworth.

Mackie, J. (1977) *Ethics: Inventing Right and Wrong.* Penguin Books, Harmondsworth.

MacIntyre, A. (2nd edn, 1985) *After Virtue—A Study in Moral Theory.* Duckworth, London.

Macpherson, C. (1987) *The Rise and Fall of Economic Justice.* Oxford University Press, Oxford.

MacRae, G. (1974) *Weber.* Fontana, London.

Mahoney, J. (1988) *Business Ethics: Oil and Water?* (three public lectures delivered in King's College, London in June, 1988). Gresham College, Iremonger Lane, London.

Marsh, P. D. (1980) *Business Ethics.* Associated Business Press, London.

Mayo, E. (1949) *The Social Problems of an Industrial Civilisation.* Routledge and Kegan Paul Ltd, London.

Milgram, S. (1965) Some conditions of obedience and disobedience to authority. *Human Relations* (February).

Mill, J, S. (1861/1962) In Warnock, Mary (Ed.) *Utilitarianism.* Fontana, London.

Miller, E. and Rice, A. (1967) *Systems of Organization.* Tavistock, London.

Mintzberg, H. (1975) The manager's job: folklore and fact. *Harvard Business Review* (July–August).

Mishan, E. (1967) *The Costs of Economic Growth.* Penguin Books, Harmondsworth.

Mishan, E. (1981) *Introduction to Normative Economics.* Oxford University Press, New York/Oxford.

Mitchell, B. (1967) *Law, Morality and Religion in a Secular Society.* Oxford University Press, London, New York, Toronto.

Mitchell, B. (1968) *Neutrality and Commitment.* Clarendon Press, Oxford (Inaugural Lecture).

Moore, G. (1903) *Principia Ethica.* Cambridge University Press, Cambridge.

Morgan, G. (1986) *Images of Organization.* Sage, Beverley Hills.

Mowat, C. L. (1962) *Britain Between The Wars.* Methuen, London.

National Economic Development Office (1975) *Management Training in Industrial Relations.* National Economic Development Office, London.

Newbiggin, E. (1984) *Stanley Adams.* Case Clearing House of Great Britain and Northern Ireland, Cranfield Institute of Technology.

Norton-Taylor, R. (1985) £400,000 Whistleblower on the Dole. *The Guardian*, 16.12.85.

Nowell-Smith, P. (1954) *Ethics.* Penguin Books, Harmondsworth.

Office of Manpower Economics (1973) *Measured Daywork.* HMSO, London.

Paine, T. (1791/1984) *Rights of Man.* Penguin American Library, Harmondsworth.

Parkinson, C. N. (1981) *The Law.* Penguin Books, Harmondsworth.

Paton, H. (1948/1965) *The Moral Law.* Hutchinson, London.

Passmore, J. (1957) *A Hundred Years of Philosophy.* Duckworth, London.

Pearson, G. (1986) Corporate culture as a management tool. *Management Accounting* (November).

Peter, L. J. (1986) *The Peter Pyramid (or Will We Ever Get The Point?)* Unwin Paperbacks, London, Sydney.

Pettigrew, A. (1973) *The Politics of Organizational Decision-Making.* Tavistock, London.

Plamenatz, J. (1965) *Man and Society*, Vol. 1, Longmans, London.

Plato (Ed. Lee, H. D. P.) (1955) *The Republic.* Penguin Classics, Harmondsworth.

Popper, Sir K. (1957/1962) *The Logic of Scientific Discovery.* Hutchinson, London.

Pugh, D. (Ed.) (1971/1987) *Organization Theory*. Penguin, Harmondsworth.

Quine, W. (1953) *From a Logical Point of View*. Harvard University Press, Cambridge, Mass.

Rawls, J. (1964) Justice as fairness. In Laslett, P. and Runciman, W. (Eds) *Philosophy, Politics and Society* (second series).

Rawls, J. (1971) *A Theory of Justice*. Harvard University Press, Cambridge, Mass.

Rex, J. (1961) *Key Problems of Sociological Theory*. Routledge and Kegan Paul, London.

Robbins, Lord (1935) *An Essay on the Nature and Significance of Economic Science*. Macmillan, London.

Robinson, R. (1950) *Definitions*. Oxford University Press, Oxford.

Roethlisberger, F. and Dickson, W. (1939a) *Management and the Worker*. Harvard University Press, Cambridge, Mass.

Roethlisberger, F. and Dickson, W. (1939b) *Management and Morale*. Harvard University Press, Cambridge, Mass.

Rogaly, J. (1977) *Grunwick*. Penguin, Harmondsworth.

Ross, Sir D. (1939) *The Foundations of Ethics*. Oxford University Press, London.

Rousseau, J.-J. (1762/1984) *The Social Contract*. Penguin American Library, Harmondsworth.

Routh, G. (1982, 2nd edn) *Occupational Pay in Great Britain*. Cambridge University Press, Cambridge.

Routh, G. (1984) *Economics: An Alternative Text*. Macmillan, London.

Ryan, L. (1988) The wave of the future (A Moral Agenda for Business: 5). *The Tablet*, 10.12.88, London.

Ryle, G. (various editions since 1949) *The Concept of Mind*. Penguin Books, Harmondsworth.

Sabine, G. (1935, 3rd edn, 1951) *A History of Political Theory*. Harrap, London.

Scheffler, S. (Ed.) (1987) *Consequentialism and its Critics*. Oxford University Press, Oxford.

Schlegelmilch, B. and Houston, J. (1988) *Corporate Codes of Ethics in Large UK Companies*. Department of Business Studies, University of Edinburgh.

Schumpeter, J. (1961) *Capitalism, Socialism and Democracy*. George Allen and Unwin, London.

Sen, A. (1985) The moral standing of the market. In *Social Philosophy and Policy*, 2.2 Spring, 1985.

Sen, A. (1987) *On Ethics and Economics*. Basil Blackwell, Oxford.

Sheldrake, J. (1985) The Local Government Comparability Dispute of 1980. In Donaldson, J. and Philby, P. (Eds) *Pay Differentials*, Gower Publishing Co. Ltd., Aldershot.

Sheldrake, J. (1988a) *The Origins of Public Sector Industrial Relations*. Gower/ Avebury, Aldershot.

Sheldrake, J. (1988b) The neglect of ethics in the teaching of industrial relations. Unpublished paper given at the Seminar on the Teaching of Business Ethics, King's College, London.

Silverman, D. (1970) *The Theory of Organizations*. Heinemann, London.

Singer, P. (1986) *Applied Ethics*. Oxford University Press, Oxford.

Smiles, S. (1869/1986) *Self-Help*. Penguin Books, Harmondsworth.

Sofer, C. (1972) *Organizations in Theory and Practice*. Hutchinson, London.

Stevenson, C. L. (1937) Persuasive Definitions. *Mind*. Vol. 47.

Strawson, P. (1952) *An Introduction to Logical Theory*. Methuen, London.

Strawson, P. (1956) In defence of a dogma (see Grice and Strawson, 1956).

Tawney, R. (1922/1961) *Religion and the Rise of Capitalism*. Penguin Books, Harmondsworth.

Tawney, R. (1931/1964) *Equality*. George Allen and Unwin, London.

Taylor, C. (1967/1978) Neutrality in political science. In Laslett, P. and Runciman, W. (Eds) *Philosophy, Politics and Society (3rd series)*.

Taylor, F. (1910) *Scientific Management*. Harper and Row, London, (1947 edn).

The Times (1982) Weasel Words. *The Times*. Editorial, 7.9.82.

Titmuss, R. (1960) *The Irresponsible Society* (Fabian Tract 323). The Fabian Society, London.

Unilever (1981) *The Responsibilities of Unilever*. Unilever Information Division, London.

Van Dam, C. and Stallaert, L. (Eds) (1978) *Trends in Business Ethics*. Nijenrode Studies in Business, Leiden and Boston.

Velasquez, M. (1988) *Business Ethics: Concepts and Cases*, 2nd edn. Prentice-Hall, Englewood Cliffs, New Jersey.

Waismann, F. (1953) Language strata. In Flew, A. (Ed.) *Logic and Language*. Basil Blackwell, Oxford.

Wallis, G. (1898) *The Life of Francis Place*. George Allen and Unwin, London.

Walton, R. and McKersie, R. (1965) *A Behavioral Theory of Labor Negotiations*. McGraw-Hill, New York.

Ward, G. (1977) *Fort Grunwick*. Temple Smith, London.

Warnock, G. (1967) *Contemporary Moral Philosophy*. Macmillan, London.

Warnock, M. (1960) *Ethics Since 1900*. Oxford/HUL, London.

Warnock, M. (1967) *Existentialist Ethics*. Macmillan, New York.

Weber, M. (1920) *The Protestant Ethic and the Spirit of Capitalism*. Tr. Henderson, A, and Parsons, T. (1947) In *Collection of Essays*. The Free Press, New York.

Webley, S. (1988) *Company Philosophies and Codes of Business Ethics. A Guide to their Drafting and Use*. Institute of Business Ethics, London.

Weston, C. (1989) Dons Warned on Boycott. *The Guardian*, 2.2.89, London.

Williams, O. (1987) Business ethics: A Trojan horse? *California Management Review*, Vol. XXIV, No. 4.

Winch, D. (1972) *Economics and Policy*. Fontana, London.

Winch, P. (1958) *The Idea of a Social Science*. Humanities Press, New York.

Wittgenstein, L. (1963) *Philosophical Investigations*. Basil Blackwell, Oxford.

Wittgenstein, L. (1964) *Remarks on the Foundations of Mathematics*. Blackwell, Oxford.

Woodward, J. (1965) *Industrial Organizations: Theory and Practice*. Oxford University Press, London.

Subject Index

221

Name Index